FOR DUMMIES
BESTSELLING BOOK SERIES

Networking For Dummies
4th Edition

Sheet

My Network and Welcome to It

Write down important stuff about your own network in the spaces provided below.

Network server type: _____ NetWare

(check one) _____ Windows NT Server

✔ Windows 95 or 98

Account information

My user ID: _____

My password: **Don't Write It Here!**

Name of NetWare Server
or Windows NT Domain: _____

Network administrator

Name: _____

Phone number: _____

E-mail name: _____

Favorite snack food: _____

My Network Drives

Drive letter   Description

_____   _____

_____   _____

_____   _____

_____   _____

My Network Printers

Printer name   Description

_____   _____

_____   _____

_____   _____

_____   _____

Coax Cabling Rules

- Segment limited to 185 meters (600 feet).
- Uses BNC connectors.
- T-connectors used to connect cable to computers.
- Terminators required at both ends of segment.

Twisted-Pair Cabling Rules

- Maximum cable length: 100 meters (330 feet).
- All computers cabled to central wiring hub.
- Terminators not required.
- RJ-45 connector wired as follows:
  - Pin 1   White/green
  - Pin 2   Green/white
  - Pin 3   White/orange
  - Pin 4   Orange/white
- Up to three hubs may be daisy chained together.
- Some hubs may also be linked using thin or thick coax.

Networking For Dummies, 4th Edition

Cheat Sheet

Secrets to Network Happiness

- Back up religiously.
- Document your network layout and keep your documentation up-to-date.
- Keep an adequate supply of spare parts and tools on hand.
- Never turn off or restart the server while users are logged in.
- Don't be afraid, Luke.

E-Mail Shorthand

BTW	By The Way
FWIW	For What It's Worth
IMO	In My Opinion
IMHO	In My Humble Opinion
IOW	In Other Words
PMJI	Pardon Me for Jumping In
ROFL	Rolling On the Floor Laughing
ROFL,PP	Rolling On the Floor Laughing, Peeing my Pants
TIA	Thanks In Advance
TTFN	Ta Ta For Now
TTYL	Talk To You Later
<g>	Grin
<bg>	Big Grin

Help, Mr. Wizard!

Before calling the network guru, try this:

- Make sure that everything is plugged in.
- Make sure that the network cable is properly attached. For twisted-pair cable, the little light on the back of your computer where the cable plugs in should be glowing.
- If your computer is frozen solid, try restarting it by pressing Ctrl+Alt+Del.
- Press Ctrl+S if error messages fly by so fast that you can't read them. Press it again to resume.
- Try the Windows 95 or 98 Network Troubleshooter. (Click Start⇨Help, and then look under "Trouble-shooting.")
- If all else fails, try restarting the entire network.

...For Dummies®: Bestselling Book Series for Beginners

TM

References for the Rest of Us!®

BESTSELLING BOOK SERIES

Are you intimidated and confused by computers? Do you find that traditional manuals are overloaded with technical details you'll never use? Do your friends and family always call you to fix simple problems on their PCs? Then the *...For Dummies*® computer book series from IDG Books Worldwide is for you.

...For Dummies books are written for those frustrated computer users who know they aren't really dumb but find that PC hardware, software, and indeed the unique vocabulary of computing make them feel helpless. *...For Dummies* books use a lighthearted approach, a down-to-earth style, and even cartoons and humorous icons to dispel computer novices' fears and build their confidence. Lighthearted but not lightweight, these books are a perfect survival guide for anyone forced to use a computer.

> *"I like my copy so much I told friends; now they bought copies."*
> — Irene C., Orwell, Ohio

> *"Quick, concise, nontechnical, and humorous."*
> — Jay A., Elburn, Illinois

> *"Thanks, I needed this book. Now I can sleep at night."*
> — Robin F., British Columbia, Canada

Already, millions of satisfied readers agree. They have made *...For Dummies* books the #1 introductory level computer book series and have written asking for more. So, if you're looking for the most fun and easy way to learn about computers, look to *...For Dummies* books to give you a helping hand.

IDG BOOKS WORLDWIDE

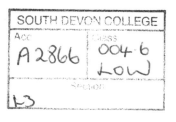

NETWORKING FOR DUMMIES®
4TH EDITION

by Doug Lowe

IDG Books Worldwide, Inc.
An International Data Group Company

Foster City, CA ◆ Chicago, IL ◆ Indianapolis, IN ◆ New York, NY

Networking For Dummies®, 4th Edition

Published by
IDG Books Worldwide, Inc.
An International Data Group Company
919 E. Hillsdale Blvd.
Suite 400
Foster City, CA 94404
www.idgbooks.com (IDG Books Worldwide Web site)
www.dummies.com (Dummies Press Web site)

Library of Congress Catalog Card No.: 99-62476

ISBN: 0-7645-0498-3

Printed in the United States of America

10 9 8 7 6 5 4 3

4B/RY/QY/ZZ/IN

Distributed in the United States by IDG Books Worldwide, Inc.

Distributed by CDG Books Canada Inc. for Canada; by Transworld Publishers Limited in the United Kingdom; by IDG Norge Books for Norway; by IDG Sweden Books for Sweden; by IDG Books Australia Publishing Corporation Pty. Ltd. for Australia and New Zealand; by TransQuest Publishers Pte Ltd. for Singapore, Malaysia, Thailand, Indonesia, and Hong Kong; by Gotop Information Inc. for Taiwan; by ICG Muse, Inc. for Japan; by Norma Comunicaciones S.A. for Colombia; by Intersoft for South Africa; by Eyrolles for France; by International Thomson Publishing for Germany, Austria and Switzerland; by Distribuidora Cuspide for Argentina; by LR International for Brazil; by Galileo Libros for Chile; by Ediciones ZETA S.C.R. Ltda. for Peru; by WS Computer Publishing Corporation, Inc., for the Philippines; by Contemporanea de Ediciones for Venezuela; by Express Computer Distributors for the Caribbean and West Indies; by Micronesia Media Distributor, Inc. for Micronesia; by Grupo Editorial Norma S.A. for Guatemala; by Chips Computadoras S.A. de C.V. for Mexico; by Editorial Norma de Panama S.A. for Panama; by American Bookshops for Finland. Authorized Sales Agent: Anthony Rudkin Associates for the Middle East and North Africa.

For general information on IDG Books Worldwide's books in the U.S., please call our Consumer Customer Service department at 800-762-2974. For reseller information, including discounts and premium sales, please call our Reseller Customer Service department at 800-434-3422.

For information on where to purchase IDG Books Worldwide's books outside the U.S., please contact our International Sales department at 317-596-5530 or fax 317-596-5692.

For consumer information on foreign language translations, please contact our Customer Service department at 1-800-434-3422, fax 317-596-5692, or e-mail rights@idgbooks.com.

For information on licensing foreign or domestic rights, please phone +1-650-655-3109.

For sales inquiries and special prices for bulk quantities, please contact our Sales department at 650-655-3200 or write to the address above.

For information on using IDG Books Worldwide's books in the classroom or for ordering examination copies, please contact our Educational Sales department at 800-434-2086 or fax 317-596-5499.

For press review copies, author interviews, or other publicity information, please contact our Public Relations department at 650-655-3000 or fax 650-655-3299.

For authorization to photocopy items for corporate, personal, or educational use, please contact Copyright Clearance Center, 222 Rosewood Drive, Danvers, MA 01923, or fax 978-750-4470.

About the Author

Doug Lowe has written more than 20 computer books, including *PowerPoint 97 For Windows For Dummies* and *Internet Explorer 5 For Windows For Dummies*. Doug enjoys presenting boring technostuff in a style that is both entertaining and enlightening.

ABOUT IDG BOOKS WORLDWIDE

Welcome to the world of IDG Books Worldwide.

IDG Books Worldwide, Inc., is a subsidiary of International Data Group, the world's largest publisher of computer-related information and the leading global provider of information services on information technology. IDG was founded more than 30 years ago by Patrick J. McGovern and now employs more than 9,000 people worldwide. IDG publishes more than 290 computer publications in over 75 countries. More than 90 million people read one or more IDG publications each month.

Launched in 1990, IDG Books Worldwide is today the #1 publisher of best-selling computer books in the United States. We are proud to have received eight awards from the Computer Press Association in recognition of editorial excellence and three from Computer Currents' First Annual Readers' Choice Awards. Our best-selling ...*For Dummies*® series has more than 50 million copies in print with translations in 31 languages. IDG Books Worldwide, through a joint venture with IDG's Hi-Tech Beijing, became the first U.S. publisher to publish a computer book in the People's Republic of China. In record time, IDG Books Worldwide has become the first choice for millions of readers around the world who want to learn how to better manage their businesses.

Our mission is simple: Every one of our books is designed to bring extra value and skill-building instructions to the reader. Our books are written by experts who understand and care about our readers. The knowledge base of our editorial staff comes from years of experience in publishing, education, and journalism — experience we use to produce books to carry us into the new millennium. In short, we care about books, so we attract the best people. We devote special attention to details such as audience, interior design, use of icons, and illustrations. And because we use an efficient process of authoring, editing, and desktop publishing our books electronically, we can spend more time ensuring superior content and less time on the technicalities of making books.

You can count on our commitment to deliver high-quality books at competitive prices on topics you want to read about. At IDG Books Worldwide, we continue in the IDG tradition of delivering quality for more than 30 years. You'll find no better book on a subject than one from IDG Books Worldwide.

John J. Kilcullen
John Kilcullen
Chairman and CEO
IDG Books Worldwide, Inc.

Steven Berkowitz
Steven Berkowitz
President and Publisher
IDG Books Worldwide, Inc.

IDG is the world's leading IT media, research and exposition company. Founded in 1964, IDG had 1997 revenues of $2.05 billion and has more than 9,000 employees worldwide. IDG offers the widest range of media options that reach IT buyers in 75 countries representing 95% of worldwide IT spending. IDG's diverse product and services portfolio spans six key areas including print publishing, online publishing, expositions and conferences, market research, education and training, and global marketing services. More than 90 million people read one or more of IDG's 290 magazines and newspapers, including IDG's leading global brands — Computerworld, PC World, Network World, Macworld and the Channel World family of publications. IDG Books Worldwide is one of the fastest-growing computer book publishers in the world, with more than 700 titles in 36 languages. The "...For Dummies®" series alone has more than 50 million copies in print. IDG offers online users the largest network of technology-specific Web sites around the world through IDG.net (http://www.idg.net), which comprises more than 225 targeted Web sites in 55 countries worldwide. International Data Corporation (IDC) is the world's largest provider of information technology data, analysis and consulting, with research centers in over 41 countries and more than 400 research analysts worldwide. IDG World Expo is a leading producer of more than 168 globally branded conferences and expositions in 35 countries including E3 (Electronic Entertainment Expo), Macworld Expo, ComNet, Windows World Expo, ICE (Internet Commerce Expo), Agenda, DEMO, and Spotlight. IDG's training subsidiary, ExecuTrain, is the world's largest computer training company, with more than 230 locations worldwide and 785 training courses. IDG Marketing Services helps industry-leading IT companies build international brand recognition by developing global integrated marketing programs via IDG's print, online and exposition products worldwide. Further information about the company can be found at www.idg.com.

1/24/99

Dedication

To Debbie, Rebecca, Sarah, and Bethany.

Author's Acknowledgments

The list of thank-yous for this book is long and goes back several years. I'd like to first thank John Kilcullen, David Solomon, Janna Custer, Erik Dafforn, Greg Robertson, and Ray Marshall for all their help with the first edition. Then came the second edition, for which I would like to thank Tim Gallan, Mary Goodwin, and Joe Salmeri. For the third edition, I'd like to thank Jennifer Ehrlich, Constance Carlisle, and Jamey L. Marcum.

For this fourth edition, I'd like to thank project editor Jeanne S. Criswell who did a great job of putting this book together in spite of missed deadlines, copy editor Ted Cains who made sure the i's were dotted and the t's were crossed, and technical editor Jamey L. Marcum who made many pertinent suggestions throughout. And, as always, thanks to all the behind-the-scenes people who chipped in with help I'm not even aware of.

Publisher's Acknowledgments

We're proud of this book; please register your comments through our IDG Books Worldwide Online Registration Form located at http://my2cents.dummies.com.

Some of the people who helped bring this book to market include the following:

Acquisitions, Editorial, and Media Development

Project Editor: Jeanne S. Criswell
     (Previous Edition: Jennifer Ehrlich)

Acquisitions Editors: Steven H. Hayes, Joyce Pepple
     (Previous Edition: Michael Kelly)

Copy Editor: Ted Cains
     (Previous Edition: Constance Carlisle)

Technical Editor: Jamey L. Marcum

Editorial Manager: Rev Mengle

Editorial Assistant: Jamila Pree

Production

Project Coordinator: Tom Missler

Layout and Graphics: Linda M. Boyer, Thomas R. Emrick, Angela F. Hunckler, Dave McKelvey, Brian Torwelle, Brent Savage, Jacque Schneider, Janet Seib, Rashell Smith, Michael A. Sullivan

Proofreaders: Laura Bowman, Vicki Broyles, Sarah Fraser, Brian Massey, Toni Settle, Janet M. Withers

Indexer: Donald Glassman

Special Help
     Barry Childs-Helton, Kim Darosett, Nicole Haims, Jade Williams

---

General and Administrative

IDG Books Worldwide, Inc.: John Kilcullen, CEO; Steven Berkowitz, President and Publisher

IDG Books Technology Publishing Group: Richard Swadley, Senior Vice President and Publisher; Walter Bruce III, Vice President and Associate Publisher; Steven Sayre, Associate Publisher; Joseph Wikert, Associate Publisher; Mary Bednarek, Branded Product Development Director; Mary Corder, Editorial Director

IDG Books Consumer Publishing Group: Roland Elgey, Senior Vice President and Publisher; Kathleen A. Welton, Vice President and Publisher; Kevin Thornton, Acquisitions Manager; Kristin A. Cocks, Editorial Director

IDG Books Internet Publishing Group: Brenda McLaughlin, Senior Vice President and Group Publisher; Diane Graves Steele, Vice President and Associate Publisher; Sofia Marchant, Online Marketing Manager

IDG Books Production for Dummies Press: Michael R. Britton, Vice President of Production; Debbie Stailey, Associate Director of Production; Cindy L. Phipps, Manager of Project Coordination, Production Proofreading, and Indexing; Shelley Lea, Supervisor of Graphics and Design; Debbie J. Gates, Production Systems Specialist; Robert Springer, Supervisor of Proofreading; Laura Carpenter, Production Control Manager; Tony Augsburger, Supervisor of Reprints and Bluelines

Dummies Packaging and Book Design: Patty Page, Manager, Promotions Marketing

◆

The publisher would like to give special thanks to Patrick J. McGovern, without whom this book would not have been possible.

◆

Contents at a Glance

Cartoons at a Glance

By Rich Tennant

page 7

page 187

page 71

page 137

page 227

page 279

Fax: 978-546-7747 • E-mail: the5wave@tiac.net

Table of Contents

Introduction

Welcome to the fourth edition of *Networking For Dummies,* the book that's written especially for people who have this nagging feeling in the back of their minds that they should network their computers but haven't a clue as to how to start or where to begin.

Do you often copy a spreadsheet file to a floppy disk and give it to the person in the next office so that he or she can look at it? Are you frustrated because you can't use the fancy laser printer that's on the financial secretary's computer? Do you wait in line to use the computer that has the customer database? You need a network!

Or maybe you already have a network, but you have just one problem: They promised that the network would make your life easier, but instead, it's turned your computing life upside down. Just when you had this computer thing figured out, someone popped into your office, hooked up a cable, and said, "Happy networking!" Makes you want to scream.

Either way, you've found the right book. Help is here, within these humble pages.

This book talks about networks in everyday — and often irreverent — terms. The language is friendly; you don't need a graduate education to get through it. And the occasional potshot will help unseat the hallowed and sacred traditions of networkdom, bringing just a bit of fun to an otherwise dry subject. The goal is to bring the lofty precepts of networking down to earth where you can touch them and squeeze them and say, "What's the big deal? I can do this!"

About This Book

This isn't the kind of book you pick up and read from start to finish, as if it were a cheap novel. If I ever see you reading it at the beach, I'll kick sand in your face. This book is more like a reference, the kind of book you can pick up, turn to just about any page, and start reading. You have 32 chapters, and each one covers a specific aspect of networking — such as printing on the network, hooking up network cables, or setting up security so that bad guys can't break in. Just turn to the chapter you're interested in and start reading.

Each chapter is divided into self-contained chunks, all related to the major theme of the chapter. For example, the chapter on hooking up the network cable contains nuggets like these:

- Defining Ethernet
- Finding out about the different types of network cable
- Using coax cable
- Using twisted-pair cable
- Mixing coax and twisted-pair cable on the same network
- Adding professional touches to your cabling

You don't have to memorize anything in this book. It's a "need-to-know" book: You pick it up when you need to know something. Need to know what 10baseT is? Pick up the book. Need to know how to create good passwords? Pick up the book. Otherwise, put it down and get on with your life.

How to Use This Book

This book works like a reference. Start with the topic you want to find out about. Look for it in the table of contents or in the index to get going. The table of contents is detailed enough that you should be able to find most of the topics you're looking for. If not, turn to the index, where you can find even more detail.

After you've found your topic in the table of contents or the index, turn to the area of interest and read as much as you need or want. Then close the book and get on with it.

Of course, the book is loaded with information, so if you want to take a brief excursion into your topic, you're more than welcome. If you want to know the big security picture, read the whole chapter on security. If you just want to know how to make a decent password, read just the section on passwords. You get the idea.

If you need to type something, you'll see the text you need to type like this:

TYPE THIS STUFF

In this example, you type **TYPE THIS STUFF** at the keyboard and press Enter. An explanation usually follows, just in case you're scratching your head and grunting, "Huh?"

Whenever I describe a message or information that you see on the screen, I present it as follows:

A message from your friendly network

This book rarely directs you elsewhere for information — just about everything you need to know about networks is right here. For more information about the latest version of Windows, try *Windows 98 For Dummies,* by Andy Rathbone (IDG Books Worldwide, Inc.). For more NetWare information, you can get a copy of *NetWare For Dummies,* 4th Edition, by Ed Tittel, James E. Gaskin, and Earl Follis. And you can find other ...*For Dummies* books that cover just about every program known to humanity.

What You Don't Need to Read

Much of this book is skippable. I've carefully placed extra-technical information in self-contained sidebars and clearly marked them so that you can steer clear of them. Don't read this stuff unless you're really into technical explanations and want to know a little of what's going on behind the scenes. Don't worry; my feelings won't be hurt if you don't read every word.

Foolish Assumptions

I'm going to make only two assumptions about who you are: (1) You're someone who works with a PC, and (2) you either have a network or you're thinking about getting one. I hope that you know (and are on speaking terms with) someone who knows more about computers than you do. My goal is to decrease your reliance on that person, but don't throw away his or her phone number quite yet.

Is this book useful for Macintosh users? Absolutely. Although the bulk of this book is devoted to showing you how to link Windows-based computers to form a network, you can find information about how to network Macintosh computers as well.

How This Book Is Organized

Inside this book, you find chapters arranged in six parts. Each chapter breaks down into sections that cover various aspects of the chapter's main subject. The chapters are in a logical sequence, so reading them in order (if you want to read the whole thing) makes sense. But the book is modular enough that you can pick it up and start reading at any point.

Here's the lowdown on what's in each of the six parts:

Part I: The Absolute Basics (A Network User's Guide)

The chapters in this part present a layperson's introduction to what networking is all about. This is a good place to start if you're clueless about what a network is. It's also a great place to start if you're a hapless network user who doesn't give a whit about optimizing network performance, but you want to know what the network is and how to get the most out of it.

Part II: Building Your Own Network

Uh, oh. The boss just gave you an ultimatum: Get a network up and running by Friday or pack your things. The chapters in this section cover everything you need to know to build a network, from picking the network operating system to understanding a mail-order advertisement to installing the cable.

Part III: The Dummies Guide to Network Management

I hope that the job of managing the network doesn't fall on your shoulders, but in case it does, the chapters in this part can help you out. You find out all about backup, security, performance, dusting, mopping, and all the other stuff network managers have to do.

Part IV: Webifying Your Network

After you get your network up and running, the first thing your users do is bang on your door and demand Internet access. The chapters in this part show you how to grant their request. Not only that, but you find out how to set up your own Web server so you can create a Web site of your own. And you discover how to turn your network into an intranet so your LAN users can access information on a local Web server.

Part V: More Ways to Network

The chapters in this part describe some interesting things you can do with your network after you get the basic network up and running — things like dialing in to your network from your computer at home or from a laptop computer while you're on the road; networking a Microsoft Access database; setting up a network at home; and welcoming Macintosh computers and older MS-DOS computers into your network fold.

Part VI: The Part of Tens

This wouldn't be a ...*For Dummies* book without a collection of lists of inter-esting snippets: ten network commandments, ten network gizmos only big networks need, ten things to look forward to in Windows 2000, and more!

Icons Used in This Book

 Hold it — technical stuff is just around the corner. Read on only if you have your pocket protector.

 Pay special attention to this icon; it lets you know that some particularly useful tidbit is at hand — perhaps a shortcut or a little-used command that pays off big.

 Did I tell you about the memory course I took?

 Stop the presses! This icon highlights information that may help you avert disaster.

 Information specific to NetWare. Skip this stuff if you don't use, or plan not to use, NetWare.

 Information specific to Windows 98-based networks is in the vicinity.

 Windows NT Server info ought to be within visual range.

Where to Go from Here

Yes, you can get there from here. With this book in hand, you're ready to plow right through the rugged networking terrain. Browse through the table of contents and decide where you want to start. Be bold! Be courageous! Be adventurous! And above all, have fun!

Part I

The Absolute Basics (A Network User's Guide)

The 5th Wave   By Rich Tennant

In this part . . .

One day the Network Thugs barge into your office and shove a gun in your face. "Don't move until we've hooked you up to the network!" one of them says while the other one rips open your PC, installs a sinister-looking electronic circuit card, closes the PC back up, and plugs a cable into its back. "It's done," they say as they start to leave. "Now . . . don't call the cops. We know who you are!"

If this has happened to you, you'll appreciate the chapters in this part. They provide a gentle introduction to computer networks written especially for the reluctant network user.

What if you don't have a network yet, and you're the one who's supposed to do the installing? Then the chapters in this part clue you in to what a network is all about. That way, you're prepared for the unfortunately more technical chapters contained in Part II.

Chapter 1

Networks Will Not Take Over the World, and Other Network Basics

- -

- -

Computer networks get a bad rap in the movies. In *War Games,* a kid with zits nearly starts World War III by playing games on a computer network. In *Sneakers,* the mob tries to take over the country by stealing a fancy black box that can access any computer network in existence. And in the *Terminator* movies, a computer network of the future called Skynet takes over the planet, builds deadly terminator robots, and sends them back through time to kill everyone unfortunate enough to have the name Sarah Connor.

Fear not. These bad networks exist only in the dreams of science fiction writers. Real-world networks are much more calm and predictable. They don't think for themselves, they can't evolve into something you don't want them to be, and they won't hurt you — even if your name is Sarah Connor.

Now that you're over your fear of networks, you're ready to breeze through this chapter. It's a gentle introduction to computer networks, superficial even, with a slant toward the concepts that can help you use a computer that's attached to a network. This chapter isn't very detailed; the really detailed and boring stuff comes later.

What Is a Network?

A *network* is nothing more than two or more computers connected by cable so that they can exchange information.

Of course, other ways to exchange information between computers exist besides networks. Most of us have used what computer nerds call the *sneakernet*. That's where you copy a file to a diskette and walk the diskette to someone else's computer. The term *sneakernet* is typical of computer nerds' attempts at humor.

The whole problem with the sneakernet is that it's slow; plus, it wears a trail in your carpet. One day, some penny-pinching computer geeks discovered that connecting computers together with cables was actually cheaper than replacing the carpet every six months. Thus, the modern computer network was born.

To create a computer network, you hook all the computers in your office together with cables, install a special *network adapter card* (an electronic circuit card that goes inside your computer — ouch!) in each computer so that you have a place to plug in the cable, set up your computer's operating system software to make the network work, and voilà, you have a working network. That's all there is to it.

Figure 1-1 shows a typical network with four computers. You can see here that all four computers are connected with a network cable to a central network device called a *hub*. You can also see that Ward's computer has a fancy laser printer attached to it. Because of the network, June, Wally, and the Beaver can also use this laser printer. (Also, you can see that the Beaver has stuck yesterday's bubble gum to the back of his computer. Although not recommended, the bubble gum shouldn't adversely affect the network.)

Computer networking has its own strange vocabulary. Fortunately, you don't have to know every esoteric networking term. Here are a few basic buzzwords to get you by:

- ✔ Networks are often called LANs. *LAN* is an acronym that stands for local area network. It's the first *TLA*, or three-letter acronym, that you see in this book. You don't need to remember it, or any of the many TLAs that follow. In fact, the only three-letter acronym you need to remember is TLA.

- ✔ You may guess that a four-letter acronym is called an FLA, but you'd be dead wrong. A four-letter acronym is called an *ETLA*, which stands for *extended three-letter acronym.*

- ✔ Every computer connected to the network is said to be *on the network*. The technical term (which you can forget) for a computer that's on the network is a *node*.

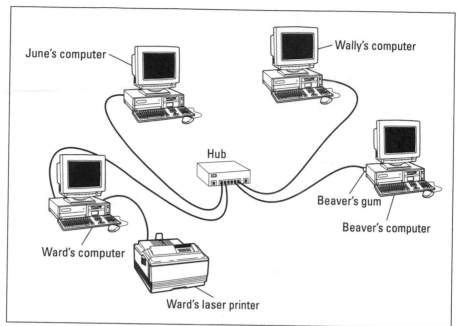

June's computer

Wally's computer

Hub

Beaver's gum

Beaver's computer

Ward's computer

Figure 1-1:
A typical
network.

Ward's laser printer

✔ When a computer is turned on and can access the network, the computer is said to be *online*. When the computer can't access the network, it's *offline*. A computer can be offline for several reasons. It can be turned off, it can be broken, the cable that connects it to the network can be unplugged, or a wad of gum can be jammed into the disk drive.

✔ When a computer is turned on and working properly, it's said to be *up*. When a computer is turned off or broken, it's said to be *down*. Turning off a computer is sometimes called *taking it down*. Turning it back on is sometimes called *bringing it up*.

TIP

✔ Don't confuse local area networks with the Internet. The *Internet* is a huge amalgamation of computer networks strewn about the entire planet. Networking the computers in your home or office so that they can share information with one another and connecting your computer to the worldwide Internet are two entirely separate things. If you want to use your local area network to connect your computers to the Internet, you can consult Chapter 18 for instructions.

Why Bother?

Frankly, computer networks are a bit of a pain to set up. So, why bother? Because the benefits of having a network make the pain of setting one up bearable. You don't have to be a Ph.D. to understand the benefits of networking. In fact, you learned everything you need to know in kindergarten: Networks are all about sharing. Specifically, networks are about sharing three things: files, resources, and programs.

- ✓ **Sharing files.** Networks enable you to share information with other computers on the network. Depending on how you set up your network, you can share files in one of three ways. The most direct way is to send the file from your computer directly to your friend's computer. The second way is to send your file to an intermediate-resting place, where your friend can pick it up later, kind of like dropping a bag full of ransom money in a phone booth. A third way is to store the file permanently at that intermediate place, where both of you can get at the file whenever you want. One way or the other, the data travels to your friend's computer over the network cable, not on a floppy disk as it does in a sneakernet.

- ✓ **Sharing resources.** You can set up certain computer resources — such as a disk drive or a printer — so that all the computers on the network can access them. For example, the laser printer attached to Ward's computer in Figure 1-1 is a shared resource, which means that anyone on the network can use it. Without the network, June, Wally, and the Beaver would have to buy their own laser printers.

  Disk drives can be shared resources, too. In fact, you must set up a disk drive as a shared resource in order to share files with other users. Suppose Wally wants to share a file with the Beaver, and a shared disk drive has been set up on June's computer. All Wally has to do is copy his file to the shared disk drive in June's computer and tell the Beaver where he put it. Then, when the Beaver gets around to it, he can copy the file from June's computer to his own. (Unless, of course, Eddie Haskell deletes the file first.)

  You can share other resources, too, such as modems (which enable you to access the Internet) or CD-ROM drives (those devices that store megabytes of data and are most useful for large clip-art libraries and encyclopedias and for playing tunes while you're supposed to be working).

- ✓ **Sharing programs.** Rather than keeping separate copies of the programs on each person's computer, sometimes putting programs on a shared disk that everyone uses is best. For example, if you have ten computer users who all use a particular program, you can purchase and install ten copies of the program — one on each computer — or you can purchase a ten-user license for the program and then install just one copy of the program on a shared disk. Each of the ten users can then access the program from the shared disk.

  In most cases, however, running a shared copy of a program over the network is unacceptably slow. A more common way of using a network to share programs is to use a copy of a program installed onto a shared network disk to then install separate copies of the program onto each user's local disk. For example, Microsoft Office enables you to do this, if you purchase a license from Microsoft for each computer on which you install Office. The advantage of installing Office from a shared network drive is that you don't have to lug around the installation disks or CDs to each user's computer. And the system administrator can customize the network installation so that the software is installed the same way on each user's computer.

Remember that purchasing a single-user copy of a program and putting it on a shared disk, so that everyone on the network can access it, is illegal. If you have five people who use the program, you need to either purchase five copies of the program or purchase a network license that specifically allows five or more users.

Servers and Clients

The network computer that contains the disk drives, printer, or other resources that are shared with other network computers is called a *server*. That term comes up repeatedly, so you have to remember it. Write it on the back of your left hand.

Any computer that's not a server is called a *client*. You have to remember this term, too. Write it on the back of your right hand.

Only two kinds of computers are on a network: servers and clients. Look at your left hand and then look at your right hand. Don't wash your hands until you have these terms memorized.

The distinction between servers and clients in a network would be somewhat fun to study in a sociology class. It's kind of like the distinction between the haves and the have-nots in society.

✔ Usually, the most powerful and expensive computers in a network are the servers. That makes sense because every user on the network shares their resources.

✔ The cheaper and less powerful computers are the clients. They're the computers used by individual users for everyday work. Because clients' resources don't have to be shared, they don't have to be as fancy.

✔ In most networks, more clients exist than servers. For example, a network with ten clients can probably get by with one server.

✔ In many networks, a clean line of segregation exists between servers and clients. In other words, a computer is either a server or a client, not both. A server can't become a client, nor can a client become a server.

✔ Other networks are more progressive, allowing any computer in the network to be a server and allowing computers to be both server and client at the same time. The network illustrated in Figure 1-1 is this type of network.

Dedicated Servers and Peers

In some networks, a server computer is a server computer and nothing else. It's dedicated solely to the task of providing shared resources, such as disk drives and printers, to be accessed by the network client computers. Such a server is referred to as a *dedicated server* because it can perform no other task besides network services.

The more modern approach to networking enables any computer on the network to function both as a client and as a server. Thus, any computer can share its printers and disk drives with other computers on the network. And while that computer is working as a server, you can still use that same computer for other functions such as word processing. This type of network is called a *peer-to-peer network,* because all the computers are thought of as peers, or equals.

Here are some points to ponder concerning the difference between dedicated server networks and peer-to-peer networks while you're walking the dog tomorrow morning:

- ✔ Peer-to-peer networking features are built into Microsoft Windows 95 and 98. Thus, if your computer runs Windows, you don't have to buy any additional software to make your computer become a server. All you have to do is enable the Windows server features.

- ✔ The network server features that are built into Windows aren't very efficient. If you're going to dedicate a computer to the task of being a full-time server, you should use a special network operating system instead of the standard Windows operating system. A network operating system, also known as an *NOS,* is specially designed to handle networking functions efficiently. The two most commonly used network operating systems are Microsoft's Windows NT Server and Novell's NetWare. I describe them both in the next section, "The NOS Choice."

- ✔ Many networks are both peer-to-peer and dedicated server networks at the same time. These networks have one or more server computers that run Windows NT Server or some other NOS, as well as client computers that use the server features of Windows to share their resources with the network.

- ✔ Besides being dedicated, it's helpful if your servers are also sincere.

The NOS Choice

All computers require an operating system to function. In addition, the network itself requires its own software operating system to coordinate the sharing of information among the networked computers. This special network software is called a *network operating system* or *NOS.*

Historical stuff that's not worth reading

Networks are nothing new. In the dinosaur era of computing, known as the Mainframerassic Period, the computing world was dominated by big, overgrown systems called *time-sharing systems.*

Time-sharing systems enabled you to use a mainframe computer via a dumb terminal, which consisted only of a monitor and a keyboard. A dumb terminal looked superficially like a PC, but it didn't have its own processor. With dumb terminals, hundreds or even thousands of users could access a single mainframe computer all at the same time.

How did this work? Through the magic of time-sharing, which divided the mainframe computer's time into slices, allocating time slices to the users one at a time. The slices were short, but long enough to maintain the illusion that the terminal user had the mainframe computer all to himself or herself.

In the 1970s, big time-sharing systems were replaced by smaller minicomputer systems, which used the time-sharing concept on a smaller scale. Not until the invention of the PC in the late 1970s did networks develop into what we think of as networks today.

Although you have several network operating systems to choose from, the two most popular are NetWare and Windows NT Server.

- ✔ One of the most popular network operating systems is NetWare, from a company called Novell. NetWare is very advanced but also very complicated. So complicated, in fact, that it has an intensive certification program that rivals the Bar. The lucky ones that pass the test are awarded the coveted title Certified NetWare Engineer, or CNE, and a lifetime supply of pocket protectors. Fortunately, a CNE is really required only for large networks with dozens or even hundreds of computers attached. Building a NetWare network with just a few computers isn't too difficult.

- ✔ Windows NT Server is a special network server version of the Windows NT operating system, which is itself a more advanced version of the popular Windows operating system from Microsoft. Windows NT Server is a bit easier to set up and use than NetWare thanks to its familiar Windows interface.

- ✔ Other network operating system choices include UNIX and IBM's OS/2 Warp Server. Apple also makes its own network operating system called Mac OS X Server, designed specially for Macintosh computers.

What Makes a Network Tick?
(You Should Probably Skip This)

To use a network, you don't really have to know much about how it works.
Still, you may feel a little better about using the network if you realize that it
doesn't work by voodoo. A network may seem like magic, but it isn't.
Following is a list of the inner workings of a typical network:

- **Network interface cards.** Inside any networked computer is a special
  electronic circuit card called a network interface card. The TLA (three-
  letter acronym!) for network interface card is *NIC*. **Important note:**
  Using your network late into the evening is not the same as watching
  NIC at night.

- **Network cable.** The network cable is what actually connects the computers together. It plugs into the network interface card at the back of
  your computer. One common type of cable, *coaxial* (sometimes called
  coax), is similar to the cable used to bring Nick at Nite to your TV. The
  cable used for cable TV is not the same as the cable used for computer
  networks, though. So, don't try to replace a length of broken network
  cable with TV cable. It won't work.

  Another common type of network cable looks like telephone cable. In
  fact, in some offices, the computer network and the phone system can
  share the same cable. Beware, though, that ordinary phone cable won't
  work for a computer network. For a computer network, each pair of
  wires in the cable must be twisted in just a certain way. That's why this
  type of cable is called *twisted-pair cable*. Standard phone cable doesn't
  have the right twists.

  For the complete lowdown on networking cables, refer to Chapter 10.

- **Network hub.** If your network is set up using twisted-pair cable, your
  network probably also has a network hub. The hub is a small box with a
  bunch of cable connectors. Each computer on the network is connected
  by cable to the hub. The hub, in turn, connects all the computers to
  each other. If your network uses coax cable, the cable goes directly from
  computer to computer, so a network hub isn't used.

- **Network software.** Of course, the software really makes the network
  work. To make any network work, a whole bunch of software has to be
  set up just right. For peer-to-peer networking with Windows, you have to
  play with the Control Panel to get networking to work. And network
  operating systems such as Windows NT Server or Novell's NetWare
  require a substantial amount of tweaking to get them to work just right.
  For more information about choosing which network software to use for
  your network, refer to Chapter 8. To find out what you need to know to
  configure the software so that your network runs smoothly, refer to
  Chapters 12 through 16.

Bogus buzzword drivel you should skip

An introductory chapter on networking concepts wouldn't be complete if it didn't include a definition for one of the computer industry's most popular networking buzzwords — *client/server.* Unfortunately, nobody really knows what client/server means, not even the experts who made up the term. The lowest-common-denominator definition is: "A computer network in which a PC (the client) can request information from a computer that can share resources (the server)." In other words, a network.

A more technically precise definition is "A computer application in which a significant portion of the application's processing is performed on the server computer rather than on the client computer." This definition is a bit much to swallow at this stage of your network education, so don't worry too much about it.

Very few networks fit this last technical definition of client/server, but client/server is such a trendy buzzword that most computer vendors want to be able to claim they do client/server. Hence the third definition, one more suitable for the real world: "Any computer product, hardware or software, that the manufacturer's marketing department feels will sell more if this trendy buzzword appears in its advertising."

If you really want to know more about client/server computing, check out my book, *Client/Server Computing For Dummies*, 3rd Edition (IDG Books Worldwide, Inc).

It's Not a Personal Computer Anymore!

If there's one thing I want you to remember from this chapter more than anything else, it's that once you hook up your personal computer (PC) to a network, it's not a personal computer anymore. You are now a part of a network of computers, and in a way, you've given up one of the key things that made PCs so successful in the first place: independence.

I got my start in computers back in the days when mainframe computers ruled the roost. Mainframe computers are big, complex machines that used to fill whole rooms and had to be cooled with chilled water. My first computer was a water-cooled Binford Power-Proc Model 2000. Argh argh argh. (I'm not making up the part about the water. A plumber was frequently required to install a mainframe computer. In fact, the really big ones were cooled by liquid nitrogen. I am making up the part about the Binford 2000.)

Mainframe computers required staffs of programmers and operators just to keep them going. They had to be carefully managed. A whole bureaucracy grew up around managing mainframes.

Mainframe computers used to be the dominant computer in the workplace. Personal computers changed all that. Personal computers took the computing power out of the big computer room and put it on the user's desktop, where it belongs. PCs severed the tie to the centralized control of the mainframe computer. With a PC, a user could look at the computer and say, "This is mine . . . all mine!" Mainframes still exist, but they're not nearly as popular as they once were.

Networks change everything all over again. In a way, it's a change back to the mainframe computer way of thinking. True, the network isn't housed in the basement and doesn't have to be installed by a plumber. But you can no longer think of your PC as your own. You're part of a network, and like the mainframe, the network has to be carefully managed.

Here are a few ways in which a network robs you of your independence:

- ✔ You can't just indiscriminately delete files from the network. They may not be yours.

- ✔ Just because Wally sends something to Ward's printer doesn't mean it immediately starts to print. The Beave may have sent a two-hour print job before that. Wally just has to wait.

- ✔ You may try to retrieve a Lotus 1-2-3 spreadsheet file from a network disk, only to discover that someone else is using it. Like Wally, you just have to wait.

- ✔ If you copy that 150MB database file to a server's disk, you may get calls later from angry coworkers complaining that no room is left on the server's disk for their important files.

- ✔ If you want to access a file on Ward's computer but Ward hasn't come in and turned his computer on yet, you have to go into his office and turn it on yourself. To add insult to injury, you have to know Ward's password if Ward decided to password-protect his computer. (Of course, if you're the Beave, you probably already know Ward's password and everyone else's. If you don't, you can always ask Eddie Haskell.)

- ✔ If your computer is a server, you can't just turn it off when you're finished using it. Someone else may be accessing a file on your hard disk or printing on your printer.

- ✔ Why does Ward always get the best printer? If *Leave It to Beaver* were made today, I bet the good printer would be on June's computer.

The Network Manager

Because so much can go wrong, even with a simple network, designating one person as the *network manager* (sometimes also called the *network administrator* or *supervisor*) is important. That way, someone is responsible for making sure that the network doesn't fall apart or get out of control.

The network manager doesn't have to be a technical genius. In fact, some of the best network managers are complete idiots when it comes to technical stuff. What's important is that the manager be organized. The manager's job is to make sure that plenty of space is available on the file server, the file server is backed up regularly, new employees can access the network, and so on.

The network manager's job also includes solving basic problems that the users themselves can't solve, and knowing when to call in an expert when something really bad happens.

- ✔ Part III of this book is devoted entirely to the hapless network manager. So if you're nominated, read that section. If you're lucky enough that someone else is nominated, celebrate by buying him or her a copy of this book.

- ✔ In small companies, picking the network manager by drawing straws is common. The person who draws the shortest straw loses and becomes manager.

- ✔ Of course, the network manager can't really be a complete technical idiot. I was lying. (For those of you in Congress, that means I was "testifying.") I exaggerated to make the point that organizational skills are more important than technical skills. The network manager needs to know how to do various maintenance tasks. This knowledge requires at least a little technical know-how, but the organizational skills are more important.

What Have They Got That You Don't Got?

With all this stuff to worry about, you may begin to wonder if you're smart enough to use your computer after it's attached to the network. Let me assure you that you are. If you're smart enough to buy this book because you know you need a network, you're more than smart enough to use the network after it's put in. You're also smart enough to install and manage a network yourself. This isn't rocket science.

I know people who use networks all the time. And they're no smarter than you are. But they do have one thing that you don't have: a certificate. And so, by the powers vested in me by the International Society for the Computer Impaired, I present you with the certificate in Figure 1-2, confirming that you've earned the coveted title, Certified Network Dummy, better known as *CND*. This title is considered much more prestigious in certain circles than the more stodgy CNE badge worn by real network experts.

Congratulations, and go in peace.

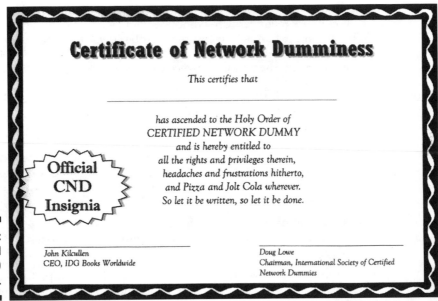

Figure 1-2:
Your official
CND
certificate.

Chapter 2

Life on the Network

● ●

In This Chapter

▶ Using local resources and network resources

▶ Playing the name game

▶ Logging in to the network

▶ Mapping network drives

▶ Using shared folders

▶ Using a network printer

▶ Logging off the network

● ●

*A*fter you hook up your PC to a network, it's not an island anymore, separated from the rest of the world like some kind of isolationist fanatic waving a "Don't tread on me" flag. The network connection changes your PC forever. Now your computer is a part of a "system," connected to "other computers" on the "network." You have to worry about annoying network details, such as using local and shared resources, logging in and accessing network drives, using network printers, logging off, and who knows what else.

Bother.

This chapter brings you up to speed on what living with a computer network is like. Unfortunately, the chapter gets a little technical at times, so you may need your pocket protector.

Distinguishing Local Resources from Network Resources

In case you didn't catch this in Chapter 1, one of the most important differences between using an isolated computer and using a network computer is the distinction between *local resources* and *network resources*. Local resources are things such as disk drives, printers, modems, and CD-ROM drives that are connected directly to your computer. You can use local resources whether you're connected to the network or not. Network resources are the disk drives, printers, modems, and CD-ROM drives that are connected to the network's server computers. You can use network resources only after your computer is connected to the network.

The whole trick to using a computer network is knowing which resources are local resources (they belong to you) and which are network resources (they belong to the network). In most networks, your C drive is a local drive. And if a printer is sitting next to your PC, it's probably a local printer. You can do anything you want with these resources without affecting the network or other users on the network (as long as the local resources aren't shared on the network).

- ✔ You can't tell whether a resource is a local resource or a network resource just by looking at it. The printer that sits right next to your computer is probably your local printer, but then again, it may be a network printer. The same holds for disk drives: The hard disk in your PC is probably your own, but it may be a network disk, which can be used by others on the network.

- ✔ Because dedicated network servers are full of resources, you may say they aren't only dedicated (and sincere) but also resourceful. (Groan. Sorry, this is but another in a tireless series of bad computer-nerd puns.)

What's in a Name?

Just about everything on a computer network has a name: The computers themselves have names, the people that use the computers have names, and the disk drives and printers that can be shared on the network have names. Knowing all the names that are used on your network isn't essential, but you do need to know some of them.

- ✔ Every person who can use the network has a user identification (*user ID* for short). You need to know your user ID in order to log in to the network. You also need to know the user IDs of your buddies, especially if you want to steal their files or send them nasty notes. More about user IDs and logging in later.

- ✔ Letting the folks on the network use their first names as their user IDs is tempting, but not a good idea. Even in a small office, you eventually run into a conflict. (And what about that Mrs. McCave, made famous by Dr. Seuss when she had 23 children and named them all Dave?) I suggest that you come up with some kind of consistent way of creating user IDs. For example, you may use your first name plus the first two letters of your last name. Then Wally's user ID would be wallycl and Beaver's would be beavercl. Or you may use the first letter of your first name followed by your complete last name. Then Wally's user ID would be wcleaver and Beaver's would be bcleaver. (Note that in most networks, capitalization does matter in the user name. Thus, bcleaver is different from BCleaver.)

- ✔ Every computer on the network must have a unique computer name. You don't have to know the names of all the computers on the network, but it helps if you know your own computer's name and the names of any server computers you need to access. The computer name is often the same as the user ID of the person who uses the computer most often. Sometimes the names indicate the physical location of the computer, such as OFFICE-12 or BACK-ROOM. Server computers often have names that reflect the group that uses the server most, like ACCTNG-SERVER or CAD-SERVER.

- ✔ Then again, some network nerds like to assign techie-sounding names like BL3K5-87A.

- ✔ Or you may want to use names from science fiction movies. HAL, Colossus, M5, and Data come to mind. Cute names such as Herbie are not allowed. (However, Tigger and Pooh are entirely acceptable. Recommended, in fact. Tiggers like networks.)

- ✔ Network resources such as disk drives and printers have names, too. For example, a network server may have two printers, named LASER and INKJET (to indicate the type of printer), and two disk drives, named C-DRIVE and D-DRIVE.

- ✔ In NetWare, disk drives' names are called volume names. Often, they are names such as SYS1, SYS2, and so on. NetWare administrators frequently lack sufficient creativity to come up with more interesting volume names.

- ✔ Networks that use a network operating system such as Windows NT Server or Novell's NetWare have a user ID for the network administrator. If you log in using the administrator's ID, you can do anything you want: add new users, define new network resources, change Wally's password, anything. The supervisor's user ID is usually something very clever, such as ADMINISTRATOR.

Logging In to the Network

To use network resources, you must connect your computer to the network, and you must go through a super-secret process called *logging in*. The purpose of logging in is to let the network know who you are so that it can decide if you're one of the good guys.

Logging in is a little like cashing a check: The process requires two forms of identification. The first is your *user ID,* the name by which the network knows you. Your user ID is usually some variation of your real name, like "Beave" for "The Beaver." Everyone who uses the network must have a user ID.

Your *password* is a secret word that only you and the network know. If you type the right password, the network believes you are who you say you are. Every user has a different password, and the password should remain a secret.

In the early days of computer networking, you had to type a LOGIN command at a stark MS-DOS prompt and then supply your user ID and password. In the days of Windows 95 and 98, however, you log in to the network through a special network logon dialog box, which appears when you start your computer, as shown in Figure 2-1.

Figure 2-1:
You must
enter your
user ID and
password to
gain access
to your
network.

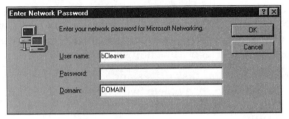

If you're not using Windows 95 or 98, you may still have to type a LOGIN command to access your network. Your network administrator can cheerfully show you how to do this. (If he or she grumbles, offer a jelly doughnut.)

Here are some more points to ponder:

✔ The terms *user name* and *login name* are sometimes used instead of user ID. They mean the same thing.

✔ As long as we're talking about words that mean the same thing, *log in* and *log on* mean the same thing.

✔ As far as the network is concerned, you and your computer aren't the same thing. Your user ID refers to you, not to your computer. That's why you have a user ID and your computer has a computer name. You can log in to the network using your user ID from any computer that's attached to the network. And other users can log in at your computer using their own user IDs.

When others log in at your computer using their own user IDs, they can't access any of your network files that are protected by your password. However, they *will* be able to access any local files that you haven't protected. So be careful which people you let use your computer.

✔ Your computer may be set up so that it logs you in automatically whenever you turn it on. In that case, you don't have to type your user ID and password. This setup makes the task of logging on more convenient, but takes the sport out of it. And it's a terrible idea if you're the least bit worried about bad guys getting into your network or personal files.

>   ✔ Guard your password with your life. I'd tell you mine, but then I'd have
>   to shoot you.

Understanding Shared Folders

Before Network (B.N.), your computer probably had just one disk drive, known as drive C. Maybe two, C and D. Either way, these drives are physically located inside your PC. They are local drives.

Now that you're on a network, you probably have access to disk drives that aren't located inside your PC but are located instead in one of the other computers on the network. These network drives can be located on a dedicated server computer or, in the case of a peer-to-peer network, on another client computer.

In some cases, you can access an entire network drive over the network. But in most cases, you can't access the entire drive. Instead, you can access only certain folders (*directories* in old MS-DOS lingo) on the network drives. Either way, the shared drives or folders are known in Windows terminology as *shared folders*.

Shared folders can be set up with restrictions on how you may use them. For example, you may be granted full access to some shared folders, so that you can copy files to or from them, delete files on them, create or remove folders on them, and so on. On other shared folders, your access may be limited in certain ways. For example, you may be able to copy files to or from the shared folder, but not delete files, edit files, or create new folders. You may also be asked to enter a password before you can access a protected folder. For more information about file-sharing restrictions, refer to Chapter 13.

Keep in mind that in addition to accessing shared folders that reside on other people's computers, you can also designate your computer as a server to enable other network users to access folders that you share. To learn how to share folders on your computer with other network users, refer to Chapter 4.

Welcome to the Network 'Hood

Windows enables you to access network resources, such as shared folders, by opening the Network Neighborhood icon that resides on your desktop (shown in the margin). When you first open the Network Neighborhood, you're greeted by icons that represent the computers that are connected to your local network workgroup, plus an icon representing the entire network, as shown in Figure 2-2.

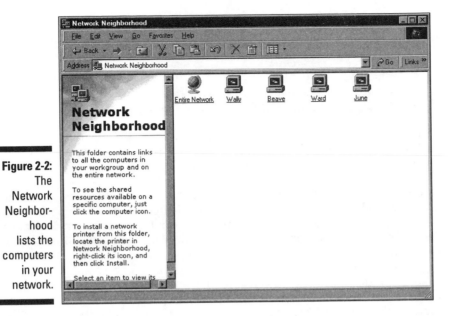

Figure 2-2:
The
Network
Neighbor-
hood
lists the
computers
in your
network.

To access shared folders that reside on another computer, open the icon that represents the computer in the Network Neighborhood. This action displays the folders that are designated as shared folders on that computer, as shown in Figure 2-3.

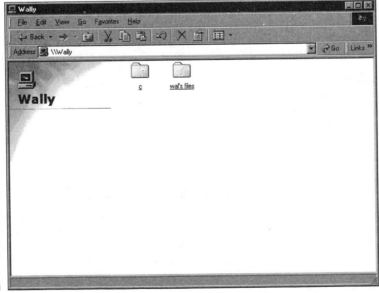

Figure 2-3:
Shared
folders on
Wally's
computer.

If the computer you want to access isn't listed in the Network Neighborhood window, open the Entire Network icon. Doing so lists all the computers that are available on your network.

As Figure 2-3 shows, Wally has designated two shared folders on his computer: one, named c, is his entire C drive. The other, named wal's files, is a folder containing files he wants to share. You can open either of these folders and then access the files within them as if they were located on your local disk drives.

You can also access the Network Neighborhood from any Windows application program. For example, suppose that you're working with Microsoft Word and would like to open a document file that has been stored in a shared folder on your network. All you have to do is choose the File⇨Open command to bring up an Open dialog box. Near the top of the Open dialog box is a list box labeled Look In. From the list, choose the Network Neighborhood icon shown in Figure 2-4 to access network computers. Then, locate the document file that you want to open on the network.

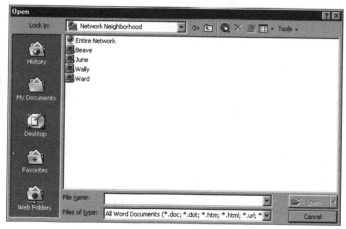

Figure 2-4: You can access the Network Neighborhood from any Windows program.

Mapping Network Drives

If you find yourself accessing a particular shared folder frequently, you may want to use a special trick called *mapping* to access the shared folder more efficiently. Mapping assigns a drive letter to a shared folder. Then you can use the drive letter to access the shared folder as if it were a local drive. In this way, you can access the shared folder from any Windows program without having to navigate through the Network Neighborhood.

For example, you can map a shared folder named \Wal's Files to drive G on your computer. Then, to access files stored in the shared \Wal's Files folder, you would look on drive G.

To map a shared folder to a drive letter, follow these steps:

1. **Use the Network Neighborhood to locate the shared folder you want to map to a drive.**

   If you're not sure how to do this, refer to the section "Welcome to the Network 'Hood" earlier in this chapter.

2. **Right-click the shared folder and then choose the M̲ap Network Drive command from the pop-up menu that appears.**

   This action summons the Map Network Drive dialog box, shown in Figure 2-5.

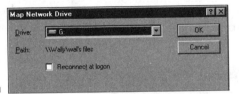

3. **Change the drive letter if you want to.**

   You probably don't have to change the drive letter that Windows selects (in Figure 2-5, drive G:). But if you're picky, you can select the drive letter from the D̲rive drop-down list.

4. **If you want this network drive to be automatically mapped each time you log on to the network, check the Reconnec̲t at logon option.**

   If you leave the Reconnec̲t at logon option unchecked, the drive letter is available only until you shut down Windows or log off from the network. If you check this option, the network drive automatically reconnects each time you log on to the network.

5. **Click OK.**

   That's it! You're done.

 Your network administrator already may have set up your computer with one or more mapped network drives. If so, you can ask him or her to tell you which network drives have been mapped. Or you can just open My Computer and have a look. (Mapped network drives are listed in My Computer using the icon shown in the margin.)

✔ Assigning a drive letter to a network drive is called *mapping the drive* or *linking the drive* by network nerds. "Drive H is mapped to a network drive," they'll say.

✔ The drive letter you use to map a drive on a network server doesn't have to be the same drive letter that the server uses to access the file. For example, suppose that you use drive H to link to the server's C drive. This is confusing, so have another cup of coffee. In this scenario, drive H on your computer is the same drive as drive C on the server computer. This shell game is necessary for one simple reason: You can't access the server's C drive as drive C because your computer has its own drive C! You have to pick an unused drive letter and map or link it to the server's C drive.

✔ Network drive letters don't have to be assigned the same way for every computer on the network. For example, a network drive that is assigned drive letter H on your computer may be assigned drive letter Q on someone else's computer. In that case, your drive H and the other computer's drive Q are really the same drive. This can be very confusing. If your network is set up this way, put pepper in your network administrator's coffee.

Four Good Uses for a Shared Folder

After you know which shared network folders are available, you may be wondering what you're supposed to do with them. Here are four good uses for a network folder.

Use it to store files that everybody needs

A shared network folder is a good place to store files that more than one user needs to access. Without a network, you have to store a copy of the file on everyone's computer, and you have to worry about keeping the copies synchronized (which you can't do, no matter how hard you try). Or you can keep the file on a diskette and pass it around. Or you can keep the file on one computer and play musical chairs — whenever someone needs to use the file, he or she goes to the computer that contains it.

With a network, you can keep one copy of the file in a shared folder on the network, and everyone can access it.

If you're trying to share a file that's accessed by an older program — for example, an ancient DOS version of a spreadsheet program like Lotus 1-2-3 — you may have a problem. You have to make sure that two people don't try to update the file at the same time. For example, suppose that you retrieve a spreadsheet file and start to work on it and then another user retrieves the same file a few minutes later. That user won't see the changes you've made so far because you haven't saved the file back to disk yet. Now, suppose you finish making your changes and you save the file while the other user is still staring at the screen. Guess what happens when the other user saves his or her changes a few minutes later? All the changes you made are gone, forever in the Black Hole of Unprotected Concurrent Access.

The root cause of this problem is that older programs don't *reserve* the file while they're working on it. As a result, other programs aren't prevented from working on the file at the same time. The result is a jumbled mess. Fortunately, most newer application programs tend to be more tolerant of networks, so they do reserve files when you open them. These programs are much safer for network use.

Use it to store your own files

You can also use a shared network folder as an extension of your own disk storage. For example, if you've filled up all the free space on your disk drive with pictures, sounds, and movies you've downloaded from the Internet, but the network server has billions and billions of gigabytes of free space, you have all the disk space you need. Just store your files on the network drive!

Here are a few guidelines for storing files on network drives:

- Using the network drive for your own files works best if the network drive is set up for private storage that other users can't access. That way, you don't have to worry about the nosy guy down in Accounting who likes to poke around in other people's files.

- Don't overuse the network drive. Remember that other users have probably filled up their disks, so they want to use the space on the network drive, too.

- Before you store personal files on a network drive, make sure that you have permission. A note from your mom will do.

Use it as a pit stop for files on their way to other users

"Hey, Wally, could you send me a copy of last month's baseball stats?"

"Sure, Beave." But how? If the baseball stats file resides on Wally's local drive, how does Wally send a copy of the file to Beaver's computer? One way is for Wally to copy the file to a network folder. Then Beaver can copy the file to his local drive.

Here are some tips to keep in mind when you use a network drive to exchange files with other network users:

✔ Don't forget to delete files that you've saved to the network folder after they've been picked up! Otherwise, the network folder quickly fills up with unnecessary files.

✔ Creating a directory on the network drive just for holding files en route to other users is a good idea. Call this directory PITSTOP or something similar to suggest its function.

✔ Most electronic mail packages also enable you to deliver files to other users. This is called "sending a file attachment." The advantage of sending a file via e-mail is that you don't have to worry about details like where to leave the file on the server and who's responsibility it is to delete the file.

Use it to back up your local disk

If enough disk space is on the file server, you can use it to store backup copies of the files on your hard disk. Just copy the files you want to back up to a shared network folder.

Obviously, copying all your data files to the network drive can quickly fill up the network drive. You'd better check with the network manager before you do it. He or she may request that you use a special program such as PKZip to compress your files before you copy them to the network drive or that you copy your backup files to a particular network drive on which all files are automatically compressed to save space.

Using a Network Printer

Using a network printer is much like using a network disk drive. If you're using Windows 95 or 98, you can print to a network printer by choosing File⇨Print to call up a Print dialog box from any program and choosing a network printer from the list of available printers.

If you're using MS-DOS or an earlier version of Windows (such as Windows 3.11), the network uses smoke and mirrors to trick your MS-DOS and Windows into believing that the network printer is actually attached to your own computer as a local printer. After the smoke and mirrors are in place, use your program's regular printing functions to print to the network printer.

With or without Windows 95 or 98, however, printing on a network printer isn't exactly the same as printing on a local printer. When you print on a local printer, you're the only one who is using that printer. But when you print to a network printer, you're sharing that printer with other network users. This complicates things in several ways:

✔ If several users print to the network printer at the same time, the network has to keep the print jobs separate from one another. If it didn't, the result would be a jumbled mess, with your 35-page report being mixed up with the payroll checks. That would be bad. Fortunately, the network takes care of this situation by using a fancy feature called print spooling.

✔ Invariably, when I get in line at the hardware store, the person in front of me is trying to buy something that doesn't have a product code on it. I end up standing there for hours waiting for someone in Plumbing to pick up the phone for a price check. Network printing can be like that. If someone sends a two-hour print job to the printer before you send your half-page memo, you have to wait. Network printing works on a first-come, first-served basis, unless you know some of the tricks I discuss in Chapter 3.

✔ Before you were forced to use the network, your computer probably had just one printer attached to it. Now, you may have access to a local printer and several network printers. You may want to print some documents on your cheap (oops, I mean local) inkjet printer but use the network laser printer for really important stuff. To do that, you have to find out how to use your application programs' functions for switching printers.

✔ Network printing is really too important a subject to squeeze into this chapter. So Chapter 3 goes into the topic in more detail.

Logging Off of the Network

After you finish using the network, you should log off. Logging off the network makes the network drives and printers unavailable. Your computer is still physically connected to the network (unless you cut the network cable with pruning shears — bad idea! Don't do it!), but the network and its resources are unavailable to you.

✔ After you turn off your computer, you're automatically logged off of the network. After you start your computer, you have to log in again. Logging off of the network is a good idea if you're going to leave your computer unattended for a while. As long as your computer is logged in to the network, anyone can use it to access the network. And because unauthorized users can access it under your user ID, you get the blame for any damage they do.

✔ In Windows, you can log off the network by clicking the Start button and choosing the Log Off command. This process logs you off the network without restarting Windows. (In some versions of Windows 95, you must choose the Start⇨Shut Down command to log off the network.)

Chapter 3

Using a Network Printer

*I*f there's one thing you come to hate about using a network, it's using a network printer. Oh, for the good ol' days when your slow but simple dot-matrix printer sat on your desk right next to your computer for you and nobody else but you to use. Now you have to share the printer down the hall. It may be a neat printer, but now you can't watch it all the time to make sure it's working.

Now you send an 80-page report to the printer, and when you go check on it 20 minutes later, you discover that it hasn't printed yet because someone else sent an 800-page report before you. Or the printer's been sitting there for 20 minutes because it ran out of paper. Or your report just disappeared into Network-Network Land.

What a pain. This chapter can help you out. It clues you in to the secrets of network printing and gives you some Network Pixie Dust (NPD) to help you find those lost print jobs. (It may also convince you to spend $300 of your own money to buy your own printer so you won't have to mess around with the network printer!)

What's So Special about Network Printing?

Why is network printing such a big deal? In Chapter 2, I talk about sharing network disk drives and folders and show that sharing is really pretty simple. After everything is set up right, using a network drive is hardly different from using a local disk drive.

The situation would be great if sharing a printer were just as easy. But it isn't. The problem with network printing is that printers are slow and finicky devices. They run out of paper. They eat paper. They run out of toner or ink. And sometimes they just croak. Dealing with all these problems is hard enough when the printer is right next to the computer on your desk, but using the printer that's accessed remotely via a network is even harder.

A printer in every port

Start with some printing basics. A *port* is a connection on the back of your computer. You use ports to connect devices to the computer. You plug one end of a cable into the port and plug the other end of the cable into a connector on the back of the device you want to connect. Most computers have two devices connected to ports: a printer and a mouse. Some computers have other devices, such as a modem or a scanner.

Ports come in two varieties: *parallel* and *serial*. Parallel ports are the type most often used for printers. Certain types of older printers used serial port connections, but most of these printers have long since been used to make beehives. The serial port is used nowadays mostly to connect a mouse or a modem to the computer. (Actually, serial ports are making a comeback in the form of a new, improved version called a *USB*. See the sidebar "Hop on the Universal Serial Bus" for more information.)

Another type of port that your computer may or may not have is a SCSI port. *SCSI* (pronounced *skuzzy*), which stands for *Small Computer System Interface*, is a special type of high-speed parallel port that's used mostly to connect disk drives, tape drives, CD-ROM drives, and other devices, such as scanners, to your computer. Because you don't use the SCSI port to connect a printer, you can ignore it for now.

Here are some additional points to ponder concerning the mysteries of printer ports:

✔ After the introduction of the first IBM Personal Computer way back in 1492, the names LPT1, LPT2, and LPT3 were assigned to the parallel ports (LPT stands for "Line Printer"). The first parallel port (and the only parallel port on most computers) is LPT1. LPT2 and LPT3 are the

Hop on the Universal Serial Bus

In 1997, a new type of serial bus called the *Universal Serial Bus*, or *USB*, became available on new computers. The USB may eventually replace *all* the external connections required by your computer. Windows 98 provides full support for USB.

Think about all the external devices that you may have to connect to a typical computer: keyboard, monitor, mouse, printer, and perhaps a modem, scanner, or tape drive. Each of these devices needs its own type of cable, and you must plug each into the correct receptacle at the back of the computer.

If USB catches on, the back of your computer will have only one type of receptacle: USB. You can plug any USB-compatible device into a receptacle. And many USB devices enable you to daisy chain other USB devices, so that you can (at least in theory) connect all your computer's external devices to your computer through a single USB receptacle.

Besides saving you the hassle of untangling a multitude of cables and connectors, USB devices also automatically configure themselves after you attach them to your computer. You no longer have to fuss with IRQ settings or other configuration details. You can even add or remove USB devices without turning off your computer or restarting Windows. Windows 98 automatically recognizes USB devices after you connect them.

We all have to wait and see if USB catches on. But if it does, your next computer and printer may well use USB rather than parallel ports, which has been the norm for printer connections since the first IBM PC rolled off the assembly line back in 1984.

second and third parallel ports. Even today, Windows 98 uses these same names.

✔ LPT1 has a pseudonym: PRN. The names LPT1 and PRN both refer to the first parallel port and are used interchangeably.

✔ COM1, COM2, COM3, and COM4 are the names used for the four serial ports. (COM stands for "communications," a subject the people who came up with names like LPT1 and COM1 needed to study more closely.)

✔ Hopefully, the name assigned to each port on your computer is printed next to the port's connector on the back of your computer. If not, you have to check your computer's manual to find out which port is which.

Printer configuration

All you have to do to use a printer is plug the printer into the parallel port on the back of your computer, right? Nope. You must also configure Windows to work with the printer. To do so, you must install a special piece of software called a *printer driver*, which tells Windows how to print to your printer.

Each different type of printer has its own printer driver. Drivers for the most common printers come with Windows. For printers that are more exotic — or for newer printers that weren't available at the time you purchased Windows — the printer manufacturer supplies the driver on a disk that comes with the printer.

To find out what printers are already configured for your computer, click the Start button and then choose the Settings⇨Printers command. The Printers folder appears, as shown in Figure 3-1.

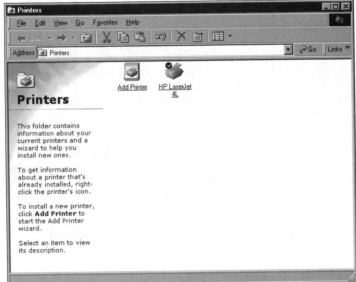

Figure 3-1:
The Printers
folder.

The Printers folder shows an icon for each printer installed on your computer. In the case of Figure 3-1, only one printer has been installed: a Hewlett-Packard LaserJet 4L. If you have more than one printer installed on your computer, you see a printer icon for each printer.

You can configure a new printer for your computer by clicking the Add Printer icon. Doing so starts the Add Printer Wizard, which adds a printer driver for a new printer to your computer. For more information about using this Wizard, see the section "Adding a Network Printer" later in this chapter.

Spooling and the print queue

Printers are far and away the slowest part of any computer. As far as your computer's central processing unit (CPU) is concerned, the printer takes an eternity to print a single line of information. To keep the CPU from twiddling its microscopic thumbs, computer geeks invented *spooling*.

Spooling is really pretty simple. Suppose that you use Microsoft Word to print a 200-page report. Without spooling, Word would send the report directly to the printer. You'd have to play Solitaire until the printer finished printing.

With spooling, Word doesn't send the report directly to the printer. Instead, Word sends the report to a disk file. Because the disk drives are so much faster than printers, you have to wait only a few seconds for the print job to finish. After your 200-page report is sent to the spool file, you can continue to use Word for other work, even though the printer hasn't actually finished your report yet.

Suppose you turn right around and send another 200-page report to the printer, while the printer is still busy printing the first 200-page report. The second report must wait for the printer to finish the first report. The place where the report waits is called the *print queue.* Print queue is the computer-nerd term for the line in which your print job has to wait while other print jobs that reached the line sooner are printed. Your print job isn't actually printed until it gets to the front of the line; that is, until it gets to the front of the queue.

Here are a few more spooling tidbits:

- The people who invented network printing way back in the 1960s thought calling the line that print jobs wait in a "line" would be uncool. The Beatles and anything British were popular back then, so they picked the British-sounding word *queue* instead.

- Although considered rude, cutting to the front of the queue is possible. You find out how to do that later in this chapter. This trick is good to know, especially if you're the only one who knows.

- Brits always use too many letters. They like to throw extra ones into words like *colour.* The word *queue* is pronounced like "cue," not "cue-you." "Cue-you" is spelled "queueue" and is often used by Certified Network Dummies as an insult.

- Believe it or not, the word *spool* is actually an acronym — a five-letter acronym, or EETLA ("Expanded Extended Three-Letter Acronym") to be precise. Brace yourself, because this acronym is really nerdy: Spool stands for "Simultaneous Peripheral Output On-Line."

What is a print job?

I've used the term *print job* several times without explaining what it means, so you're probably already mad at me. I'd better explain before it's too late. A print job is a collection of printed pages that are kept together and treated as a set. If you print a 20-page document from Word, the entire 20-page printout is a single print job. Every time you use Word's Print command (or any other program's Print command), you create a print job.

How does the network know when one print job ends and the next one begins? Because the programs that do the printing send out a special code at the end of each Print command that says, "This is the end of the print job. Everything up to this point belongs together, and anything I print after this point belongs to my next print job."

Analogy alert! You can think of this code as kind of like the little stick you use at the grocery-store checkout stand to separate your groceries from the groceries that belong to the person in line behind you. The stick tells the clerk that all the groceries in front of the stick belong together, and the groceries behind the stick belong to the next customer.

When you print over a network, you can do lots of neat stuff with print jobs. You can tell the print server to print more than one copy of your job, to print a full-page banner at the beginning of the job, to make finding it in a stack of print jobs easy, or to stop printing when your job gets to the front of the line so that you can change from plain paper to preprinted invoices or checks. You handle these tricks from the standard Windows Print dialog boxes.

Adding a Network Printer

Before you can print to a network printer, you have to configure your computer to access the network printer that you want to use. From the Start menu, choose the Settings⇨Printers command to open the Printers folder. If your computer is already configured to work with a network printer, an icon for the network printer appears in the Printers folder (see the icon in the margin). You can tell a network printer from a local printer by the shape of the printer icon. Network printer icons have a pipe attached to the bottom of the printer.

If you use Windows 95 or 98 and you don't have a network printer configured for your computer, you can add one by using the Add Printer Wizard. Open the Add Printer icon in the Printers folder to start the Add Printer Wizard. When the Wizard asks whether you want to add a local or a network printer, choose network. Then, when the Wizard asks you to type the path for the network printer, click the Browse button. A dialog box similar to the one in Figure 3-2 appears, showing the computers and shared resources available on your Network Neighborhood.

Sniff around in this dialog box until you find the printer you want to use from your computer. Click this printer and then click OK to return to the Add Printer Wizard.

Next, the Wizard copies the correct printer driver for the network printer to your computer. Depending on the operating system your computer uses and the Windows version you use, you may be asked to insert your Windows CD-ROM so that Windows can locate the driver files, or you may have to insert the driver disk that came with the printer. In many cases, however, Windows copies the driver files directly from the server computer that the printer is attached to, so you won't have to bother with the Windows CD or the printer's driver disks.

Figure 3-2:
The Add
Printer
Wizard
wants to
know which
network
printer you
want to use.

Finally, the Add Printer Wizard asks for a name that you want to give to the network printer and whether you want to designate the printer as your default printer, as shown in Figure 3-3. Type a name that distinguishes the printer from other printers that you may have installed on your computer and then click Next to continue. As its final duty, the Add Printer Wizard offers to print a test page so that you can make sure the network connection and printer configuration are working properly.

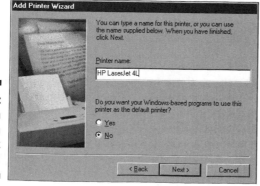

Figure 3-3:
Choosing a
name for a
network
printer.

Using a Network Printer

After the network printer is installed in Windows, printing to the network printer is a snap. You can print to the network printer from any Windows program by using the File⇔Print command to summon the Print dialog box. For example, Figure 3-4 shows the Print dialog box for WordPad, the free word processing program that comes with Windows. Near the top of this dialog box is a drop-down list entitled Name, which lists all the printers that installed on your computer. Choose the network printer from this list and then click OK to print your document. That's all there is to it!

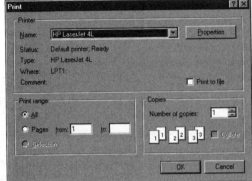

Figure 3-4:
A typical
Print
dialog box.

Playing with the Print Queue

After you send your output to a network printer, you usually don't have to worry about it. You just go to the network printer and voilà! Your output is waiting for you.

That's what happens in the ideal world. In the real world where you and I live, all sorts of things can happen to your print job between the time you send it to the network printer and the time it actually prints:

  ✔ You discover that someone else already sent a 50-trillion-page report ahead of you that isn't expected to finish printing until the national debt is completely paid off.

  ✔ The price of framis valves goes up $2 each, rendering foolish the recommendations you made in the report.

  ✔ Your boss calls and tells you that his brother-in-law will be attending the meeting, so won't you please print an extra copy of the proposal for him. Oh, and a photocopy won't do. Originals only, please.

> ✔ You decide to take lunch, so you don't want the output to print until you get back.

Fortunately, your print job isn't totally beyond your control just because you've already sent it to the network printer. You can easily change the status of jobs you've already sent. You can change the order in which jobs print, hold a job so that it won't print until you say so, or cancel a job altogether.

You can probably make your network print jobs do other tricks, too — such as shake hands, roll over, and play dead. But the basic tricks — hold, cancel, and change the print order — are enough to get you started.

Using Windows Print Queue Tricks

To play with the printer queue, choose Settings⇔Printers from the Start menu and then open the icon for the printer you want to manage. A window similar to the one shown in Figure 3-5 appears. If you happen to be Wally, you can see the bad news: Some user named Beave has slipped in a 166-page report from Microsoft Word before your little one-page memo.

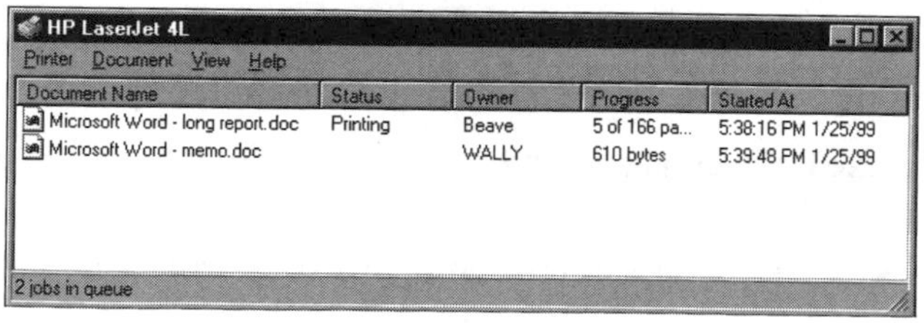

Figure 3-5:
Managing a
print queue.

Document Name	Status	Owner	Progress	Started At
Microsoft Word - long report.doc	Printing	Beave	5 of 166 pa...	5:38:16 PM 1/25/99
Microsoft Word - memo.doc		WALLY	610 bytes	5:39:48 PM 1/25/99

HP LaserJet 4L — Printer Document View Help — 2 jobs in queue

To manipulate the print jobs that appear in the print queue or the printer itself, use the following tricks:

✔ To temporarily stop a job from printing, select the job and use the Document⇔Pause Printing command. Choose the same command again to release the job.

✔ To delete a print job, select the job and choose the Document⇔ Cancel Printing command.

✔ To stop the printer, choose the Printer⇔Pause Printing command. To resume, choose the command again.

✔ To delete all print jobs, choose the Printer⇔Purge Print Documents command.

✔ To cut to the front of the line, drag the print job you want to print to the top of the list.

The best thing about Windows printer management is that it shelters you from the details of working with different network operating systems. Whether you print on a NetWare printer, a Windows NT printer, or a Windows 95 or 98 shared printer, the Printer window icon manages all print jobs the same.

What to Do When the Printer Jams

The only three sure bets in life are (1) the original *Rocky* will always be Sylvester Stallone's best movie, (2) *Star Wars* and *Star Trek* fans will never get along, and (3) the printer will always jam shortly after your job reaches the front of the queue.

What do you do when you walk in on your network printer while it's printing all 133 pages of your report on the same line?

1. **Start by yelling "Fire!"**

   No one will save you if you yell "Printer!"

2. **Find the printer's online button and press it.**

   This step takes the printer offline so that the server stops sending information to it and the printer stops. This doesn't cure anything, but it stops the noise. If you must, turn the printer off.

3. **Pull out the jammed paper and reinsert the good paper into the printer. Nicely.**

4. **If necessary, restart the job that was printing, from the beginning.**

   Depending on your printer, this step may not be necessary. Some printers resume printing automatically after you clear the jam.

5. **Press the online button so that the printer resumes printing.**

Chapter 4

Becoming a Server

• •

• •

*A*s you probably know, two types of computers exist on any network: client computers and server computers. In the economy of computer networks, client computers are the consumers — the ones who use network resources such as shared printers and disk drives. Servers are the providers — the ones who offer their own printers and disk drives to the network so that client computers can use them.

This chapter shows you how to turn your humble Windows client computer into a server computer, so that other computers on your network can use your printer and any folders that you decide you want to share. In this way, your computer functions as both a client and a server computer at the same time. It's a client computer when you send a print job to a network printer or when you access a file stored on another server's disk. It's a server computer when someone else sends a print job to your printer or accesses a file stored on your computer's disk.

Enabling File and Printer Sharing

Before you can share your files or your printer with other network users, you must set up a Windows feature known as *File and Printer Sharing*. Without this feature installed, your computer can be a network client but not a server.

If you are lucky, File and Printer Sharing is already set up on your computer. To find out, double-click My Computer on your desktop. Select the icon for your C drive and then click File in the menu bar to reveal the File menu. If the menu includes a Sharing command, File and Printer Sharing is already set up, so you can skip the rest of this section. If you can't find a Sharing command in the File menu, you have to install File and Printer Sharing before you can share a file or a printer with other network users.

To install File and Printer Sharing on your computer, follow these steps:

1. **From the Start menu, choose Settings⇨Control Panel.**

   The Control Panel comes to life.

2. **Double-click the Network icon (shown in the margin).**

   The Network dialog box appears, as shown in Figure 4-1.

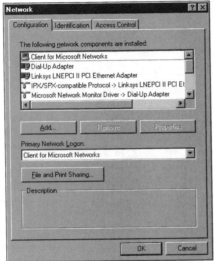

Figure 4-1:
The
Network
dialog box.

3. **Click the File and Print Sharing button.**

   This summons the File and Print Sharing dialog box, as shown in Figure 4-2.

Figure 4-2:
The File
and Print
Sharing
dialog box.

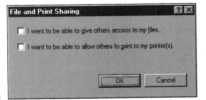

4. **Click the File and Print Sharing options you want to enable for your computer.**

   The first option enables you to share your files with other network users; the second allows you to share your printer. To share your files and your printer, check both options.

5. **Click OK to dismiss the File and Print Sharing dialog box.**

   You return to the Network dialog box.

6. **Click OK to dismiss the Network dialog box.**

   The Network dialog box vanishes, and a Copy Progress dialog box appears to let you know that Windows is copying the files required to enable File and Print Sharing. If you're prompted to insert the Windows CD-ROM, do so with a smile.

   After all the necessary files have been copied, you see a dialog box informing you that you must restart your computer for the new settings to take effect.

7. **Click Yes to restart your computer.**

   Your computer shuts down and then restarts. Your computer may take a minute or so to restart, so be patient. When your computer comes back to life, you're ready to share files or your printer.

Sharing a Disk Drive or Folder

To enable other network users to access files that reside on your hard drive, you must designate either the entire drive or a folder on the drive as a shared drive or folder. If you share an entire drive, other network users can access all the files and folders on the drive. If you share a folder, network users can access only those files that reside in the folder you share. (If the folder you share contains other folders, network users can access files in those folders, too.)

I recommend against sharing an entire disk drive, unless you want to grant everyone on the network the freedom to sneak a peek at every file on your disk. Instead, you should share just the folder or folders that contain the specific documents that you want others to be able to access. For example, if you store all your Word documents in the My Documents folder, you can share your My Documents folder so that other network users can access your Word documents.

To share a folder, follow these steps:

1. **Double-click the My Computer icon on your desktop.**

   The My Computer window comes to center stage.

2. **Select the folder you want to share.**

   Click the icon for the disk drive that contains the folder you want to share and then find the folder itself and click it.

3. Choose the File⇨Sharing command.

The Properties dialog box for the folder you want to share appears. Notice that the sharing options are grayed out as long as the Not Shared option is selected.

4. Click the Shared As option button.

After you do, the rest of the sharing options come alive, as shown in Figure 4-3.

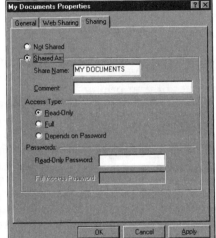

Figure 4-3:
The Sharing options come to life when you check the Shared As option.

5. Change the Share Name if you don't like the name Windows proposes.

The Share Name is the name that other network users use to access the shared folder. You can use any name you wish, but the name can be no more than 12 characters in length. Upper- and lowercase letters are treated the same in a share name, so "My Documents" is the same as "MY DOCUMENTS."

Windows proposes a share name for you based on the actual folder name. If the folder name is 12 or fewer characters, the proposed share name is the same as the folder name. But if the folder name is longer than 12 characters, Windows abbreviates it. For example, "Multimedia Files" becomes "MULTIMEDIA F."

If the name Windows chooses doesn't make sense or seems cryptic, change the share name to something better. For example, I would probably use "MEDIA FILES" instead of "MULTIMEDIA F."

6. Type a Comment for the folder if you wish.

The Comment field lets you provide more information about the shared folder.

7. **Use the Access Type settings to indicate the level of access you want to allow other users to have.**

   You have three options for the Access Type settings:

   - **Read Only:** Network users can open files in the shared folder, but they can't change, rename, delete, or create new files in the shared folder.

   - **Full:** Network users can open, modify, rename, delete, and create new files in the shared folder.

   - **Depends on Password:** You can grant some users read-only access, while users who know the right password get full access.

8. **If you want to protect the folder with a password, type the password in the password field.**

   If you selected Read Only in Step 7, you can type a password in the Read-Only Password field. Then, anyone who attempts to access the folder has to type the password before Windows allows him or her to read the files in the folder.

   If you selected Full in Step 7, you can type a password in the Full-Access Password field. Once again, Windows requires that anyone who wants to access the folder must first type in the correct password.

   If you chose Depends on Password in Step 7, you can type a password in both the Read-Only Password and Full-Access Password fields. Then, whether a user attempting to access the folder is granted read-only or full access to the folder depends on which password the user types.

9. **Click OK.**

   If you typed a password in either password field in Step 8, Windows displays the dialog box shown in Figure 4-4 so that you can confirm the passwords. Type each password again and then click OK.

Figure 4-4:
Windows
asks you to
confirm your
passwords.

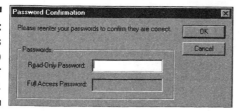

The Properties dialog box vanishes, and a hand is added to the icon for the folder to show that the folder is shared, as shown in the margin.

If you change your mind and decide you want to stop sharing a folder, double-click My Computer, select the folder or drive you want to stop sharing, and choose the File⇨Sharing command to summon the Properties dialog box. Click the Not Shared option and then click OK.

Sharing a Printer

Sharing a printer is much more traumatic than sharing a disk drive. When you share a disk drive, other network users access your files from time to time. When they do, you hear your disk click a few times, and your computer may hesitate for a half second or so. The interruptions caused by other users accessing your disk are sometimes noticeable, but rarely annoying.

But when you share a printer, your coworker down the hall is liable to send a 40-page report to your printer just moments before you try to print a one-page memo that has to be on the boss's desk in two minutes. The printer may well run out of paper or, worse yet, jam during someone else's print job — and you'll be expected to attend to the problem.

As annoying as these interruptions can be, sharing your printer makes a lot of sense in some situations. If you have the only decent printer in your office or workgroup, everyone is going to be bugging you to let them use it anyway. You may as well share the printer on the network. At least that way, they won't be lining up at your door asking you to print their documents for them.

To designate your printer as a shared printer, follow the bouncing ball through these steps:

1. **From the Start menu, choose the Settings⇨Printers command.**

   The Printers folder appears, as shown in Figure 4-5. In this example, the Printers folder lists a single printer, named HP Deskjet 855C.

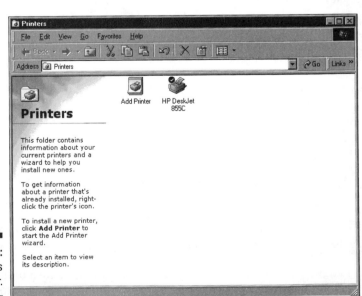

Figure 4-5:
The Printers folder.

2. **Select the printer you want to share.**

   Click the icon for the printer to select the printer.

3. **Choose the File⇨Sharing command.**

   You're right: It doesn't make sense. You're sharing a printer, not a file, but the Sharing command is found under the File menu. Go figure.

   When you choose the File⇨Sharing command, the Properties dialog box for the printer appears.

4. **Click the Shared As option button.**

   Figure 4-6 shows how the Printer Properties dialog box appears after you click the Shared As option button.

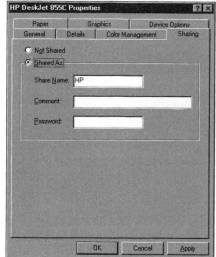

Figure 4-6:
The Properties dialog box for a shared printer.

5. **Change the Share Name if you don't like the name suggested by Windows.**

   Other computers use the share name to identify the shared printer, so choose a meaningful or descriptive name.

6. **Type a Comment for the printer if you wish.**

   The comment field lets you provide more information about the shared printer.

7. **If you want to password-protect the printer, type a password in the Password field.**

   If you leave the Password field blank, any network user can access your printer. If you type a password in the Password field, anyone who tries to access your printer is asked to enter the password.

8. Click OK.

You return to the Printers folder, where a hand is added to the printer icon, as shown in the margin, to show that the printer is now a shared network printer.

To take your shared printer off the network so that other network users can't access it, follow the above procedure through Step 3 to call up the Printer Properties dialog box. Check Not Shared instead of Shared As and then click OK. The hand disappears from the printer icon to indicate that the printer is no longer shared.

Chapter 5

Mr. McFeeley's Guide to E-Mail

● ●

In This Chapter

▶ Using e-mail

▶ Reading and sending e-mail messages

▶ Scheduling and conferencing electronically

▶ Watching smileys and e-mail etiquette

● ●

Do you often return to your office after a long lunch to find your desk covered with those little pink "While You Were Out" notes and your computer screen plastered with stick-on notes?

If so, maybe the time has come for you to bite the bullet and find out how to use your computer network's electronic mail, or *e-mail*, program. Most computer networks have one. If yours doesn't, bug the network manager until he or she gets one.

This chapter introduces you to what's possible with a good e-mail program. So many e-mail programs are available that I can't possibly show you how to use all of them, so I'm focusing on Microsoft Outlook, the e-mail program that comes with Microsoft Office. Other e-mail programs are similar.

E-Mail and Why It's So Cool

E-mail is nothing more than the computer-age equivalent of Mr. McFeeley, the postman from *Mr. Rogers' Neighborhood.* E-mail enables you to send messages to and receive messages from other users on the network. Instead of writing the messages on paper, sealing them in an envelope, and giving them to Mr. McFeeley to deliver, e-mail messages are stored on disk and electronically delivered to the appropriate user.

Sending and receiving e-mail

To send an e-mail message to another network user, you must activate the e-mail program, compose the message by using a text editor, and provide an address — usually the network user ID of the user you want the message sent to. Most e-mail programs also require that you create a short comment that identifies the subject of the message.

When you receive a message from another user, the e-mail program copies the message to your computer and displays it on-screen so you can read it. You then can delete the message, print it, save it to a disk file, or forward it to another user. You can also reply to the message by composing a new message to be sent back to the user who sent the original message.

Here are some additional thoughts about sending and receiving e-mail:

- ✔ When someone sends a message to you, most e-mail programs immediately display a message on your computer screen or make a sound to tell you to check your e-mail. If your computer isn't on the network when the message is sent, then you're notified the next time you log on to the network.

- ✔ Most e-mail packages can be set up to check for new e-mail automatically when you log on to the network.

- ✔ Besides sending text messages, most e-mail packages enable you to attach a file to your message. You can use this feature to send a word processing document, a spreadsheet, or a program file to another network user.

- ✔ Most e-mail programs enable you to keep a list of users you commonly send e-mail to in an address book. That way you don't have to retype the user ID every time.

- ✔ Most programs also enable you to address a message to more than one user — the electronic equivalent of a carbon copy. Some programs also enable you to create a list of users and assign a name to the list. Then you can send a message to each user in the list by addressing the message to the list name. For example, June may create a list including WARD, WALLY, and BEAVER, and call the list BOYS. To send e-mail to all the boys on her family network, she simply addresses the message to BOYS.

Understanding the post office

Most e-mail programs use a network server as an electronic post office where messages are stored until they can be delivered to the recipient. This post office is sometimes called a *mail server*. A network server used as a mail server doesn't have to be dedicated to that purpose, although in larger networks it sometimes is. In smaller networks, the network file server doubles as the mail server.

The following paragraphs describe some additional details you should know about the post office:

✔ Depending on the e-mail program, setting up more than one mail server on a network is possible. In that case, you must check e-mail on all the servers. If you check just one of the mail servers, you won't be notified of any e-mail that's waiting for you on the other mail servers.

✔ Disk space on a mail server is often at a premium. Be sure to delete unneeded messages as you read them.

✔ Windows 98 comes with a simple post-office program called Workgroup Postoffice for Windows 98, which you can use to set up a post office on a Windows 98 computer to provide e-mail for a small network that doesn't have a dedicated server running Windows NT Server or NetWare. Unfortunately, Workgroup Postoffice is not automatically installed when you install Windows 98. You can find the Workgroup Postoffice on the Windows 98 CD-ROM, in a folder named \tools\oldwin95\exchange. To install Workgroup Postoffice on your computer, insert the Windows 98 CD-ROM in your CD-ROM drive, open the \tools\oldwin95\exchange folder in a My Computer window, and then double-click the icons for the exupdusa.exe and wgpoupd.exe program files and follow the instructions that appear on the screen.

Microsoft Outlook

Because it comes free with Microsoft Office, Microsoft Outlook is one of the most popular programs for accessing e-mail. Although many other e-mail programs are available, most of them work much like Outlook for the basic chores of reading e-mail messages and creating messages of your own.

Windows 98 comes with a scaled-back version of Outlook called Outlook Express. Outlook Express is designed to work only with e-mail that you send and receive over the Internet, not for e-mail that you exchange with other users over a local area network. As a result, Outlook Express is generally not used as an e-mail program for network users. (However, if each network user has an Internet connection and an Internet e-mail account, Outlook Express works fine.)

The following sections describe some basic procedures for using Microsoft Outlook to send and receive e-mail.

Sending e-mail

To send an e-mail message to another network user, start Microsoft Outlook by choosing Microsoft Outlook from the Start➪Programs menu. Outlook appears in its own window, as shown in Figure 5-1.

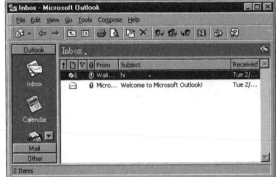

Figure 5-1:
Microsoft
Outlook.

To create a message to send to another user, click the New Mail Message button (shown in the margin). A window appears in which you may type the e-mail address of the recipient (usually the recipient's network user ID), the subject of the message, and the message itself.

Figure 5-2 shows a message composed and ready to be delivered.

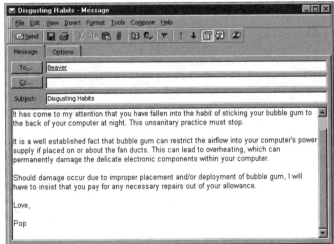

Figure 5-2:
Creating an
e-mail
message.

 After you finish typing the message, click the Send button. The message is delivered to the user listed in the To field.

Here are a few additional points about sending e-mail:

✔ The recipient must run Outlook or another e-mail program on his or her computer to check for incoming e-mail. When the recipient runs his or her e-mail program, your message is delivered.

> ✔ You can keep a personalized address list using the Address Book, which is available from the Tools menu in Outlook.
>
> ✔ You can use Outlook to send e-mail to other users of your local network and to send and receive e-mail to Internet users. However, a modem is necessary to send e-mail to an Internet e-mail address.

Reading your e-mail

To read e-mail sent to you by other users, simply start Microsoft Outlook by choosing Microsoft Outlook from the Start⇨Programs menu. After you start Outlook, the program automatically checks to see if you have any new e-mail and automatically checks for new messages on a regular basis. Any new messages you receive appear in the main Outlook window, highlighted with boldface type. In addition, Outlook plays a special sound to inform you whenever you receive new e-mail.

To read a message that has been sent to you, just double-click the message in the Outlook main window. The text of the message appears in a separate window.

After you read the message, you have several options for handling it.

 If the message is worthy of a reply, click the Reply button. A new message window appears, enabling you to compose a reply. The new message is automatically addressed to the sender of the original message, and the text of the original message is inserted at the bottom of the new message.

 If the message was addressed to more than one recipient, the Reply to All button lets you send a reply that is addressed to all the recipients listed on the original message.

 If the message was intended for someone else, or if you think that someone else should see it (maybe it contains a juicy bit of gossip), click the Forward button. A new message window appears, enabling you to type the name of the user you want the message forwarded to.

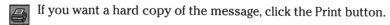 If you want a hard copy of the message, click the Print button.

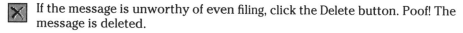 If the message is unworthy of even filing, click the Delete button. Poof! The message is deleted.

If you have more than one message waiting, you can read the next message in line by clicking the Next button.

Electronic Scheduling

Scheduling software takes advantage of the communication features of e-mail to enable you to schedule meetings with other network users. You tell the scheduling program the people you want at the meeting, as well as when and where you want the meeting to occur. The program takes your information and checks the people's schedules to see whether they can make the meeting. If so, the scheduling program notifies everyone of the meeting by sending an e-mail note. If not, the scheduling program suggests an alternate meeting time.

Outlook includes an excellent group scheduling function that makes it easy to schedule meetings. Here are a few final points on scheduling software:

- ✔ Most scheduling programs keep track of room usage so that they don't schedule two meetings at the same place and time.

- ✔ For scheduling software to work, everyone must use it religiously. If Bob forgets to tell the scheduling program about his Friday golf match, the program may well schedule a meeting for him on Friday morning.

- ✔ Scheduling software is most appropriate for large offices. Purchasing and maintaining the software for an office of three isn't worth the money.

Electronic Conferencing

Windows 98 comes with a nifty program called NetMeeting, which enables you to hold online meetings with two or more participants. NetMeeting sports the following features for online conferencing:

- ✔ **Chat:** Two or more users can type messages to one another. Unlike e-mail messages, any chat message you type appears immediately on the other users' computers.

- ✔ **Whiteboard:** This is a drawing area in which all participants in a conference can doodle, much like a networked version of Windows Paint.

- ✔ **File transfer:** You can send files to other NetMeeting users.

- ✔ **Application sharing:** Other NetMeeting users can see on their screens an application that you're running on your computer. You can also share applications so that several NetMeeting users can work together on a single document over the Internet.

- ✔ **Voice conference:** If your computer is equipped with a sound card and microphone, you can have a voice conference with another user whose computer also has a sound card and microphone.

- ✔ **Video conference:** Similarly, if you have attached a video camera to your computer, you can engage in a video conference with other NetMeeting users who also have video cameras on their computers.

E-Mail Etiquette

Communicating with someone via e-mail is different from talking with that person face-to-face or over the telephone. You need to be aware of these differences, or you may end up insulting someone without meaning to. Of course, if you do mean to insult someone, pay no attention to this section.

The following paragraphs summarize the salient points of e-mail etiquette:

- Always remember that e-mail isn't as private as you'd like it to be. It's not that difficult for someone to electronically steam open your e-mail and read it. Be careful what you say, to whom you say it, and about whom you say it.

- Don't forget that all the rules of social etiquette and office decorum apply to e-mail, too. If you wouldn't pick up the phone and call the CEO of the company, don't send him or her e-mail, either.

- When you reply to someone else's e-mail, keep in mind that the person you're replying to may not remember the details of the message he or she sent to you. Providing some context for your reply is polite. Most e-mail systems (including Outlook) do this for you by automatically tacking on the original message at the end of the reply. If yours doesn't, be sure to provide some context — such as including a relevant snippet of the original message in quotation marks — so that the recipient knows what you're talking about.

- E-mail doesn't have the advantage of voice inflections. This limitation can lead to all kinds of misunderstandings. You have to be careful that people know when you're joking and when you mean it. E-mail nerds have developed a peculiar way to convey tone of voice: They string together symbols on the computer keyboard to create smileys. Table 5-1 shows some of the more commonly used (or abused) smileys.

Table 5-1	Commonly Used and Abused Smileys
Smiley	*What It Means*
:-)	Just kidding
;-)	Wink
:-(	Bummer
:-0	Well, I never!
:-x	My lips are sealed.

✔ If you don't get it, tilt your head to the left and look at the smiley sideways.

✔ E-mail nerds also like to use shorthand abbreviations for common words and phrases, like FYI for "For Your Information" and ASAP for "As Soon As Possible." Table 5-2 lists the more common ones.

Table 5-2	Common E-Mail Abbreviations
Abbreviation	*What It Stands For*
BTW	By The Way
FWIW	For What It's Worth
IMO	In My Opinion
IMHO	In My Humble Opinion
IOW	In Other Words
PMJI	Pardon Me for Jumping In
ROFL	Rolling On the Floor, Laughing
ROFL,PP	Rolling On the Floor Laughing, Peeing my Pants
TIA	Thanks In Advance
TTFN	Ta Ta For Now (quoting Tigger)
TTYL	Talk To You Later
<g>	Grin
<bg>	Big Grin
<vbg>	Very Big Grin

✔ Note that the abbreviations referring to gestures or facial expressions are typed between a less-than sign and a greater-than sign: <g>. Other gestures are spelled out, like <sniff>, <groan>, or <sigh>.

✔ You're not able to italicize or underline text on many e-mail programs (although you can in Exchange, Outlook, or Outlook Express). Type an asterisk before and after a word you *wish* you could italicize. Type an underscore _before_ and _after_ a word you'd like to underline.

✔ Be aware that if you do use italic, underlining, or other formatting features that are available in Exchange, Outlook, or Outlook Express, the person receiving your mail may not be able to see the formatting if they use a different e-mail program.

✔ Capital letters are the electronic equivalent of SHOUTING. TYPING AN ENTIRE MESSAGE IN CAPITAL LETTERS CAN BE VERY ANNOYING AND CAN CAUSE YOU TO GET THE ELECTRONIC EQUIVALENT OF LARYNGITIS.

Chapter 6

Help! The Network's Down!

• •

• •

*F*ace it: Networks are prone to break.

They have too many "C" parts. Cables. Connectors. Concentrators. Cards. All these parts must be held together in a delicate balance; the network equilibrium is all-too-easy to disturb. Even the best-designed computer networks sometimes act as if they're held together with baling wire and chewing gum.

To make matters worse, networks breed suspicion. After your computer is attached to a network, you're tempted to blame the network every time something goes wrong, regardless of whether the problem has anything to do with the network. Can't get columns to line up in a Word document? Must be the network. Your spreadsheet doesn't add up? The @#$% network's acting up again.

This chapter doesn't begin to cover everything that can go wrong with a computer network. If it did, you'd take this book back and demand a refund after you got about 40 pages into "Things that can go wrong with IPX.COM."

Instead, this chapter focuses on the most common things that can go wrong with a network that an ordinary network user (that's you) can fix. And best of all, you're pointed in the right direction when you come up against a problem that you can't fix yourself.

When Bad Things Happen to Good Computers

What do you do when your computer goes on the blink? Here are some general ideas for finding out what the problem really is and deciding whether you can fix it yourself. I explain each suggestion in detail later in the chapter:

1. **Make sure that your computer and everything attached to it is plugged in.**

   Computer geeks love it when a user calls for help and they get to tell the user that the computer isn't plugged in. They write it down in their geek logs so that they can tell their geek friends about it later. They may even want to take your picture so that they can show it to their geek friends. (Most "accidents" involving computer geeks are a direct result of this kind of behavior.)

2. **Make sure that your computer is properly connected to the network.**

3. **Note any error messages that appear on the screen.**

4. **Try the built-in Windows network troubleshooter.**

5. **Do a little experimenting to find out whether the problem is indeed a network problem or a problem with just your computer.**

6. **Try restarting your computer.**

7. **Try restarting the entire network.**

8. **If none of these steps corrects the problem, scream for help.**

   Have a suitable bribe prepared to encourage your network guru to work quickly. (You can find a handy list of suitable bribes at the end of this chapter.)

My Computer's Dead!

If your computer seems totally dead, here are some things to check:

- Is it plugged in?

- If your computer is plugged into a surge protector or a power strip, make sure that the surge protector or power strip is plugged in and turned on. If the surge protector or power strip has a light, it should be glowing.

- Make sure that the computer's On/Off switch is turned on. This sounds too basic to include even here, but many computers are set up so that the computer's actual power switch is always left in the "On" position and the computer is turned on or off by means of the switch on the surge protector or power strip. Many computer users are surprised to find out that their computers have On/Off switches on the back of the cases.

✔ If you think your computer isn't plugged in but it looks like it is, listen for the fan. If the fan is turning, the computer is getting power and the problem is more serious than an unplugged power cord. (If the fan isn't running, but the computer is plugged in and power is on, the fan may be out to lunch.)

✔ If the computer is plugged in, turned on, and still not running, plug a lamp into the outlet to make sure that power is getting to the outlet. You may need to reset a tripped circuit breaker.

✔ The monitor has a separate power cord and switch. Make sure that the monitor is plugged in and turned on. (The monitor actually has two cables that must be plugged in. One runs from the back of the monitor to the back of the computer; the other is a power cord that comes from the back of the monitor and must plug into an electrical outlet.)

✔ Your keyboard, monitor, mouse, and printer are all connected to the back of the computer by cables. Make sure that these cables are all plugged in securely.

✔ Make sure that the other ends of the monitor and printer cables are plugged in properly, too.

✔ Most monitors have knobs that you can use to adjust the contrast and brightness of the monitor's display. If the computer is running but your display is dark, try adjusting these knobs. They may have been turned all the way down.

Ways to Check Your Network Connection

Network gurus often say that 95 percent of all network problems are cable problems. The cable that connects your computer to the rest of the network is a finicky beast. It can break at a moment's notice, and by "break," I don't necessarily mean "physically break in two." Sure, sometimes the problem with the cable is that Eddie Haskell got to it with pruning shears. But cable problems aren't usually visible to the naked eye.

✔ If your network uses twisted-pair cable (the cable that looks something like phone wire and is sometimes called "10baseT" cable), you can quickly tell whether the cable connection to the network is good by looking at the back of your computer. A small light is near where the cable plugs in. If this light is glowing steadily, the cable is good. If the light is dark or if it's flashing intermittently, you have a cable problem.

If the light is not glowing steadily, try removing the cable from your computer and reinserting it. This action may cure the weak connection.

✔ Detecting a cable problem in a network that's wired with coax cable, the kind that looks like cable-TV cable, is more difficult. The connector on the back of the computer forms a T. The base end of the T plugs into your computer. One or two coax cables plug into the outer ends of the T. If you use only one coax cable, you must use a special plug called a *terminator* in place of a cable at the other end of the T. If you can't find a terminator, try conjuring one up from the twenty-first century. ***Warning:*** Do not do this if your name happens to be Sarah Connor.

Don't unplug a coax cable from the network while the network is running. Data travels around a coax network the way the baton travels around the track in a relay race. If one person drops it, the race is over. The baton never gets to the next person. Likewise, if you unplug the network cable from your computer, the network data never gets to the computers that are "down the line" from your computer. (Well, actually, Ethernet — see Chapter 10 — isn't dumb enough to throw in the towel at the first sign of a cable break. You can disconnect the cable for a few seconds without permanently scattering network messages across the galaxy, and you can disconnect the T connector itself from the network card so long as you don't disconnect the cables from the T connector. But don't attempt either unless you have a good reason and a really good bribe for the network manager, who is sure to find out that you've been playing with the cables.)

✔ Some networks are wired so that your computer is connected to the network with a short (six feet or so) patch cable. One end of the patch cable plugs into your computer, and the other end plugs into a cable connector mounted on the wall. Try quickly disconnecting and reconnecting the patch cable. If that doesn't do the trick, try to find a spare patch cable that you can use.

If you can't find a spare patch cable, try borrowing a fellow network user's patch cable. If the problem goes away when you use your neighbor's patch cable, you can assume that yours has gone south and needs to be replaced.

✔ If you come in late at night while no one is around, you can swap your bad patch cable with someone else's good cable, and no one will ever know. The next day, that neighbor will want to borrow this book from you so that he or she can find out what's wrong with the network. The day after that, someone else will need the book. You may never get your book back. You'd better buy a copy for everyone now.

Notice: Neither the author nor the publisher endorses such selfish behavior. We mention it here only so that you'll know what happened when one day someone down the hall has a network problem, and you suddenly have a network problem the next day.

✔ In some networks, computers are connected to one another via a small box called a *concentrator,* or *hub.* The concentrator is prone to cable problems, too — especially those concentrators that are wired in a "professional manner" involving a rat's nest of patch cables. Don't touch the rat's nest. Leave problems with the rat's nest to the rat — er, that is, the network guru.

A Bunch of Error Messages Flew By!

Did you notice any error messages on your computer screen when you started your computer? If so, write them down. They are invaluable clues that can help the network guru solve the problem.

If you see error messages when you start up your computer, keep the following points in mind:

- ✔ Don't panic if you see lots of error messages fly by. Sometimes a simple problem that's easy to correct can cause a plethora of error messages when you start your computer. The messages may look as if your computer is falling to pieces, but the fix may be very simple.

- ✔ If the messages fly by so fast that you can't see them, press your computer's Pause key. Your computer comes to a screeching halt, giving you a chance to catch up on your error-message reading. After you've read enough, press the Pause key again to get things moving. (On some computers, the Pause key is labeled "Hold." On computers that don't have a Pause key, pressing Ctrl+Num Lock or Ctrl+S does the same thing.)

- ✔ If you missed the error messages the first time, restart your computer and watch them again.

- ✔ Better yet, press F8 when you see the message `Starting MS-DOS` or `Starting Windows`. This processes each line of your CONFIG.SYS and AUTOEXEC.BAT files separately, enabling you to see the messages displayed by each command before proceeding to the next command.

The Windows 98 Networking Troubleshooter

Windows 98 comes with a built-in troubleshooter that can often help you pin down the cause of a network problem. To use it, click the Start button and then choose Help. Click Troubleshooting and then click Windows 98 Troubleshooters. Finally, click Networking to start the networking troubleshooter as shown in Figure 6-1. Answer the questions asked by the troubleshooter and click Next to move from screen to screen. The networking troubleshooter can't solve all networking problems, but it does point out the causes of the most common problems.

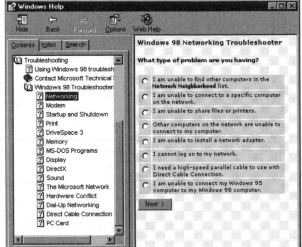

Figure 6-1:
The
Windows 98
Networking
Trouble-
shooter.

Time to Experiment

If you can't find some obvious explanation for your troubles — like the computer's unplugged — you need to do a little experimenting to narrow down the possibilities. Design your experiments to answer one basic question: Is this a network problem or a local computer problem?

Here are some ways you can narrow down the cause of the problem:

- ✓ Try performing the same operation on someone else's computer. If no one on the network can access a network drive or printer, something is probably wrong with the network. On the other hand, if you're the only one having trouble, the problem is with your computer alone. Your computer may not be reliably talking to the network or configured properly for the network, or the problem may have nothing to do with the network at all.

- ✓ If you're able to perform the operation on someone else's computer without problems, try logging on to the network with someone else's computer but using your own user ID. Then see whether you can perform the operation without error. If you can, the problem is probably on your computer rather than on the server computer. Your network guru will want to know.

- ✓ Try the operation without using the network. Log off the network by using the Start⇨Logoff command. Then try the operation again.

  If the symptoms of the problem remain the same whether your computer is logged on to the network or not, the problem is probably not with the network.

✔ What if you simply can't perform the operation without the network? For example, what if the data files are on a network drive? Try copying the files to your local drive. Then log off the network and try the operation again, this time using the files on your local drive.

How to Restart Your Computer

Sometimes trouble gets your computer so tied up in knots that the only thing to do is reboot. In some cases, your computer just starts acting weird. Strange characters appear on the screen, or Windows goes haywire and won't let you exit a program. Sometimes your computer gets so confused that it can't even move. It just sits there, like a deer staring at oncoming headlights. It won't move, no matter how hard you press the Esc key or the Enter key.

When your computer starts acting like this, you need to reboot. To restart your computer, follow these steps:

1. **Save your work if you can.**

   Use the File⇨Save command, if you can, to save any documents or files you were editing when things started to go haywire. If you can't use the menus, try clicking the Save button in the toolbar. If that doesn't work, try pressing Ctrl+S — the standard keyboard shortcut for the Save command.

2. **Close any running programs if you can.**

   Use the File⇨Exit command or click the Close button in the upper-right corner of the program window. Or press Alt+F4.

3. **Choose the Start⇨Shut Down command from the taskbar.**

   The Shut Down Windows dialog box appears.

4. **Select the Restart option and then click OK.**

   Your computer restarts itself.

If restarting your computer doesn't seem to fix the problem, you may need to turn your computer all the way off and then turn it on again. To do so, follow the previous procedure until Step 4. Choose the Shut Down option instead of the Restart option and then click OK. Depending on your computer, Windows either turns off your computer or displays a message that says `It is now safe to turn off your computer.` If Windows doesn't turn the computer off for you, flip the On/Off switch to turn your computer off. Wait a few seconds and then turn the computer back on.

Here are a few things to try if you have trouble restarting your computer:

- ✔ If your computer refuses to respond to the Start⇨Shut Down command, try pressing the Ctrl, Alt, and Del keys at the same time. This is called the "three-finger salute." It's appropriate to say "Queueue" as you do it.

    When you press Ctrl+Alt+Del, Windows 95 or 98 displays a dialog box that enables you to close any running programs or shut down your computer entirely. In Windows 3.1, Windows for Workgroups, or plain old MS-DOS, pressing Ctrl+Alt+Del automatically restarts your computer.

- ✔ If Ctrl+Alt+Del doesn't do anything, you've reached the last resort. The only thing left to do is press the button labeled Reset on your computer.

- ✔ Pressing the Reset button (or in Windows 3.1, Windows for Workgroups, or MS-DOS, pressing Ctrl+Alt+Del) is a drastic action that you should take only after your computer becomes completely unresponsive. Any work you haven't yet saved to disk is lost. (Sniff.) (If your computer doesn't have a Reset button, turn the computer off, wait a few moments, then turn the computer back on again.)

- ✔ If at all possible, save your work before restarting your computer. Any work you haven't saved is lost. Unfortunately, if your computer is totally tied up in knots, you probably can't save your work. In that case, you have no choice but to jump off the digital cliff.

How to Restart the Network

If you think the network is causing your trouble, you can restart the network to see whether the problem goes away.

Restarting a NetWare or Windows NT server is not a good idea unless your network administrator has shown you how to do it and has given you permission to do so. If you don't know what you're doing, you may not be able to get the server running again. In that case, you have to tuck your tail between your legs, call the network administrator, and apologize profusely for messing with the network when you know you shouldn't have.

Here is the basic procedure for restarting a network. Keep in mind that for NetWare or Windows NT servers, you may need to take additional steps to get things going again. Check with your network administrator to be sure.

1. **Have all users log off the network and turn off their computers.**

2. **After you're sure the users have logged off the network and shut down their computers, shut down the network server (assuming you have a dedicated server).**

You want to do this behaving as a good citizen if possible, decently and in order. If you use Novell NetWare, type DOWN at the server's keyboard and then reboot the server. For Windows NT Server, use the Start⇨ Shut Down command.

3. **Reboot the server computer or turn it off and then on again. Watch the server start up to make sure that no error messages appear.**

4. **Turn on each computer one at a time, making sure that each computer starts up without error.**

Remember the following when you consider restarting the network:

✔ Restarting the network is even more drastic than restarting your individual computer. Make sure that everyone saves his or her work and logs off the network before you do it! You can cause major problems if you blindly turn off the server computer while users are logged on.

✔ Obviously, restarting the network is a major inconvenience to every network user. Better offer treats.

✔ Restarting the network is a job for the network guru. Don't do it yourself unless the network guru isn't around, and even then, do it only after asking his or her permission in writing, preferably in triplicate.

The Care and Feeding of Your Network Guru

Your most valuable asset when something goes wrong with the network is your network guru. If you're careful to stay on good terms with your guru, you're way ahead of the game when you need his or her help.

Make an effort to solve the problem yourself before calling in the cavalry. Check the network connection. Try rebooting. Try using someone else's computer. The more information you can provide the guru, the more appreciation you get.

Be polite, but assertively tell your guru what the problem is, what you tried to do to fix it, and what you think may be causing the problem (if you have a clue). Say something like this:

"Hi, Joe. I've got a problem with the network: I can't log in from my computer. I tried a few things to try to figure out the problem. I was able to log in from Wally's computer using my user ID, so I think the problem may be just with my computer.

"To be sure, I checked some other things. The green light on the back of my computer where the network cable plugs in is glowing, so I don't think it's a cable problem. I also rebooted my computer, but I still couldn't log on. Then I had everyone log off, and I restarted the server, but still no luck. My guess is that something may be wrong with my computer's network driver."

Blow into your guru's ear like that, and he or she will follow you anywhere. (Of course, that may be an undesirable result.)

Here are a few other ways you can be nice to your computer guru, if you are so inclined:

- Always remember your manners. No one likes to be yelled at, and even computer geeks have feelings (believe it or not). Be polite to your network guru, even if you're mad or you think the problem's his or her fault. This suggestion may sound obvious, but you want your guru to like you.

- Don't call your guru every time the slightest little thing goes wrong. Computer experts hate explaining that the reason the computer is only printing in capital letters is that you pressed the Caps Lock key.

- Read the manual. It probably won't help, but at least your guru thinks you tried. Gurus like that.

- Humor your network guru when he or she tries to explain what's going on. Nod attentively when she describes what the bindery is or when he says something is wrong with the File Allocation Table. Smile appreciatively when she tries to simplify the explanation by using a colorful metaphor. Wink when he thinks you understand.

- Mimick your guru's own sense of humor, if you can. For example, most computer geeks like the old *Saturday Night Live* routine with the copier guy. So say something like, "It's Joe, fixin' the network. Crimpin' the cable. Jumpin' Joe, the Net-o-Rama, rentin' an apartment at eight oh two dot three Ethernet Lane. Captain Joe of the Good Ship NetWare, goin' down with the server." Don't worry if it's not funny. He'll think it is.

Computer Bribes for Serious Network Trouble

A *...For Dummies* book wouldn't be complete without a bribe list. You probably know already about the common foodstuffs most computer gurus respond to: Cheetos, Doritos, Jolt Cola, Diet Coke (I wish they made Diet Jolt — twice the caffeine, twice the NutraSweet), Twinkies, and so on.

Bribes of this sort are suitable for small favors. But if you're having a serious problem with your network, you may need to lay it on a bit thicker. More serious bribes include the following:

- Computer games, especially 3-D shoot-em-ups such as Quake.

- Videotapes of any Pink Panther, Monty Python, or Mel Brooks movie.

- T-shirts with strange stuff written on them or T-shirts from computer companies.

- *Star Trek* paraphernalia. A high percentage of computer gurus are also Trekkies, or as they sometimes prefer to be called, Trekkers. Most of them like the original *Star Trek, The Next Generation,* and *Deep Space Nine.* Most don't care for *Voyager.*

If you want to really impress a guru, use the three-letter acronyms for each series: *TOS* for The Original Series, *TNG* for *The Next Generation,* and *DS9* for *Deep Space Nine. (VOY* is for *Voyager,* but since nobody likes *Voyager,* it doesn't matter.)

- Digitized sounds. You can never have enough digitized sounds. Anything from a Pink Panther movie ("Does your dog bite?"), *Saturday Night Live* ("All right, have a beer, make some copies, havin' a party!"), or *Home Improvement* ("Say, Al, do you suppose they call these coping saws because they're good at handling stress?") will do. Clips from a favorite *Star Trek* show are good bribes, too.

Don't give your guru a digitized recording of the famous "I've fallen and I can't get up" line. He or she already has five of those.

You can find an ample supply of digitized sounds on the Internet. If you don't have access to the Internet, getting it may be worth the cost just for the constant supply of bribes these files can provide.

Part II
Building Your Own Network

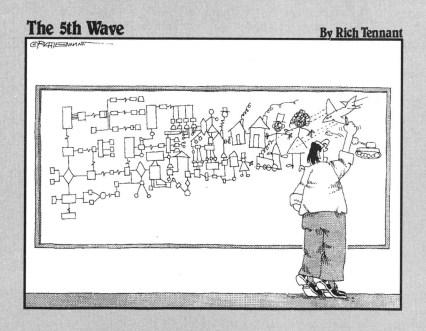

In this part . . .

You discover how to build a network yourself, which includes planning it and installing it. You find out what choices are available for cable types, network operating systems, and all the other bits and pieces that you have to contend with.

Yes, some technical information is included in these chapters. But fear not! I bring you tidings of great joy! Lo, a working network is at hand, and you, yea even you, can design it and install it yourself.

Chapter 7

The Bad News: You Have to Plan Ahead

*O*kay, so you're convinced you need to network your computers. What now? Do you stop by Computers-R-Us on the way to work, install the network before morning coffee, and expect the network to be fully operational by noon?

I don't think so.

Networking your computers is just like any other worthwhile endeavor: To do it right requires a bit of planning. This chapter helps you think through your network before you start spending money. It shows you how to come up with a networking plan that's every bit as good as the plan a network consultant would charge you $1,000 for. See? This book is already saving you money!

Making a Network Plan

If you pay a consultant or a company that specializes in network design to study your business and prepare a networking plan, the result is a 500-page proposal with the sole purpose, aside from impressing you with bulk, of preventing you from understanding just exactly what the consultant is proposing.

Truth is, you don't have to be a computer science major to make a good network plan. Despite what computer consultants want you to think, designing a small computer network isn't rocket science. You can do it yourself. Just follow these simple guidelines:

- ✔ Don't rush through the planning phase. The most costly networking mistakes are the ones you make before you put the network in. Think things through and consider alternatives.

- ✔ Write down the network plan. The plan doesn't have to be a fancy, 500-page document. (If you want to make it look good, pick up a ½-inch, three-ring binder. The binder is big enough to hold your network plan with room to spare.)

- ✔ Ask someone else to read your network plan before you buy anything, preferably someone who knows more about computers than you do.

Taking Stock

One of the most challenging parts of planning a network is figuring out how to work with the computers you already have. In other words, how do you get there from here? Before you can plan how to get "there," you have to know what "here" is. In other words, you have to take a thorough inventory of your current computers.

What you need to know

You need to know the following information about each of your computers:

- ✔ **The processor type and, if possible, its clock speed.** Hope that all your computers are 200 MHz Pentiums or better. But in most cases, you find a mixture of Pentium and 486 processors with perhaps even some archaic 386, 286, and (heaven forbid) 8088 processors, with clock speeds ranging anywhere from 25 MHz to 200 MHz.

  You can't usually tell what kind of processor a computer has just by looking at the computer's case. Most computers, however, display the processor type when you turn them on or reboot them by pressing Ctrl+Alt+Del. If the information on the startup screen scrolls away too quickly for you to read it, try pressing the Pause key to freeze the information. When you finish reading it, press the Pause key again so that your computer can continue booting.

- ✔ **The size of the hard disk and the arrangement of its partitions.** Some really old computers have a 40MB hard disk divided into two partitions, so that the partitions appear to be two separate hard disks. That's okay, as long as you know how the partitions are set up.

On a Windows 95 or 98 computer, you can find out the size of a hard disk by opening the My Computer window, right-clicking the drive icon, and choosing the Properties command from the shortcut menu that appears. Figure 7-1 shows the Properties dialog box for a 1.99GB disk drive that has 431MB of free space.

If your computer runs MS-DOS (with or without Windows), you can use the CHKDSK command to display the size of your disk drives and the amount of free space.

Figure 7-1:
The Properties dialog box for a disk drive shows the drive's total capacity and the amount of free space available on the drive.

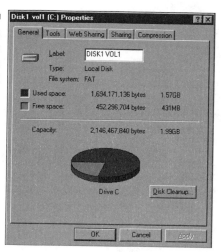

The amount of memory. In Windows, you can find out this information easily enough by right-clicking the My Computer desktop icon and choosing the Properties command. The amount of memory on your computer appears in the resulting dialog box. For example, Figure 7-2 shows the System Properties dialog box for a computer running Windows 98 with 64MB of RAM.

If you're working with an older DOS-based computer, you have to fuss with two different kinds of memory: conventional and extended. Use the CHKDSK command to find out how much conventional memory a computer has. If you have DOS Version 4.0 or later, you can type MEM to find out how much extended memory you have.

Some ancient 8088 or 286 computers have an antiquated type of memory known as *expanded memory.* Expanded memory doesn't affect the network much, so don't worry about it.

The operating system version. If you are running Windows 95 or 98, you can determine the version by checking the System Properties dialog box. For example, Figure 7-2 shows the System Properties dialog box for a Windows 98 computer. The actual Windows version for this computer is 4.10.1998.

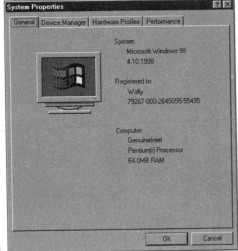

Figure 7-2:
Finding
out what
version of
Windows
you have.

For an older, DOS-based computer, you can determine the DOS version by typing the VER command at a DOS prompt. If any of your computers are running a DOS version lower than 3.3, you should upgrade them: DOS versions older than 3.3 have poor network support.

In Windows 3.x, you can determine the Windows version by choosing the Help⇨About command from Program Manager.

Once upon a time, Microsoft offered a networked version of its original Windows operating system, known as Windows for Workgroups. Windows for Workgroups was sophisticated for its time, but if you still have any computers running Windows for Workgroups, you really should upgrade them to Windows 98 before you put in a network or expand an existing network. Networking with Windows 98 is much easier than with Windows for Workgroups.

✔ **What kind of printer, if any, is attached to the computer.**

✔ **What software is used on the computer.** Microsoft Office? WordPerfect? Lotus 1-2-3? Make a complete list, including version numbers.

Programs that gather information for you

Gathering information about your computers is a lot of work if you have more than a few computers to network. Fortunately, several available software programs can automatically gather the information for you. These programs inspect various aspects of a computer, such as the CPU type and speed, amount of RAM, and the size of the computer's disk drives. Then they show the information on the screen and give you the option of saving the information to a disk file or printing it.

Windows 98 comes with just such a program, called Microsoft System Information. Microsoft System Information gathers and prints information about your computer. You can start Microsoft System Information by choosing Start⇨Programs⇨Accessories⇨System Tools⇨System Information.

When you fire up Microsoft System Information, you see a window similar to the one shown in Figure 7-3. Initially, Microsoft System Information displays basic information about your computer, such as the version of Microsoft Windows you use, the processor type, the amount of memory on the computer, and the free space on each of the computer's disk drives. You can obtain information that is more detailed by clicking Hardware Resources, Components, Software Environment, and Applications in the left side of the window.

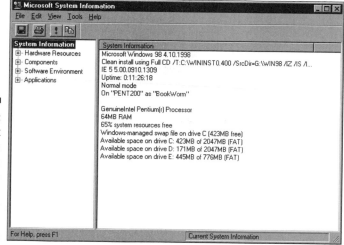

Figure 7-3:
Microsoft
System
Information
displays
information
about your
computer.

If you don't have Windows 98, don't panic. You may have an older version of Microsoft System Information anyway: Microsoft included it free with Office 95 and 97. To start Microsoft System Information from any of the Office programs (Word, Excel, or PowerPoint), choose the Help⇨About command. When the About dialog box appears, click the System Info button.

MS-DOS 6 (including 6.0, 6.2, and 6.22) includes a similar program called *MSD*, which stands for *Microsoft Diagnostics*. To run it, just type **MSD** at a DOS command prompt and press Enter.

Considering Why You Need a Network, Anyway

An important step in planning your network is making sure that you understand why you want the network in the first place. Here are some of the more common reasons for needing a network, all of them quite valid:

- ✔ My coworker and I exchange files using a floppy disk just about every day. With a network, we could trade files without using the floppies.

- ✔ I don't want to buy everyone a laser printer when I know the one we have now just sits there taking up space most of the day. Wouldn't buying a network be better than buying a laser printer for every computer?

- ✔ Someone figured out that we're destroying seven trees a day by printing interoffice memos on real paper, so we want to save the rain forest by setting up an e-mail system.

- ✔ Business is so good that one person typing in orders eight hours each day can't keep up. With a network, I can have two people entering orders, and I won't have to pay either one overtime.

- ✔ My brother-in-law just put in a network at his office, and I don't want him to think I'm behind the times.

Make sure that you identify all the reasons you think you need a network and write them down. Don't worry about winning the Pulitzer Prize for your stunning prose. Just make sure that you write down what you expect a network to do for you.

If you were making a 500-page networking proposal, you'd place the description of why a network is needed in a tabbed section labeled "Justification." In your ½-inch network binder, file the description under "Why."

As you consider the reasons you need a network, you may conclude that you don't need a network after all. That's okay. You can always use the binder for your stamp collection.

Making Three Basic Network Decisions That You Can't Avoid

When you plan a computer network, you're confronted with three inescapable network decisions. You can't install the network until you make these decisions. The decisions are weighty enough that I devote a separate section in this chapter to each one.

Stupid stuff about printer switches

If your only reason for networking is to share a printer, a cheaper way may exist: Buy a switch box instead of a network. Switch boxes let two or more computers share a single printer. Instead of running a cable directly from computer to printer, you run cables from each computer to the switch box and then run one cable from the switch box to the printer. Only one of the computers has access to the printer at a time; the switch decides which one.

You can find two kinds of printer switches:

Manual printer switches have a knob on the front that enables you to select which computer is connected to the printer. When you use a manual switch, you first must make sure that the knob is set to your computer before you try to print. Turning the knob while someone else is printing probably will cost you a bag of doughnuts.

Automatic printer switches have a built-in electronic ear that listens to each computer. When it hears one of the computers trying to talk to the printer, the electronic ear automatically connects that computer to the printer. The switch also has an electronic holding pen called a *buffer* that can hold printer output from one computer if another computer is using the printer. Automatic switches aren't foolproof, but they work most of the time.

Naturally, a good automatic switch costs more than a manual switch. For example, a manual switch that can enable four computers to share one printer costs about $20. A decent automatic switch to enable four computers to share a printer can set you back about $75. Still, that's a lot cheaper and easier to set up than a full-blown network.

I haven't introduced a new TLA (three-letter acronym) in a while, so I call these basic network decisions BNDs, which stands for — you guessed it — "basic network decisions."

BND 1: What network operating system will you use?

You have many network operating systems from which to choose, but from a practical point of view, your choices are limited to the following:

- ✔ Novell NetWare, the most popular network operating system for large networks. NetWare requires that you dedicate at least one computer to act as a network server, and it can be a challenge for a novice user to install. With NetWare, the client computers can run DOS or any version of Windows. Plus, you can easily connect Macintosh computers to a NetWare network.

- ✔ Windows NT Server, a special version of Windows that, like NetWare, requires that you dedicate one or more computers to act as network servers. Windows NT Server is best used when all the client computers run some version of Windows — preferably Windows 95 or 98. However, you can make Windows NT Server work with DOS and Macintosh client computers.

✔ If you don't want to dedicate a computer to function as a server, you can build the entire network using Windows 95 or 98 on your client computers.

✔ If you want to build a simple peer-to-peer network, but the networking features of Windows aren't enough for you, consider using Artisoft's LANtastic. LANtastic offers many peer-to-peer networking features that Windows doesn't provide, such as sharing modems and fax machines. In addition, LANtastic does a better job of welcoming older DOS-based computers into your network than Windows networking does.

✔ You can start with a simple peer-to-peer network using Windows 95 or 98 now and then upgrade to NetWare or Windows NT Server later. All the networks listed in this section use the same cable, network interface cards, hubs, and so on. Changing from one to another is a matter of reconfiguring the software. (Of course, to change from a peer-to-peer network to NetWare or Windows NT Server, you must have a dedicated server computer.)

✔ You can also build a peer-to-peer network using Windows 95 or 98 and then upgrade to LANtastic later. If all your computers run Windows 95 or 98, I recommend this approach. After all, in Windows, you already have all the software you need to get a network up and running. Spend your time and money getting the network interface cards and cables working. Then you can add LANtastic later if you find that Windows networking isn't enough for your needs.

✔ Chapter 8 describes the advantages and disadvantages of each of these systems so that you can decide which is the best choice for your network.

BND 2: What arrangement of server computers will you use?

A peer-to-peer network built with Windows 95 or 98 does not require you to use dedicated server computers. This doesn't mean that dedicated server computers can and should be used only with NetWare or Windows NT Server. On the contrary, if you can possibly afford it, a dedicated server computer is almost always the way to go, no matter what network operating system you use.

✔ Using a dedicated server computer even on a peer-to-peer network makes the network faster, easier to work with, and more reliable. Consider what happens when the user of a server computer doubling as a workstation decides to turn the computer off, not realizing that someone else is accessing files on his or her disk drive.

- You don't necessarily have to use your biggest and fastest computer as your server computer. I've seen networks where the slowest computer on the network is the server. This is especially true when the server is used mostly to share a printer.

- When you plan your server configuration, you must also plan how your data and program files will be dispersed on the network. For example, will all users have copies of Microsoft Office on their local drives, or will one copy of Office be stored on the server drive? (Within the limits of your software license, of course.)

- Planning your server configuration also means assigning network drive letters for computers requiring you to map drive letters to network drives. Be consistent about this so that a particular network drive is accessed by using the same drive letter from every computer.

- Server configuration is heady enough to merit its own chapter: Chapter 9.

BND 3: How will you cable the network?

The third basic networking decision is how to connect your computers.

- You must choose between two basic types of network cabling: Twisted-pair cable (called UTP or 10baseT) and standard coax cable (called thinnet). Each has advantages and disadvantages, and using a mixture of both is possible and sometimes desirable. (For information about the differences between these two types of cables, refer to Chapter 1.)

- You must also pick the network interface cards to install in each computer. Using the same card in each computer is best, although you can also mix and match them. The card you select must be compatible with the cable you select. For example, if you opt to use twisted-pair cable, make sure all of your network cards will work with twisted-pair cable.

- If you use twisted-pair cable, you also need a network hub.

- As you plan your network cabling, you need to draw a floor plan showing the location of each computer and the route of the cables.

- I give you the gory details of network cabling in Chapter 10.

Using a Network Starter Kit — Networks to Go

For me, one of the most fun parts of building a network is going to my local computer store and filling a shopping cart full of stuff. I love to wander the aisles and pick out a network hub, network interface cards, cables, connectors, and other goodies.

If shopping isn't your bag, you can buy in a single box all the pieces you need to network two or three computers. A typical network starter kit for two computers includes two Ethernet network interface cards, a small hub, two twisted pair cables with connectors already attached, so that you can connect both computers to the hub, and instructions for hooking everything up. A kit of this sort costs between $100 and $200, depending on where you purchase it and who manufactures the individual components in the kit.

The starter kit accommodates the first two computers in your network. For each additional computer you want to connect, you purchase an add-on kit that contains a network interface card and a cable.

Here are a couple of additional points to ponder concerning network starter kits:

- ✔ The cable that comes with the starter kit is generally 25 feet long. If your computers are farther apart than that, you have to buy a separate cable.

- ✔ The hub that comes with twisted-pair starter kits usually has ports for connecting as many as four or five computers. If you know you need to network more than that, you should probably purchase the hub and other network components separately.

Looking at a Sample Network Plan

Consider a typical family business: Cleavers' Baseball Card Emporium, which buys and sells valuable as well as worthless baseball cards and other baseball memorabilia.

The Cleavers' computer inventory

The Cleavers have four computers:

- ✔ Ward's computer is a brand-new 400 MHz Pentium III with 64MB of RAM and a 10GB disk drive. Ward runs Microsoft Windows 98 and Office 97 for spreadsheet analysis (Excel) and occasional word processing (Word). He also has a high-speed laser printer.

- ✔ June's computer is a 200 MHz Pentium II with 32MB of RAM and a 4GB hard disk. June runs Windows 95 and does most of the company's word processing with an old version of Word for Windows. She has a little inkjet printer that she bought at a garage sale for $20, but it doesn't work well, so she would like to use Ward's laser printer to print letters.

- ✔ Wally's computer is a 486 with 4MB of RAM, a 300MB hard drive, and Windows 3.1. Wally keeps the company's inventory records on his computer by using a database program he created himself using COBOL. He is sure that the database program is Y2K compliant, but Ward doesn't believe him.

✔ The Beave has a 100MHz Pentium computer with 16MB of RAM, a 2GB disk drive, and a built-in Ethernet port. The computer originally belonged to Eddie Haskell, but Beave traded a Joe DiMaggio, a Wade Boggs, and a Sammy Sosa for it.

Why the Cleavers need a network

The Cleavers want to network their computers for two simple reasons:

✔ So that everyone can access the laser printer.

✔ So that everyone can access the inventory database.

Without the second reason, the Cleavers wouldn't need a network. They could share the laser printer by purchasing a simple printer-sharing switch that would enable all four computers to access the printer (see the sidebar "Stupid stuff about printer switches" earlier in this chapter). But to give everyone access to the inventory database requires a network.

Network operating system

None of the Cleavers is a computer whiz, so they opt for a simple peer-to-peer network operating system based on Windows 95 and 98. This network operating system will enable them to share the printer and the disk drive containing the inventory database — so it adequately meets their needs.

After Ward decides that a Windows network is the way to go, he realizes that Wally's computer will have to be upgraded. Wally's computer will be upgraded to 16MB of RAM and Windows 98.

Server configuration

Because the Cleavers can't afford a separate computer to use as a server, two of the computers do double duty as both clients and servers. Ward's computer is set up as a client/server so that everyone can access his printer, and Wally's computer is set up as a client/server so that everyone can access the inventory database.

After the network is up and running, Wally considers moving the inventory database to Ward's computer. That way, only one server computer has to be managed. Because Ward doesn't use his computer often, he probably won't mind the small reduction in performance as other users access his disk.

(Of course, since Ward is both company CEO and the head of the household, he wouldn't consider trading his high-powered computer with June, who uses her computer six or seven hours every day. Sigh.)

Network cabling

For simplicity, the Cleavers opt to wire their network with twisted-pair cable. All four computers are located in the spacious den, so the floor plan presents no unusual wiring problems. The hub can be placed on a desk next to any of the four computers.

Fortunately, only three of the computers need networking cards, since Beave's computer has a built-in network port. To simplify shopping, the Cleavers decide to purchase a network starter kit for two of the computers and a one-computer add-on kit for the third. They will also take Wally's computer to the store and have the computer upgraded to 16MB of RAM and Windows 98 while they shop for the other network components. The Cleavers will have their network up and running in no more than a few hours.

Chapter 8

Choose Your Weapon
(Or Which Network Should I Use?)

* * *

* * *

*O*ne of the basic choices you must make before you go too far is which network operating system to use as the foundation for your network. This chapter provides an overview of the advantages and disadvantages of the most popular network operating systems.

Novell NetWare

NetWare is one of the most popular network operating systems, especially for large networks. You can use NetWare to build networks of thousands of computers. But you can also use NetWare for small networks consisting of just a few computers.

Novell currently sells three versions of NetWare: 3.2, 4.2, and 5. NetWare 5, the latest and greatest version, is naturally the best of the three. It sports a number of advanced features that make it suitable for larger networks. NetWare 4.2 is suitable for smaller networks. Novell continues to sell NetWare 3.2 mostly because the managers of many existing NetWare 3.x networks don't want to upgrade to a newer version.

I don't get a penny for promoting *Networking with NetWare For Dummies*

If you think NetWare is the networking system for you, be sure to get a copy of *Networking with NetWare For Dummies,* 4th Edition, by Ed Tittel, James E. Gaskin, and Earl Follis (IDG Books Worldwide, Inc.). This is a great book that shows you how to install, use, and manage your network and keep your sanity.

I thought I should get, like, a two percent commission or something for promoting *Networking with NetWare For Dummies*, 3rd Edition, here, but no such luck. Bummer. Get the book anyway.

What's so great about NetWare?

Throughout this book, I pound NetWare a bit for being overly complicated. However, a lot can be said in favor of NetWare. NetWare can be complicated to set up and administer, but it's still the most popular network operating system in use. There must be something good to say about it! So here goes:

- ✔ When Novell set out to design NetWare way back in the 1980s, the company recognized that the old DOS operating system just didn't cut it for networking. Rather than live with the limitations of DOS, Novell decided to bypass DOS altogether. NetWare file servers don't run DOS or Windows; instead, NetWare itself is the operating system for the file server. This frees NetWare from the many built-in limitations of DOS and Windows.

- ✔ Because NetWare servers don't run DOS or Windows, NetWare servers must be dedicated servers. In other words, you can't have a NetWare server double as a user's workstation. This setup costs more because you must purchase a separate server computer. However, the arrangement is more efficient because the server computer can concentrate on servicing the network.

- ✔ Clients on a NetWare network can include computers running DOS, Windows, OS/2, or the Mac OS. If you have a mix of PCs and Macintoshes, NetWare may be your best choice.

- ✔ The NetWare file server uses a more efficient structure for organizing files and directories than DOS or Windows.

- ✔ All versions of NetWare provide features for System Fault Tolerance (SFT), which keep the network running even if a hardware failure occurs.

The disadvantages of NetWare

NetWare is among the best networking systems available, but that doesn't mean it's the best choice for your network. Here are some of the disadvantages to using NetWare for small networks:

✔ A NetWare network is definitely more complicated to set up than a peer-to-peer network based on Windows. The investment of time and effort to figure it out is steep. Windows comes with an instruction manual that's so small you can almost call it a pamphlet. NetWare comes with thousands of pages of manuals.

If you figure out computer stuff pretty quickly, you can probably handle NetWare. Otherwise, using NetWare probably means you have to hire a consultant to install it for you. That's not necessarily a bad thing; just remember that installing NetWare is not a do-it-yourself project unless you're pretty good with computers.

✔ The hardware for a NetWare system costs more than for a peer-to-peer network because you must dedicate at least one computer as a file server. (However, the networking components — adapter cards, cable, and so on — don't cost any more. And if you use a dedicated file server for your peer-to-peer network, the hardware costs are the same.)

✔ Then, you have the cost of NetWare itself. If you build a peer-to-peer network based on Windows, you don't have to pay extra for the networking software, which is built into Windows. But if you opt for NetWare, you have to purchase the NetWare software for your server.

The price of the NetWare server software varies depending on how many client computers your network has. Unfortunately, you can't buy NetWare client licenses one at a time. Instead, you purchase the NetWare software, which enables you to use it for five users. Then, you purchase licenses that allow you to connect additional users 5, 10, 25, 50, 100, 250, or 500 at a time. If your network has six users, you must purchase the five-user server plus a five-user connection license.

Table 8-1 shows the prices for NetWare 5 as of February 1999. The pricing for NetWare 4.2 is a bit less. As you can see, the cost per user is smaller for larger networks. (Note that you can purchase NetWare at a discount from mail-order suppliers, software stores, or software resellers.)

This pricing scheme isn't so bad for larger networks. For a network with 50 users, NetWare costs under $100 per user. But for a five-user network, NetWare costs $239 per user. For a network that small, you probably don't need the extra expense or the added complication of NetWare.

Table 8-1	The Cost of NetWare 5		
Number of Users	**Price**	**Explanation**	**Cost Per User**
5	$1,195	5-user server	$239.00
10	$2,190	5-user server + 5 user client	$219.00
15	$2,625	5-user server + 10 user client	$175.00
30	$3,945	5-user server + 25 user client	$131.50
55	$5,320	5-user server + 50 user client	$96.73
105	$8,190	5-user server + 100 user client	$78.00
255	$14,690	5-user server + 250 user client	$57.61
505	$28,190	5-user server + 500 user client	$55.82

Network Directory Service (also known as NDS)

In the original versions of NetWare, information about the resources available on each server and the users that could log on was stored in a special file called the *bindery* on the server. Each server's bindery contained information only about the resources on that particular server. The bindery meant that, as a user, you had to log on separately to each server that contained resources you wanted to use. NetWare 3.2 still works this way.

With NetWare versions 4.2 and 5, the bindery has been replaced by a feature called the *Network Directory Service,* or NDS. NDS is like a super bindery for the entire network. With NDS, you don't have to log on to individual servers. Instead, you log on to the network just once to gain access to any of the network's resources.

NDS isn't particularly important for small networks with only one server. For large networks with dozens of servers, though, NDS is a major improvement because it dramatically simplifies management of the servers. For example, suppose your network had ten servers running NetWare 3.2. Each time a new user is added to the network, you have to add user ID and other information to each of the ten servers. With NDS, you have to add the new user information just once.

TIP

Do you have the savvy to install NetWare?

How do you know whether you have what it takes to contend with NetWare? Try this little self-test. If you know all (or most) of the answers to these questions, you probably have enough computer savvy to figure out NetWare. If not, don't feel bad. As the Good Book says (sort of), "Some are prophets, some are evangelists, some are teachers, some are NetWare administrators, some are Computer Dummies. . . ."

1. What command do you use to copy all the files, including files in subdirectories, from drive A to the current directory?

   A. FDISK

   B. DELETE A:*.*

   C. FORMAT C:

   D. XCOPY A:*.* /S

2. Which of these files is processed every time you start your computer?

   A. LETSGETGOING.BAT

   B. GETUPYOULITTLESLEEPYHEAD.COM

   C. YOURANG.LURCH

   D. AUTOEXEC.BAT

3. Which of the following bribes are appropriate when enlisting the help of a computer guru?

   A. Cheetos

   B. Doritos

   C. Doughnuts

   D. All the above

4. Who is the most dangerous man in all of France?

   A. Jacques Cousteau

   B. Marcel Marceau

   C. Big Bird

   D. Chief Inspector Jacques Clouseau

If you answered D to three or more of these questions, you probably have the savvy to install NetWare yourself, unless the one you missed was #3, in which case you don't have a prayer.

NetWare 4.2

NetWare 4.2 is the most commonly used version of NetWare. You can use 4.2 for small networks with just a dozen or so users or with huge networks with thousands of users and dozens of servers. NetWare 4 was the first version of NetWare to use Network Directory Service (NDS) to simplify the task of managing networks with more than one server.

Novell claims that NetWare 4.2 can run on any 386-based computer with at least 16MB of RAM and 105MB of free disk space. This may be possible, but I sure don't want to try it. A more realistic minimum setup for a NetWare 4.2 server computer is something like this:

- Pentium processor, at least 100MHz
- 32MB of RAM, 64MB is better
- 2GB of disk space

This setup gives you enough computing horsepower, RAM, and disk space to make NetWare run decently for a small network. For a larger network, you have to allow more RAM and disk space.

NetWare 4.2 is also available in a special Small Business edition, which includes the basic NetWare 4.2 operating system plus a collection of goodies designed to make networking easier for small businesses. Among the extras you get with NetWare for Small Business are the following:

- GroupWise, an e-mail and group scheduling program that is similar to Microsoft Outlook
- A simplified network administration program called Novell Easy Administration Tool, also known as NEAT
- A backup program to back up data on both client and server computers
- A full complement of Netscape programs for accessing the Internet and creating your own Web site

One of the best features of NetWare for Small Business is that it lets you purchase client licenses one user at a time. NetWare for Small Business costs $1,295 and lets up to five users connect to the server. But after that initial purchase, you can buy add-on client licenses one at a time for just $70 each.

NetWare 5

NetWare 5 is the newest version of NetWare, and it provides several major improvements over NetWare 4.2. Here are just a few of the new features of NetWare 5:

- A new graphical user interface based on Java, which lets you administer the server in a more friendly manner that resembles Windows.
- Better support for TCP/IP, the networking protocol used for the Internet.
- Advanced operating system features such as memory protection, virtual memory, and better multiprocessor support — up to 32 processors in a single server. (If you don't know what any of that means, count your blessings.)
- Files can be as large as 8 terabytes (that's 8,000GB), and NetWare 5 can support billions of files on a single disk.

NetWare 5 requires a beefier server computer than NetWare 4.2 does. A NetWare 5 server requires at least a Pentium processor, 64MB of RAM, and 550MB of free disk space. You probably want an even more powerful computer than that for your NetWare 5 server. Here's a recommended minimum configuration:

- ✔ 300MHz Pentium II processor
- ✔ 128MB RAM
- ✔ 10GB free disk space

Windows NT Server 4.0

Windows NT Server is Microsoft's answer to NetWare. For the longest time, Microsoft played second fiddle to Novell. Recently, however, Windows NT Server has gained ground on NetWare, and today it's a toss-up as to which to choose. If you want to stay with an all-Microsoft network, Windows NT Server is the way to go.

Windows NT Server 4.0 comes with a bunch of free Internet tools. These tools enable you to connect to the Internet and set up your own Internet Web site. In addition, you can use the Internet tools to set up an Intranet, which is simply a Web site that can be accessed only from the computers that are on your LAN.

Here's a summary of the more pertinent features of NT:

- ✔ The server processor must be at least a 486, with at least 16MB of memory. Yeah, right. I wouldn't use it on anything smaller than a 100MHz Pentium with 32MB of RAM.
- ✔ Here are some of the file-system limits:

    - Max number of users: unlimited

    - Number of volumes: 25

    - Max size of a volume: 17,000GB

    - Max disk space for server: 408,000GB

    - Largest file: 17 billion GB (Wow! That's more than the maximum disk space for a server, which is impossible!)

    - Max amount of RAM in server: 4GB

    - Max number of open files: unlimited

✔ NT Server is priced differently than NetWare. For NT Server, you buy the server with 5 client licenses for $809, 10 client licenses for $1,129, or 25 client licenses for $1,609. Then you can add additional client licenses for $39.95 apiece, or you can buy client licenses 25 at a time for $699 (which works out to $32.95 per client). For the sake of comparing prices with NetWare, Table 8-2 shows the price of NT Server for 5, 10, 25, 50, 100, 250, and 500 users.

Table 8-2	The Cost of Windows NT Server 4.0		
Number of Users	*Price*	*Explanation*	*Cost Per User*
5	$809	5-user server	$161.00
10	$1,129	10-user server	$112.90
25	$1,508	5-user server + 20-user client	$60.32
50	$2,527	10-user server + two 20-user clients	$50.54
100	$4,304	5-user server + five 20-user clients	$43.04
250	$8,119	10-user server + twelve 20-user clients	$32.48
500	$18,284	5-user server + twenty-five 20-user clients	$36.57

✔ Isn't it odd that the 25-user version of the server actually costs more than the 5-user version plus one 20-user client license? Go figure.

✔ Windows NT Server is part of a family of products from Microsoft called Microsoft BackOffice. Besides NT Server, BackOffice includes the following:

- Microsoft SQL Server, a database program
- Microsoft Exchange Server for improved electronic mail
- Microsoft Site Server for creating advanced Internet Web sites
- Microsoft SNA Server to connect to mainframe computers
- Microsoft System Management Server to manage large networks

✔ For networks with 25 or fewer PCs, Microsoft offers a special version of NT Server called Microsoft BackOffice Small Business Server, also known as SBS. SBS includes Windows NT Server and selected BackOffice features (including SQL Server and Exchange Server) and a set of wizards that simplifies the task of administering a small network.

NTFS drives

NT Server can use disk drives that are formatted in the same way as standard Windows and MS-DOS drives. (The technical term for this type of drive formatting is *FAT*, which stands for File Allocation Table.) But for better performance, Windows NT Server enables you to format your disk drives using a different type of disk format, called NTFS (for NT File System). NTFS drives have the following advantages over FAT drives:

✔ NTFS drives can be larger than FAT drives. FAT uses 32-bit disk addresses, which means that the largest disk drive can be 2GB. NTFS uses 64-bit disk addresses, which can theoretically support drives that are several million times larger than the biggest drives made today.

✔ NTFS is much more efficient at using the space on your disk drive. As a result, NTFS can cram more data onto a given disk drive than FAT.

✔ NTFS drives provide better security features than FAT drives. NTFS stores security information on disk for each file and directory. In contrast, FAT has only rudimentary security features.

✔ NTFS drives are more reliable because NTFS keeps duplicate copies of important information, such as the location of each file on the disk. If a problem develops on an NTFS drive, Windows NT Server can probably correct the problem without losing any data. In contrast, FAT drives are prone to losing information.

Windows 2000 Server

At the time of this writing, Microsoft is preparing to release a new version of Windows NT Server, known as Windows 2000 Server. Windows 2000 Server builds on the strengths of Windows NT Server 4.0, adding new features that will make Windows 2000 Server faster, easier to manage, more reliable, and easier to use for large and small networks alike.

The most significant new feature of Windows 2000 Server is called *Active Directory*, which provides a single directory of all network resources and enables program developers to incorporate the directory into their programs. Active Directory integrates various directory services, such as Novell's NDS and NT's own directory services, and enables you to manage all the directory information on your network using a single interface that resembles the Internet's World Wide Web.

Windows 2000 Server will come in three versions:

✔ **Windows 2000 Server** is the basic server, designed for small- to medium-sized networks. It includes all the basic server features, including file and print sharing and e-mail.

> ✔ **Windows 2000 Advanced Server** is the next step up, designed for larger networks. Advanced Server can support server computers that have up to 64GB of memory (not disk — RAM!) and four integrated processors instead of the single processor that desktop computers and most server computers have.
>
> ✔ **Windows 2000 Datacenter Server** is Microsoft's most ambitious operating system yet. It can support servers that have as many as 32 processors and is specially designed for large database applications.

Other Server Operating Systems

Although NetWare and NT Server are the two most popular choices for network operating systems, they're not the only available choices. The following sections briefly describe four other server choices: IBM's OS/2 Warp Server, Banyan Vines, UNIX, and Linux.

For Macintosh users, Apple offers a special server operating system called Mac OS X Server. For more information about Mac OS X Server, refer to Chapter 25.

OS/2 Warp Server

IBM's OS/2 Warp Server is one operating system that you shouldn't overlook; it's comparable in many ways to both NetWare and NT Server. OS/2 Warp Server offers advanced file- and print-server features and supports DOS, Windows 3.x, Windows 95 and 98, and Macintosh client computers.

One of OS/2 Warp Server's biggest limitations is its lack of a global directory service, such as NetWare's NDS or the Active Directory feature that will be available with Windows 2000 Server.

Banyan VINES

VINES is a sophisticated network operating system that has been around for more than a decade and is used in many large corporations. However, unless you already know a lot about VINES, I suggest you steer clear.

UNIX

UNIX originally began its life as a time-sharing operating system for mini-computers, but it has since become a popular server operating system for medium- to large-sized networks. For some types of network servers, such as those that require high-performance database access, UNIX is the server operating system of choice.

Unlike other server operating systems, UNIX comes in different variations from several vendors. No single version of "true" UNIX exists. Instead, many different versions look much the same but are not completely compatible. The best known version of UNIX is from a company called Santa Cruz Operation, or SCO.

Linux

Perhaps the most interesting operating system available today is Linux. Linux is a free operating system that is based on UNIX. Linux was started by Linus Torvalds, who thought it would be fun to write a version of UNIX in his free time, as a hobby. He enlisted help from hundreds of programmers throughout the world, who volunteered their time and efforts via the Internet. Today, Linux is a full-featured version of UNIX that its users consider to be as good or better than Windows. In fact, almost as many people now use Linux as use Macintosh computers.

Linux offers the same networking benefits of UNIX and can be an excellent choice as a server operating system.

Peer-to-Peer Networking with Windows

If you're not up to the complexity of NetWare or NT, you may want to opt for a simple peer-to-peer network based on Windows.

Why peer-to-peer networks are easier to use

Peer-to-peer networks are easier to set up and use than NetWare or NT mainly because they don't require you to jettison your familiar Windows operating system in favor of a specialized network operating system. Instead, peer-to-peer networks simply use the networking features that come built into Windows 95 and 98.

Although Windows limits the capabilities of these networks, these networks are easier to use because you don't have to find out the ins and outs of a foreign operating system. Everything you already know about Windows — even if that's not very much — can help you when you set up a peer-to-peer network.

Here are a few other things that make peer-to-peer networks easier to use than server-based networks:

- ✔ Peer-to-peer networks don't require that you use a dedicated server computer. Any computer on the network can function as both a network server and a user's workstation. (However, you can configure a computer as a dedicated server if you want to. Doing so results in better performance.)

- ✔ One reason peer-to-peer networks are easier to set up and use is that they don't provide as many advanced features as NetWare or NT. Peer-to-peer networks don't provide the same fault tolerance features; their security systems aren't as advanced; and they don't provide as many options for tweaking performance. With fewer variables to worry about, mastering the equation is easier.

Drawbacks of peer-to-peer networks

Yes, peer-to-peer networks are easier to install and manage than NetWare or NT, but they aren't without their drawbacks.

- ✔ Because peer-to-peer networks are Windows based, they're subject to the inherent limitations of Windows. Windows is designed primarily to be an operating system for a single-user, desktop computer rather than be part of a network, so Windows can't manage a file or printer server as efficiently as a real network operating system.

- ✔ If you don't set up a dedicated network server, someone (hopefully not you) may have to live with the inconvenience of sharing his or her computer with the network. With NetWare or NT Server, the server computers are dedicated to network use so that no one has to put up with this inconvenience.

- ✔ Although a peer-to-peer network may have a lower cost per computer for smaller networks, the cost difference between peer-to-peer networks and NetWare or NT is less significant in larger networks (say, 20 or more clients).

Windows 98

Windows 98, the current version of Windows at the time of this writing, includes everything you need to set up a peer-to-peer network. If all your computers run Windows 98 (or Windows 95), you only have to purchase network cards and cable to build a network.

Here are the more salient features of Windows 98 networking:

Anticipating Windows 2000 Professional

Windows 2000 is the long-awaited merging of Windows 98 and Windows NT. Windows 2000 will offer many new features, including the following:

✔ An improved Start menu and desktop interface that eliminate clutter and present the options you use most often first.

✔ A new Network Connection Wizard that simplifies the task of connecting your computer to a network.

✔ Network Places, an easier way to get around in the network.

✔ Integration with Internet Explorer 5.

✔ Windows 98 automatically detects most networking cards and configures itself to work with them.

✔ Windows 98 enables you to access the network through a desktop icon called Network Neighborhood. Using it is child's play.

✔ Windows 98 can connect to other Windows 98 or Windows 95 computers as well as to Windows NT Server or NetWare servers.

✔ Windows 98 includes a great Hearts game that you can play with other network users.

Windows NT Workstation 4.0

Although Windows NT is usually considered a server operating system, Microsoft also peddles a desktop version of NT called Windows NT Workstation 4.0. NT Workstation 4.0 sports the user-friendly Windows 95 user interface and costs only about $50 more than Windows 98. NT Workstation offers many advantages over Windows 95 or 98, the most important one being that NT Workstation does not crash as often as Windows 95 or 98.

Unfortunately, Windows NT Workstation hasn't yet caught up to the new and improved user interface of Windows 98. For that, you have to wait for Windows 2000 Professional, as I describe in the sidebar "Anticipating Windows 2000 Professional."

Artisoft's LANtastic

Back in the days when Windows did not have any built-in networking, Artisoft's LANtastic was the most popular peer-to-peer network operating system. But now that networking comes built in with Windows, LANtastic has become somewhat less popular.

Here are some of the reasons you may want to consider using LANtastic:

- ✔ LANtastic supports Windows 95 and 98, as well as older computers that run Windows 3.1 or just DOS. If your network has older computers, LANtastic may be the easiest way to get them all up and running on the network.

- ✔ LANtastic includes features that let you share modems for Internet access or network faxing. Windows 95 or 98 can't do that.

- ✔ LANtastic includes an option that enables you to dedicate a computer for use as a server. Although a dedicated LANtastic server won't operate as efficiently as a dedicated NetWare or NT server, it's more efficient than a Windows 95 or 98 server.

Chapter 9

Planning Your Servers

● ●

In This Chapter

▶ Deciding whether to use dedicated servers

▶ Making sure that you provide enough disk space

▶ Storing programs and data files on a server

▶ Using a separate print server

▶ Buying a reliable server computer

● ●

*O*ne of the key decisions you must make when networking your computers is how you make use of server computers. Even if you use a
peer-to-peer network system, such as Windows 98, you must still deal with
the question of servers.

This chapter helps you to make the best use of your network server, first by
convincing you to use a dedicated server if possible and then by suggesting
ways to use the server efficiently.

To Dedicate or Not to Dedicate

In case you haven't noticed, I'm a big believer in dedicated server computers,
even if you use a peer-to-peer network. Yes, one of the strengths of a simple
Windows 98 network is that you can use any computer on the network as
both a server computer and a user's workstation. Does that mean you should
make every computer a server? No way.

You give up a lot when your desktop computer doubles as a network server.

　　✔ Every time someone accesses data on your hard disk, your own work is
　　　temporarily suspended. If your hard disk is popular, you become
　　　annoyed with the frequent delays.

　　✔ You lose the sense of privacy that comes with having your own com-
　　　puter. Remember that nasty memo about your boss? You'd better not
　　　leave it lying around on your disk . . . someone else may lift it off the net-
　　　work. (You can set up your disk so that you have some private space

where other users can't snoop about. But make sure that you set it up right and remember to store confidential files in private space. And make sure that you know more about the networking software than anyone else in the office. Someone who knows more about networking than you do can probably figure out a way to thwart your security measures.)

✔ You lose the independence of having your own computer. You have to leave your computer on all day even when you're not using it because someone else may be. Want to turn off your computer because the noise it makes interrupts your afternoon nap? You can't. Want to delete some unnecessary files to free up some hard disk space? You can't, if the files don't belong to you.

✔ Your computer isn't immune to damage caused by other network users. What if someone accidentally deletes an important file on your disk? What if someone copies a 100MB file onto your hard disk while you aren't looking, so that no free space is available when you try saving the spreadsheet you've been working on all afternoon?

I hope that you're convinced. If you can at all afford it, set aside a computer for use as a dedicated server. Beg, borrow, or steal a computer if you must.

Here are a few other thoughts to consider about using dedicated servers:

✔ Peer-to-peer networks enable you to adjust certain configuration options for network servers. If you use a computer as both a server and a client, you must balance these options so that they provide reasonable performance for both server and client functions. But if you dedicate the computer as a server, you can skew these options in favor of the server functions. In other words, you're free to tweak the server's configuration for peak network performance. You can find details for doing this in Chapter 14.

✔ As a general rule, try to limit the number of servers on your network. Having one server sharing a 10GB drive is better than two servers sharing a 5GB drive. The fewer servers you have on your network, the less time you will have to spend administering them.

✔ In a larger network, you may want to use two dedicated server computers: one as a file server and the other as a print server. This improves the performance for file operations and network printing.

✔ If you're the greedy type, offer to donate your old 100MHz Pentium computer as the network server if the company will purchase a new 350MHz Pentium II computer for your desktop.

Actually, this idea has merit: The file server doesn't have to be the fastest computer on the block, especially if it's used mostly to store and retrieve word processing, spreadsheet, and other types of files instead of for intensive database processing.

How Much Disk Space?

The general rule for a network is that you never have enough disk space. No matter how much you have, you eventually run out. Don't delude yourself into thinking that 10GB is twice as much space as you'll ever need. Make that space available to the network, and it fills up in no time.

What then? Should you just keep adding a new disk drive to your file server every time you run out of space? Certainly not. The key to managing network disk space is just that — managing it. Someone has to sign on the dotted line that he or she will keep tabs on the network disk and let everyone know when it's about to burst its seams. And every network user must realize that disk storage on the server is a precious resource, to be used judiciously and not squandered.

Here are a few additional tips that can help you make the best use of your server disk space:

- ✔ If you use a peer-to-peer network, consider activating the Windows DriveSpace feature on the server computer. To set up DriveSpace properly, you first must quote from *Wayne's World:* Say "Ex-squeeze me," and DriveSpace politely compresses the data on your hard disk so that the disk's capacity is effectively doubled. And doing so really, really works. Only trouble is, it slows down the server a bit. For the best server performance, you're better off purchasing a larger disk drive and not compressing it.

- ✔ Encourage all network users to remember that their computers have local disk drives in addition to the network drives. Just because you have a network doesn't mean that everything has to be stored on a network drive!

- ✔ Don't try to cut costs by using *diskless clients.* Some networks are set up so that the clients have no local drives at all. For this to work, a special chip is required in the network interface card so that the computer can boot without a disk drive. Diskless clients are cheaper, but they force the user to store everything on the network. In addition, they bog down the network because routine disk accesses, such as locating DOS program files, have to travel across the network cable.

What to Put on a File Server

Of course, the only way to predict how much network disk space you need is to plan what files you're going to store on the server. You need enough space to accommodate the network itself, shared data files, private data files, and shared application programs.

The network itself

You can't make all the space on the network server's disk available to network users; you have to reserve some of it for the network operating system itself. Setting aside 100MB or more of disk space for the network operating system, print spool files, sealing wax, and other fancy stuff is not unreasonable.

A network can take up an amazing amount of disk space. Check out these numbers:

- ✔ Novell says you should allow 105MB for NetWare 4.2 and 500MB for NetWare 5. For Windows NT Server 4.0, allow 125MB.

- ✔ If you go the peer-to-peer route with Windows, the network support is built into the operating system so that you don't have to allow for additional disk space. The operating systems require a hefty amount of disk space, though. Windows 95 easily fills 70MB of disk space, and Windows 98 up to 200MB.

- ✔ If the server can support a printer, allow an additional 20MB for spool files. If you routinely print large graphics files on the network printer, you may have to allow even more spool space.

- ✔ Allow space for any additional programs that you may want to have available on the server, such as a disk repair utility like Norton Utilities.

Shared data files

Allow sufficient space on the file server for data files that network users share. One large database file or hundreds or even thousands of small word processing or spreadsheet files may take up most of this space. Either way, don't skimp on space here.

Estimate the amount of space you need for shared files. The only way you can do this is to add up the size of the files that must be shared. Double the result. If you can afford to, double it again.

Private data files

Every user wants access to network disk space for private file storage — perhaps because their own disks are getting full, they want the security of knowing that their files are backed up regularly, or they just want to try out the network.

You have two approaches to providing this private space:

✔ Create a folder for each network user on a shared network drive. For example, the Cleavers set up the following folders for private storage:

- Ward   \WARD
- June   \JUNE
- Wally   \WALLY
- Beaver   \BEAVER

Now, just tell each network user to store private files in his or her own folder. The problem with this setup is that these folders aren't really private; nothing keeps Beaver from looking at files in Wally's directory.

To make these directories more secure, you can password-protect them by using the security features in your network operating system.

✔ Create a separate network drive mapping for each private folder. For example, you can map drive P to each network user's private directory. Then you can tell each user to store private files on his or her P drive. For Wally, the P drive refers to the \WALLY folder, but for Beaver, the P drive refers to \BEAVER. This setup keeps Beaver out of Wally's files.

The net effect (groan, sorry) of this setup is that each user seems to have a separate P drive on the server. In reality, these drives are merely folders on the server drive.

Estimating the disk space required for private file storage is more difficult than estimating shared file storage. After your users figure out that they have seemingly unlimited private storage on the network server, they start filling it up.

Shared programs

If several users use the same application program, consider purchasing a network version of the program and storing the program file on the network server. The advantage of doing this rather than storing a separate copy of the program on each user's local disk is that you have to manage only one copy of the software. For example, if a new version of the software comes out, you have to update just the copy on the server rather than separate copies on each workstation.

The network version of most programs enables each network user to set the program's options according to his or her preferences. Thus, one user may run the program using the default setup with boring colors, while another user may prefer to change the screen colors so that the program displays magenta text on a cyan background. Stalin probably would have outlawed network versions.

Many application programs create temporary files that you're not aware of and don't normally need to worry about. When you use these programs on a network, be sure to configure them so that the temporary files are created on a local drive rather than on a network drive. This configuration not only gives you better performance, but also ensures that one user's temporary files don't interfere with another's.

Planning Your Network Drive Mapping

If you plan to use mapped drive letters to access network drives, you should scope out which drive letters you will use. Here are some general rules to follow:

- ✔ Be consistent. If a network drive is accessed as drive Q from one workstation, map it as drive Q from all workstations that access the same drive. Don't have one user referring to a network drive as drive Q and another using the same drive but with a different letter.

- ✔ Use drive letters that are high enough to avoid conflicts with drive letters that are used by local drives. For example, suppose that one of your computers has three disk partitions, a CD-ROM drive, and a RAM drive. This computer would already have drive letters C through G assigned. I usually start network drive assignments with drive M and continue with N, O, P, and so on.

  Novell NetWare usually begins drive assignments at drive F.

- ✔ If you use DriveSpace, be aware that DriveSpace causes drive letter crashes if you're not careful. To protect yourself, start your network before you install DriveSpace, so that DriveSpace can find its way around your network drive assignments. And always wear a helmet and safety goggles when using DriveSpace.

- ✔ With Windows 95 or 98, keep in mind that drive letter mapping isn't a requirement. Users can access any shared network drive via the Network Neighborhood icon that appears on the Windows desktop.

Sharing CD-ROM Drives

CD-ROM drives have become standard equipment on desktop computers, but if your computer is the only one in the office with a CD-ROM drive, you may have users waiting in line to borrow time on your computer so that they can use your CD-ROM drive.

Fortunately, all the network operating systems described in this book enable you to set up a CD-ROM drive as a shared network drive, so that users throughout the network can access it. In fact, sharing a CD-ROM drive is no different than sharing a regular disk drive.

But an annoying problem crops up when you share a desktop computer's CD-ROM drive with other network users. Imagine that you're using your CD-ROM drive for important work, such as browsing the latest edition of Microsoft's Cinemania to figure out what movie you should rent tonight, when some clown down in sales wants to access the master price list CD just sent from corporate headquarters. You get an annoying message that says something like `Please Insert the Master Price List CD in Drive D.` And that won't be the last of it, either. You're pestered by annoying interruptions like this all day long.

If you're going to share a CD-ROM drive, make sure that it's located on a dedicated server computer, and the drive is dedicated to a particular disk. For example, if corporate headquarters really does send you a CD containing the master price list, and network users need to access this CD frequently, dedicate an entire CD-ROM drive just for this disk. Then you won't have to contend with annoying messages about changing the disks.

If you have more than one CD to be shared, just install more than one CD-ROM drive in the server computer. With the cost of CD-ROM drives being so low — good ones cost under $100 — this solution isn't unrealistic. If you share more than a few CDs, you can even buy special CD-ROM "towers" with stacks of CD-ROM drives built in. For example, you can purchase a CD-ROM tower with seven 40-speed CD-ROM drives for under $2,000. These towers are self-contained servers with network software built in, so you can connect them directly to your network.

An alternative to a CD-ROM tower is a *jukebox*. A jukebox is a single CD-ROM drive that can hold several discs and automatically swaps discs as they are accessed. Jukeboxes are less expensive than towers, but they're slower; whenever a user accesses a disc that isn't currently in the CD-ROM drive, the jukebox must switch discs. If two users are accessing two discs simultaneously, the jukebox spends a lot of time shuttling discs back and forth. (To avoid this problem, you can get jukeboxes that have more than one CD reader built in — for more money, of course.)

If you don't want to fuss with shared CD-ROM drives, CD-ROM towers, or jukeboxes, you can always just copy the entire contents of your most popular CD-ROM disks to the server's hard disk.

Using a Separate Print Server

If you have a larger network (say, eight or more computers) and shared printing is one of the main reasons you're networking, you may want to consider using two dedicated server computers: one as a file server and the other as a print server. By using separate server computers for file and print sharing, you will improve the overall performance of your network.

Here are some thoughts to keep in mind when you use a separate print server:

- ✔ Most network operating systems have configuration options that enable you to balance disk performance against printer performance. By using separate computers for your file server and print server, you can set these options accordingly. If the same computer works as both a file and print server, you must set these options somewhere in the middle, compromising performance one way or the other.

- ✔ If the printer is used exclusively for text output, the print server can be the slowest computer on the network and you still won't notice any performance delay. If you do a lot of graphics printing on a high-quality laser printer, however, don't use a dog computer for the print server. I've seen ten-minute print jobs slowed to an hour or more by a cheap print server.

- ✔ As an alternative to dedicating a separate computer to use as a print server, you can connect most printers directly to the network via an inexpensive print server device. The most commonly used device of this type is called the HP JetDirect, made by Hewlett-Packard (the same folks who make all those great printers). An external HP JetDirect is a small box that contains an Ethernet port (RJ-45 for twisted-pair, BNC for thinnet, or both) and a parallel port to which you can attach a printer. Internal HP JetDirect cards are designed to be installed in Hewlett-Packard printers, enabling you to connect the printer directly to the network. You can get an external HP JetDirect for under $150.

Buying a Server Computer

If you have a spare computer lying around that you can use as a server, great. Most of us don't have spare computers in the closet, though. If you plan to buy a new computer to use as a network server, here are some tips for configuring it properly:

- ✔ A network server computer need not have the latest in large-screen color monitors and supercharged graphics cards. An ordinary 14- or 15-inch monitor with an inexpensive video card will do.

✔ On the other hand, don't scrimp on the processor and memory. Buy the fastest Pentium II or Pentium III processor you can afford and equip it with at least 64MB of RAM; 128MB is better. Every last byte of extra memory can be put to good use on a server.

✔ Buy the biggest disk drive you can afford. The price of disk storage has dropped so much in recent years that you can easily outfit a server computer with at least 5GB of disk storage. I've seen 10GB drives advertised for under $225, and you can get a 19GB drive for under $350.

✔ While you're at it, buy SCSI disks instead of IDE disks. SCSI offers much better performance for network servers, where several users are accessing the disk simultaneously. SCSI is more expensive than IDE, but the performance benefit is worth the increased cost. For more information about the benefits of SCSI over IDE, see Chapter 14.

✔ Have the computer built in a tower-style case that has plenty of room for expansion: several free bays for additional disk drives and a more-than-adequate power supply. You want to make sure that you can expand the server when you realize you didn't buy enough disk space.

Keeping the Power On

One feature people often overlook when setting up a network server is the power. You can simply plug the server computer into the wall, or you can plug it into a surge protector to smooth out power spikes before they damage your computer. Using a surge protector is good, but even better is connecting your server computer to a device called an *uninterruptible power supply,* or UPS.

Inside the UPS box is a battery that is constantly charged and some electronics that monitor the condition of the power coming from the wall outlet. If a power failure occurs, the battery keeps the computer running. The battery can't run the computer forever but can keep it running long enough — anywhere from ten minutes to more than an hour, depending on how much you paid for the UPS — to shut things down in familiar Presbyterian fashion (decently and in order). For most small networks, a UPS that keeps you going for ten minutes is enough. You just want to make sure that any disk in progress (I/O) has time to finish. A decent UPS can be had for about $150.

Here are a few additional thoughts about UPS:

✔ Using a UPS can prevent you from losing data when a power outage occurs. Without a UPS, your server computer can be shut down at the worst of times, such as while it's updating the directory information that tracks the location of your files. With a UPS, the computer can stay on long enough for such meticulous operations to be completed safely.

✔ In a true UPS, power is always supplied to the computer from the battery; the current from the wall outlet is used only to keep the battery charged. Most inexpensive UPS devices are actually stand-by power supplies (SPSs). An SPS runs the computer from the wall-outlet current but switches to battery within a few gazillionths of a second if a power failure occurs. With a true UPS, you have no delay between the power failure and the battery takeover. SPSs are less expensive than UPSs, though, so they're more commonly used.

✔ The ultimate power-failure protection is to attach a UPS to every computer on the network. That gets a bit expensive, though. At the very least, you should protect the server.

✔ If a power outage occurs and your server is protected by a UPS, get to the server as quickly as you can, log everyone off, and shut down the server. You should also go to each computer and turn off the power switch. Then, when power is restored, you can restart the server, restart each workstation, and assess the damage.

Location, Location, and Location

The final network server consideration to address in this chapter is where to put the server. In the old days, you put the network server in a room with glass windows all around, paid a full-time lab technician in a white coat to tend to its every need, and gave it a name like ARDVARC or SHADRAC.

Nowadays, the most likely location for a file server is in the closet. Nothing says the server has to be in a central location; it can be in the closet down at the end of the hall, atop the filing cabinets in the storage room, or in the corner office. The server can be almost anywhere, as long as it's near an electrical outlet and network cable can be routed to it.

Of course, a print server is different. It should be near the printer, which should be in an accessible location with storage space for paper, toner (for laser printers), a place to leave printouts that belong to other users, and a box to drop wasted paper so that it can be recycled.

Some bad locations for the server:

✔ In the attic. Too dusty.

✔ In the bathroom. Too much moisture.

✔ In the kitchen. Your computer gurus raid your refrigerator every time you call them. They start showing up spontaneously "just to check."

✔ In your boss's office. You don't want him or her to think of you every time the server beeps.

The good news is that you still get to name your server computer. You can call it something boring like SERVER1, or you can give it an interesting name like BERTHA or SPOCK.

Chapter 10

Oh, What a Tangled Web We Weave (Cables, Adapters, and Other Stuff)

- -

- -

*I*f you've ever installed an underground sprinkler system, you'll have no trouble cabling your network. Working with network cable is a lot like working with sprinkler pipe: You have to use the right size pipe (cable), the right valves and headers (hubs and repeaters), and the right sprinkler heads (network interface cards).

Network cables have one compelling advantage over sprinkler pipes: You don't get wet when they leak.

This chapter tells you far more about network cables than you probably need to know. I introduce you to Ethernet, the most common system of network cabling for small networks. Then you find out how to work with the cables used to wire an Ethernet network. You also find out how to select the right network interface cards, which enable you to connect the cables to your computers.

What Is Ethernet?

Ethernet is a standardized way of connecting computers to create a network. You can think of Ethernet as kind of like a municipal building code for networks: It specifies what kind of cables to use, how to connect the cables together, how long the cables can be, how computers transmit data to one another using the cables, and more.

You may have heard of two other popular network building codes: Token Ring and ARCnet. Ethernet is more commonly used than Token Ring because Ethernet is less expensive. Ethernet is used more than ARCnet because ARCnet is slower.

Some people treat Ethernet, Token Ring, and ARCnet like religions that they're willing to die for. To a Lord of the Token Ring, Ethernet represents the Antichrist. Ethernet fanatics often claim that you can hear satanic messages if you send data backward through a Token Ring network. Ethernet and Token Ring fanatics both treat ARCnet users as if they were a cult, possibly due to reports of ARCnet disciples giving away flowers at airports. Don't engage an Ethernet, Token Ring, or ARCnet Pharisee in a discussion about the merits of his or her network beliefs over opponents' beliefs. It's futile.

Without regard to the technical merits of Ethernet, Token Ring, or ARCnet, the fact is that the vast majority of small networks use Ethernet. 'Nough said.

Here are a few interesting tidbits about Ethernet standards:

- *Ethernet* is a set of standards for the infrastructure on which a network is built. All the network operating systems I discuss in this book — NetWare, Windows NT Server, and Windows 95 or 98 — can operate on an Ethernet network. If you build your network on a solid Ethernet base, you can change network operating systems later.

- Ethernet is often referred to by network gurus as 802.3 (pronounced *eight-oh-two-dot-three*), which is the official designation used by the IEEE (pronounced *eye-triple-ee*), a group of electrical engineers who wear bow ties and have nothing better to do than argue about inductance all day long. This situation is a good thing, though, because if not for them, you wouldn't be able to mix and match Ethernet components made by different companies.

- Standard Ethernet transmits data at a rate of 10 million bits per second, or 10 Mbps. Because 8 bits are in a byte, that translates into roughly 1.2 million bytes per second. In practice, Ethernet can't move information that fast because data must be transmitted in packages of no more than 1,500 bytes, called *packets*. So a 150K file has to be split into 100 packets. This

Stop me before I tell you about Token Ring!

Just in case you do get into an argument about Ethernet with a Token Ring fanatic, here's where he or she is coming from. Ethernet can get bogged down if the network gets really busy and messages start colliding like crazy. Token Ring uses a more orderly approach to sending packets through the network. Instead of sending a message whenever it wants to, a computer on a Token Ring network must wait its turn. In a Token Ring network, a special packet called the *token* is constantly passed through the network from computer to computer. A computer can send a packet of data only when it has the token. In this way, Token Ring ensures that collisions won't happen.

Sometimes, a computer with a defective network interface card accidentally swallows the token. If the token disappears for too long, the network assumes the token's been swallowed and the network burps to generate a new token.

Two versions of Token Ring are in use. The older version runs at 4 Mbps. The newer version runs at 16 Mbps, plus it allows two tokens to exist at once, which makes the network even faster.

Oh, in case you're wondering, ARCnet uses a similar token-passing scheme.

speed has nothing to do with how fast electrical signals move on the cable. The electrical signals themselves travel at about 70 percent the speed of light, or as Picard would say, "Warp factor point-seven-oh. Engage."

✔ A newer version of Ethernet, called Fast Ethernet, moves data ten times as fast as normal Ethernet. Because Fast Ethernet moves data at a whopping 100Mbps and uses twisted pair cabling, it's often called 100BaseT. Although Fast Ethernet is more expensive than standard 10 Mbps Ethernet, the cost of Fast Ethernet is coming down. If you're interested in speed, you may want to check out Fast Ethernet for your network. However, 10Mbps is plenty fast for most small networks.

Three Types of Ethernet Cable

You can construct a 10Mbps Ethernet network by using three different types of cable: *thick coax* (called *yellow cable* because it's usually yellow), *thin coax* (called *thinnet* because it's thinner than the yellow stuff or *cheapernet* because it's cheaper than the yellow stuff), or *twisted pair,* which looks like phone cable. Twisted-pair cable is sometimes called UTP or 10baseT cable, for reasons I try hard not to explain later.

Who cares what CSMA/CD stands for?

Besides specifying the mechanical and electrical characteristics of network cables, Ethernet specifies the techniques used to control the flow of information over the network cables. The technique Ethernet uses is called CSMA/CD, which stands for "carrier sense multiple access with collision detection." This phrase is a mouthful, but if we take it apart piece by piece, you get an idea of how Ethernet works (as if you want to know).

Carrier sense means that whenever a computer wants to send a message on the network cable, it first listens to the cable to see whether anyone else is already sending a message. If it doesn't hear any other messages on the cable, the computer assumes that it's free to send one.

Multiple access means that nothing prevents two or more computers from trying to send a message at the same time. Sure, each computer listens before sending. But suppose that two computers listen, hear nothing, and then proceed to send their messages? Picture what happens when you and someone else arrive at a four-way stop sign at the same time. You wave the other driver on, he or she waves you on, you wave, he or she waves, you all wave, and then you both end up going at the same time.

Collision detection means that after a computer sends a message on the network, it listens carefully to see whether the message crashed into another message. Kind of like listening for the screeching of brakes at the four-way stop. If the computer hears the screeching of brakes, it waits for a random period of time and tries to send the message again. Because the delay is random, two messages that collide are sent again after different delay periods, so a second collision is unlikely.

Wasn't that a waste of time?

The yellow stuff isn't used much for small networks, but I describe it anyway. The real choice you must make is between thinnet cable and twisted pair.

The yellow stuff

The original Ethernet networks were wired with thick, heavy cable called thick coax, or yellow cable, because of its color. Thick coax isn't used much anymore, especially for small networks, because it's expensive, heavy, and not very flexible. (I mean that literally: Making yellow cable bend around tight corners is difficult.)

Here are some of the advantages and disadvantages of thick yellow cable:

 ✔ The yellow stuff is less susceptible to interference from mongo-magnets and motors and what not, so it's still used sometimes in factories, warehouses, nuclear test sites, Frankenstein laboratories, and so on.

- ✔ You can string yellow cable for greater distances than other types of Ethernet cable. A single run of yellow cable (called a *segment*) can be as long as 500 meters.

- ✔ The way yellow cable is attached to individual computers is weird. Usually, a long length of yellow cable is run along a path that takes it near each computer on the network. Each computer must be connected to the yellow cable via a device called a *transceiver.* The transceiver usually includes a device called a *vampire tap,* a clamp-like thingamabob that taps into the yellow cable without cutting and splicing it. The transceiver is connected to the network interface card by means of an *AUI cable.* (AUI stands for *attached unit interface,* not that the information matters.)

- ✔ I think you can see why the yellow stuff isn't used much anymore.

- ✔ It's really too bad. The yellow stuff would coordinate so well with this book.

Thinnet

A more practical type of cable for Ethernet networks is thin coax cable, usually called thinnet. Thinnet is less expensive than yellow cable, not only because the cable itself is less expensive, but also because separate transceivers aren't required to attach computers to the cable. (Thinnet does use transceivers, but the transceiver is built into the adapter card.) Figure 10-1 shows a typical thinnet cable.

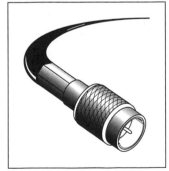

Figure 10-1:
A thinnet
cable.

Here are some salient points about thin coax cable:

✔ Thinnet is about ⅕ inch in diameter, so it's much lighter and more flexible than the yellow stuff. You can easily wrap it around corners, drape it over doorways, around potted plants, and so on.

✔ You attach thinnet to the network interface card by using a goofy twist-on connector called a BNC connector. You can purchase preassembled cables with BNC connectors already attached in lengths of 25 or 50 feet, or you can buy bulk cable on a big spool and attach the connectors yourself by using a special tool. (I suggest buying preassembled cables. Attaching connectors to bulk cable can be tricky.)

✔ Whereas yellow cable is usually wired with a single length of cable that's tapped into using vampire taps, thinnet is run with separate lengths of cable. At each computer, a T connector is used to connect two cables to the network interface card. Figure 10-2 shows a typical thinnet arrangement. One length of thinnet connects Ward's computer to June's, a second length connects June's to Wally's, and a third length connects Wally's to Beaver's.

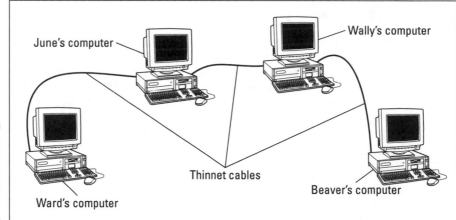

Figure 10-2:
A network
wired with
thinnet
cable.

June's computer

Wally's computer

Thinnet cables

Ward's computer

Beaver's computer

✔ A special plug called a *terminator* is required at each end of a series of thinnet cables. In Figure 10-2, terminators are required at Ward's computer and at Beaver's. The terminator prevents data from spilling out the end of the cable and staining the carpet.

✔ The cables strung end-to-end from one terminator to the other are collectively called a *segment*. The maximum length of a thinnet segment is 185 meters. You can connect as many as 30 computers on one segment. To span a distance greater than 185 meters or to connect more than 30 computers, you must use two or more segments with a funky device called a *repeater* to connect each segment.

Unshielded twisted-pair (UTP) cable

A popular alternative to thinnet cable is unshielded twisted-pair cable, or UTP. UTP cable is even cheaper than thin coax cable, and best of all, many modern buildings are already wired with twisted pair because this type of wiring is often used with modern phone systems. Figure 10-3 shows a twisted-pair cable.

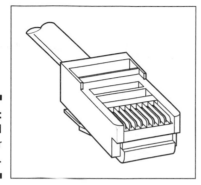

Figure 10-3:
Unshielded
twisted-pair
cable.

When you use UTP cable to construct an Ethernet network, you connect the computers in a star arrangement, as Figure 10-4 illustrates. In the center of this star is a device called a hub. Depending on the model, Ethernet hubs enable you to connect from 4 to 24 computers using twisted-pair cable. Most hubs have connectors for 8 or 12 cables. Hubs are sometimes called concentrators.

An advantage of this star arrangement is that if one cable goes bad, only the computer attached to that cable is affected; the rest of the network continues to chug along. With thinnet, a bad cable affects the entire network, not just the computer that the bad cable is connected to.

Here are a few other details you should know about twisted-pair cabling:

- ✔ UTP cable consists of pairs of thin wire twisted around each other; several such pairs are gathered up inside an outer insulating jacket. Ethernet uses two pairs of wires, or four wires all together. The number of pairs in a UTP cable varies but is often more than two.

- ✔ UTP cable comes in five grades, Category 1 through Category 5. The higher the Category number, the greater the amount of protection the cable provides from outside electrical interference. Of course, higher-Category cables are also more expensive. Ethernet networks should be cabled with Category 3 or better. Category 5 is preferable.

- ✔ If you want to sound like you know what you're talking about, say "Cat 5" instead of "Category 5."

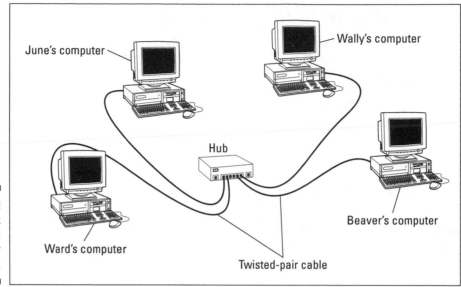

June's computer

Wally's computer

Hub

Figure 10-4:
A network
wired with
twisted-pair
cable.

Ward's computer

Beaver's computer

Twisted-pair cable

✔ UTP cable connectors look like modular phone connectors but are a bit larger. UTP connectors are officially called RJ-45 connectors.

✔ Like thinnet, UTP cable is also sold in prefabricated lengths. However, RJ-45 connectors are much easier to attach to bulk UTP cable than BNC cables are to attach to bulk coax cable. As a result, I suggest you buy bulk cable and connectors unless your network consists of just two or three computers. A basic crimp tool to attach the RJ-45 connectors costs about $50.

✔ The maximum allowable cable length between the hub and the computer is 100 meters.

✔ 100 Mbps Fast Ethernet uses Category-5 twisted-pair cabling. If you wire your 10 Mbps twisted-pair network using Cat-5 cables and connectors, you can upgrade to 100 Mbps Fast Ethernet later simply by replacing your 10 Mbps Ethernet cards with Fast Ethernet cards.

Hubs and the Network

The biggest difference between using thinnet and twisted-pair cable is that when you use twisted-pair, you also must use a separate device called a *hub*. Until recently, hubs were expensive enough that most do-it-yourself networkers building small networks opted for thinnet to avoid the expense and hassle of using hubs.

Worthless filler about network topology

A networking book wouldn't be complete without the usual textbook description of the three basic *network topologies*. The first type of network topology is called a *bus,* in which network nodes (that is, computers) are strung together in a line, like this:

A bus is the simplest type of topology but has its drawbacks. If the cable breaks somewhere in the middle, the break splits the network into two.

The second type of topology is called a *ring:*

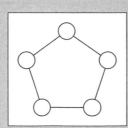

A ring is very much like a bus except with no end to the line: The last node on the line is connected to the first node, forming an endless loop.

The third type of topology is called a *star:*

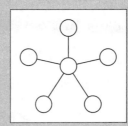

In a star network, all the nodes are connected to a central hub. In effect, each node has an independent connection to the network, so a break in one cable doesn't affect the others.

Ethernet networks are based on a bus design. However, fancy cabling tricks make an Ethernet network appear to be wired as a star when twisted-pair cable is used.

Nowadays, the cost of hubs has dropped so much that the advantages of twisted-pair cabling outweigh the hassle and cost of using hubs. With twisted-pair cabling, you can more easily add new computers to the network, move computers, find and correct cable problems, and service computers that you need to remove from the network temporarily.

If you do decide to use twisted-pair cabling, you need to know some of the ins and outs of using 10baseT hubs:

Ten base what?

The IEEE, in its infinite wisdom, has decreed that the following names shall be used to designate the three types of cable used with 802.3 networks (in other words, with Ethernet):

- 10base5 is thick coax cable (the yellow stuff).

- 10base2 is thin coax cable (thinnet).

- 10baseT is unshielded twisted-pair cable (UTP).

In each moniker, the 10 means that the cable operates at 10Mbps, and *base* means the cable is used for baseband networks as opposed to broadband networks (don't ask). The 5 in 10base5 is the maximum length of a yellow cable segment: 500 meters; the 2 in 10base2 stands for 200 meters, which is about the 185-meter maximum segment length for thinnet (for a group of engineers, the IEEE is odd; I didn't know the word *about* could be part of an engineer's vocabulary); and the T in 10baseT stands for twisted.

Of these three official monikers, 10baseT is the only one used frequently; 10base5 and 10base2 are usually just called thick and thin.

- Because you must run a cable from each computer to the hub, find a central location for the hub to which you can easily route the cables.

- The hub requires electrical power, so make sure that an electrical outlet is handy.

- When you purchase the hub, purchase one with at least twice as many connections as you need. Don't buy a four-port hub if you want to network four computers; when (and not if) you add the fifth computer, you'll have to buy another hub.

- You can connect hubs to one another as shown in Figure 10-5; this is called *daisy-chaining*. When you daisy-chain hubs, you connect a cable to a standard port on one of the hubs and the daisy-chain port on the other hub. Be sure to read the instructions that come with the hub to make sure that you daisy-chain them properly.

- You can daisy-chain no more than three hubs together. If you have more computers than three hubs can accommodate, don't panic. For a small additional cost, you can purchase hubs that have a BNC connection on the back. Then, you can string the hubs together via thinnet cable. The three-hub limit doesn't apply when you use thinnet cable to connect the hubs.

- When you shop for network hubs, you may notice that the expensive ones have network-management features that support something called SNMP. These hubs are called *managed hubs*. Unless your network is very large and you know what SNMP is, don't bother with the more expensive managed hubs. You'd be paying for a feature you'll never use.

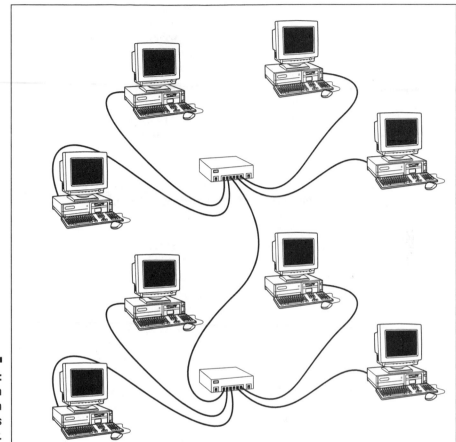

Figure 10-5:
You can
daisy-chain
hubs
together.

Network Interface Cards

Now that you know far more about network cable than you really need to, I want to point out a few things about network interface cards that you should consider before you buy:

- ✔ The network interface cards you use must have a connector that matches the type of cable you use. If you plan on wiring your network with thinnet cable, make sure that the network cards have a BNC connector. For twisted-pair wiring, make sure that the cards have an RJ-45 connector.

- ✔ Some network cards provide two or three connectors. I see them in every combination: BNC and AUI, RJ-45 and AUI, BNC and RJ-45, and all three. Selecting a card that has both BNC and RJ-45 connectors isn't a bad idea. That way, you can switch from thinnet to twisted-pair or vice versa without buying new network cards. You can get both types of connectors for a cost of only $5–$10 more per card. Don't worry about the AUI connector, though. You'll probably never need it.

✔ Long ago and far away, Novell manufactured a network interface card known as the NE2000. The NE2000 card is no longer made, but NE2000 remains a standard of compatibility for network interface cards. If a card is NE2000 compatible, you can use it with just about any network. If you buy a card that is not NE2000 compatible, make sure the card is compatible with the network operating system you intend to use.

✔ When you purchase a network card, make sure that you get one that's compatible with your computer. Most computers can accommodate cards designed for the standard 16-bit ISA bus. Newer Pentium-based computers can also accommodate cards with 32-bit PCI bus. For a Pentium computer, PCI cards are well worth the extra few bucks. Not only are PCI cards faster than ISA cards, they are also easier to configure.

✔ Make sure that the computer in which you're going to use the card has an available slot of the same type as the card you purchase. For example, suppose your computer has four ISA bus slots and three PCI bus slots, but all three of the PCI slots are already in use while two of the ISA slots are available. In this case, get an ISA card.

✔ Make sure that the card is Plug and Play compatible. This feature enables Windows to automatically configure the card so that you don't have to go through a bunch of tedious configuration gyrations just to get the card working.

✔ Network cards can be a bit tricky to set up — even Plug and Play cards. Each different card has its own nuances. You can simplify your life a bit if you use the same card for every computer in your network. Try not to mix and match network cards.

✔ If you see Ethernet cards advertised on late-night television for an unbelievably low price (like $9.95 or free with Proof of Purchase seals from three cereal boxes), make sure that the cards are 16-bit cards. You won't be satisfied with the slow performance of bargain-basement 8-bit cards unless your computer is also of the bargain-basement variety. If you have a 486 or Pentium computer, don't even think about using 8-bit cards.

Network Starter Kits

Often, the easiest way to buy the equipment you need to build a network is to purchase a network starter kit. A typical network starter kit includes everything you need to network two computers. To add additional computers, you purchase add-on kits that include everything you need to add one computer to the network.

For example, suppose you want to network three computers in a small office. You could start with a two-computer network starter kit, which would include the following items:

- Two 10baseT PCI Ethernet cards
- One 5-port Ethernet 10baseT hub
- Two 15-feet-long 10baseT twisted-pair cables
- Software for the cards
- Instructions

This kit, which should set you back about $100, connects two of the three computers. To connect the third computer, purchase an add-on kit that includes a 10baseT PCI Ethernet card, another 15-feet-long twisted-pair cable, software, and instructions, for about $40.

Professional Touches

If most of the stuff I discuss in this chapter makes sense to you, and if you want to impress your friends, consider adding the following extra touches to your network installation. These extra touches make the job look like it was done by a professional. (If you find this chapter to be hopelessly confusing, you should probably concentrate on just getting your network up and running. Worry about making it look pretty later.)

Figure 10-6 shows some of the following professional touches:

- Use 10baseT wiring; that's what most network pros are doing these days.
- Run the wiring through the ceiling and walls instead of along the floor, and mount a wall jack near each computer. Then plug each computer into the wall jack by using a short (10-foot or so) patch cable. Be sure to use top-quality Category-5 jacks and make sure each pair of wires inside the cable is twisted right up to the point where the wires attach to the jack. In other words, don't untwist the wires any more than absolutely necessary to make them easier to work with.
- When you run the wiring through the walls and ceiling, take special care to avoid power cords, fluorescent lamps, and other electrical devices that may interfere with the signals traveling inside the network cable. And don't kink the cable: Curve it gently around corners.
- To really do it right, run 10baseT cable to every possible computer location in your office, even if you don't yet have a computer there. That way, when you do move a computer to that location, the hard wiring (up in the ceiling and through the wall) is already done. All you have to do then is attach the computer to the wall jack with a patch cord.

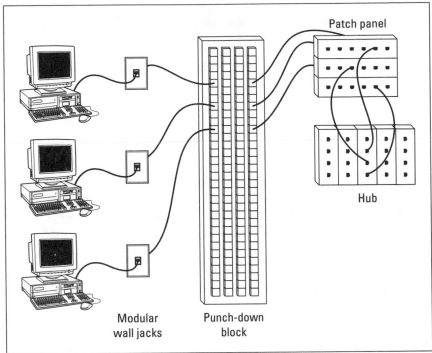

Patch panel

Hub

Figure 10-6:
A
professional
touch.

Modular
wall jacks

Punch-down
block

✔ Designate a corner of a closet or storeroom to be your wiring closet. Bundle all the cables together and attach them to a punch-down block. (A *punch-down block* is a handy gadget that lets you connect wires to one another without stripping the insulation off the wires. All you do is place the wire over one of the punch-down block connectors and punch the wire into the connector using a special punch-down tool.) After the wires are connected to the punch-down block, you can then run wires from the punch-down block to a patch panel, which is nothing more than a series of RJ-45 jacks mounted neatly in a row.

✔ Connect the appropriate jacks in the patch panel to your network hub with short patch cables. The whole thing looks a bit like a rat's nest, but you can easily reconfigure the network at a moment's notice. If someone changes locations, all you have to do is adjust the patch cables in the wiring closet accordingly.

✔ A full-fledged patch panel, like the one shown in Figure 10-6, is usually used only with large networks. For smaller networks, you can get small self-contained units that contain a punch-down block that's already con-nected to six or eight RJ-45 blocks. These boxes are a slick way to give a professional look to a small network setup.

✔ Be careful about making your network look too good. People may assume that you're a network geek and start offering you Cheetos to solve their problems.

Hints for Reading Network Ads

If you're willing to purchase your network components from a mail-order supplier, you can probably save a bunch of money. Just go to the supermarket and pick up a copy of *Computer Shopper* and browse through it until you find several companies that specialize in networking products. Figure 10-7 shows a typical mail-order advertisement for network stuff.

You can probably figure out most ads, but I want to point out a few things:

✔ The lines that have two prices (generally separated by a slash) are either listing the price if you buy one item versus the price if you buy five or more, or the price for two similar items configured differently. For example, the Fancy Dance 2000 ISA network card may be $79.95 if you buy one, but $69.95 each if you buy five or more.

✔ Some prices change too often to print, so you have to call to find out.

✔ Most mail-order networking companies are very willing to answer questions on the phone. If you're not sure what you need, give the company a call.

✔ Make sure that you understand the shipping costs and the conditions for returning damaged goods. Before you buy anything, make sure that the company has the product in stock and can ship it the same day, or the next day if you call late.

ETHERNET CARDS
Fancy Dance 2000 ISA BNC & UTP ea/5+...........$79.95/69.95
Fancy Dance 2000 PCI BNC & UTP ea/5+...........$99.95/89.95
Fast Dance 100Mbps PCI.......................................$119.95/109.95
Cheapster Combo ISA..$24.95
Cheapster Combo PCI..$29.95

10BaseT HUBS
24-Port..$229.95
16-Port..$159.95
12-Port..$139.95
8-Port..$59.95
5-Port..$49.95

NetWare
5/10 User..$659/1,439
25/50 User..$2,599/3,499
100/250 User..CALL
NetWare 4.2 Small Business..................................CALL

MICROSOFT
Windows NT Server 5/10 User..............................$599/899
Windows NT Server 20 User License Pack........$599
BackOffice 2.5..$2,199
Windows 98 Upgrade..$89.95
Office Professional Comp Upgrade......................$299.95

CABLE
Thinnet 25'/50' Patch Cable..................................$14.95/21.95
1000' Bulk Thinnet Spool......................................$149
Cat-5 10BaseT 4 Pair 500'/1000'..........................$179.95/349.95
BNC Crimp Connector...$2.89
BNC T Connector..$3.69
BNC Crimp Tool..$29.95
RJ45 Connector ea/20+...$2.49/1.89
RJ45 Crimp Tool...$29.95

Figure 10-7:
A fictional
mail-order
ad for
network
stuff.

Chapter 11

Putting It Together (Or Insert Tab A into Slot B)

*N*ow comes the fun part: putting your network together. Get ready to roll up your sleeves and dig into the bowels of your computers. Make sure that you scrub thoroughly first.

Getting the Tools You Need

Of course, to do a job right, you must have the right tools.

Start with a basic set of computer tools, which you can get for about $15 from any computer store or large office-supply store. These kits include the right screwdrivers and socket wrenches to open up your computers and insert adapter cards. (If you don't have a computer tool kit, make sure that you have several flathead and Phillips screwdrivers of various sizes.)

If all your computers are in the same room, and you're going to run the cables along the floor, and you're using prefabricated cables, the computer tool kit should contain everything you need.

If you're using bulk cable and plan on attaching your own connectors, you need the following tools in addition to the tools that come with the basic computer tool kit:

- ✔ **Wire cutters.** Big ones for thinnet cable; smaller ones are okay for 10baseT cable. If you're using yellow cable, you need the Jaws of Life.

- ✔ **A crimp tool appropriate to your cable type.** You need the crimp tool to attach the connectors to the cable.

- ✔ **Wire stripper.** You need this only if the crimp tool doesn't include a wire stripper. For thinnet, a special wire-stripper-doohickey is required because the cable's inner conductor, outer conductor, and outer insulation must be cut at precise lengths.

If you plan on running cables through walls, you need these additional tools:

- ✔ **A hammer.**

- ✔ **A bell.**

- ✔ **A song to sing.** Just kidding about these last two.

- ✔ **A keyhole saw.** This is useful if you plan on cutting holes through walls to route your cable.

- ✔ **A flashlight.**

- ✔ **A ladder.**

- ✔ **Possibly a *fish tape*.** A fish tape is a coiled-up length of stiff metal tape. To use it, you feed the tape into one wall opening and *fish* it toward the other opening, where a partner is ready to grab it when the tape arrives. Next, your partner attaches the cable to the fish tape and yells something like "Let 'er rip!" or "Bombs away!" Then you reel in the fish tape and the cable along with it. (You can find fish tape in the electrical section of most well-stocked hardware stores.)

If you plan on routing cable through a concrete subfloor, you need to rent a jackhammer and a backhoe and hire someone to hold a yellow flag while you work.

Configuring Network Interface Cards

You have to install a network interface card in each computer before you can connect the network cables. Installing a network card is a manageable task, but you have to be willing to roll up your sleeves.

Fortunately, most network cards sold these days are of the Windows 95 and 98 "Plug and Play" variety. This means that you can slap one of them into your computer and turn your computer back on, and Windows automatically configures itself to use the card. If any of the card's settings conflict with settings used by other cards already installed in your computer, Windows adjusts the settings automatically to eliminate the conflict.

Would that all network cards were Plug and Play cards. Unfortunately, not all of them are. Some network cards (especially cheaper ones) still require that you use a special installation or configuration program that comes with the card. And if you're installing a hand-me-down network card you got from your brother-in-law, you may have to contend with setting switches or jumper blocks on the card itself. Bother.

And, of course, Plug and Play is a Windows 95 and 98 feature. If you're stuck with DOS or Windows for Workgroups, you have to configure the network cards the old-fashioned way. If you're unfortunate enough to be using an older network card or a DOS, Windows 3.1, or Windows for Workgroups computer, be sure to read and follow the instructions that come with the network card.

Configuring network cards is probably the most confusing part of installing a network and also the most troublesome if you don't get it just right. So, be sure to pay attention when you're configuring your network cards. Make sure that you've had your morning coffee.

Installing the Network Card

If you've installed one adapter card, you've installed them all. In other words, installing a network card is just like installing a modem, a new video controller card, a sound card, or any other type of card. If you've ever installed one of these cards, you can probably install a network card blindfolded.

If you haven't installed a card, here's a step-by-step procedure:

1. **Shut down Windows and then turn the computer off and unplug it.**

   Never work in your computer's insides with the power on or the power cord plugged in!

2. **Remove the cover from your computer.**

   Figure 11-1 shows the screws you must typically remove to open the cover. Put the screws someplace where they won't wander off.

3. **Find an unused expansion slot inside the computer.**

   The expansion slots are lined up in a neat row near the back of the computer; you can't miss 'em. Most computers have at least five slots known as ISA slots. Each slot consists of two adjacent receptacles, one slightly longer than the other. The cards have two corresponding connectors that slide into the receptacles.

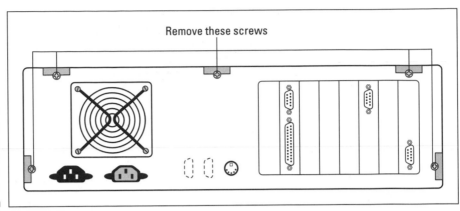

Figure 11-1:
Removing
your
computer's
cover.

Newer computers of the Pentium variety have two or three high-speed *PCI slots.* These slots are usually used for high-speed video or disk controllers, but they can also be used for network interface cards, if you purchase a network interface card designed for use in a PCI slot. The PCI slots are smaller than the regular ISA slots, so that you can't accidentally insert a PCI card into an ISA slot or vice versa.

Some really old computers have both 8-bit slots and 16-bit slots. You can tell the difference by looking at the connectors: Each 16-bit slot has two connectors, whereas each 8-bit slot has only one connector. Since a 16-bit card has two connectors, you can't possibly put a 16-bit card into an 8-bit slot. If you have an 8-bit card and your computer has both an 8-bit slot and a 16-bit slot free, slide the card into the 8-bit slot — no point in wasting a perfectly good 16-bit slot on a wimpy 8-bit card if you can avoid it.

Some computers also have other types of slots — mainly VESA and EISA slots. Standard ISA or PCI networking cards won't fit in these slots, so don't try to force them.

4. **When you find a slot that doesn't have a card in it, remove the metal slot protector from the back of the computer's chassis.**

A small retaining screw holds the slot protector in place. Remove the screw, pull the slot protector out, and put the slot protector in a box with all your other old slot protectors. Don't lose the screw. (After a while, you collect a whole bunch of slot protectors. Keep them as souvenirs.)

5. **Insert the network card into the slot.**

Line up the connectors on the bottom of the card with the connectors in the expansion slot and then press the card straight down. Sometimes you have to press uncomfortably hard to get the card to slide into the slot.

6. **Secure the network card with the screw you removed in Step 4.**

7. **Put the computer's case back together.**

   Watch out for the loose cables inside the computer; you don't want to pinch them with the case as you slide it back on. Secure the case with the screws you removed in Step 2.

8. **Turn the computer back on.**

   If you're using a Plug and Play card with Windows 95 or 98, the card automatically is configured after you start the computer again. Otherwise, you may need to run an additional software installation program. See the installation instructions that come with the network interface card for details.

Working with Cable

The hardest part about working with network cable is attaching the cable connectors. That's why the easiest way to wire a network is to buy prefabricated cables, with the connectors already attached. Thinnet cable is commonly sold in prefabricated lengths of 25, 50, or 100 feet. You can buy prefabricated twisted-pair cable, or you can attach the connectors yourself (it isn't hard to do).

Before I show you how to attach cable connectors, here are a few general tips for working with cable:

- Always use more cable than you need, especially if you're running cable through walls. Leave plenty of slack.

- When running cable, avoid sources of interference like fluorescent lights, big motors, and so on. The most common source of interference for cables run behind fake ceiling panels are fluorescent lights; be sure to give light fixtures a wide berth as you run your cable. Three feet should do it.

- If you must run cable across the floor where people walk, cover the cable so that no one trips over it. Inexpensive cable protectors are available from most hardware stores.

- When running cables through walls, label each cable at both ends. Most electrical supply stores carry pads of cable labels that are perfect for the job. These pads contain 50 sheets or so of precut labels with letters and numbers. They look much more professional than wrapping a loop of masking tape around the cable and writing on the tape with a marker.

- When several cables come together, tie them with plastic cable ties. Avoid masking tape if you can; the tape doesn't last, but the sticky glue stuff does. It's a mess a year later. Cable ties are available from electrical supply stores.

> ✔ Cable ties have all sorts of useful purposes. On my last backpacking trip, I used a pair of cable ties to attach an unsuspecting buddy's hat to a high tree limb. He wasn't impressed with my innovative use of the cable ties, but my other hiking companions were.

Attaching a BNC connector to thinnet cable

Properly connecting a BNC connector to thinnet cable is an acquired skill. You need two tools: a wire stripper that can cut through the various layers of the coax cable at just the right location and a crimping tool that crimps the connector tightly to the cable after you get the connector into position. BNC connectors have three separate pieces, as shown in Figure 11-2.

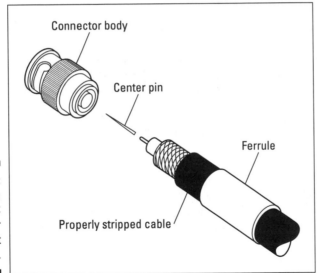

Figure 11-2:
Attaching a BNC connector to thinnet cable.

Here's the procedure, in case you ignore my advice and try to attach the connectors yourself:

1. **Slide the hollow tube portion of the connector (lovingly called the *ferrule*) over the cable.**

   Let it slide back a few feet to get it out of the way.

2. **Cut the end of the cable off cleanly.**

3. **Use the stripping tool to strip the cable.**

   Strip the outer jacket back ½ inch from the end of the cable, strip the braided shield back ¼ inch from the end, and strip the inner insulation back ³⁄₁₆ inch from the end.

4. **Insert the solid center conductor into the center pin.**

   Slide the center pin down until it seats against the inner insulation.

5. **Use the crimping tool to crimp the center pin.**

6. **Slide the connector body over the center pin and inner insulation but under the braided shield.**

   After you push the body back far enough, the center pin clicks into place.

7. **Now slide the ferrule forward until it touches the connector body.**

   Crimp it with the crimping tool.

Don't get sucked into the trap of trying to use easy "screw-on" connectors. They aren't very reliable.

Attaching an RJ-45 connector to UTP cable

RJ-45 connectors for UTP wiring are much easier to connect than thinnet connectors. The only trick is making sure that you attach each wire to the correct pin. Each pair of wires in a UTP cable has complementary colors. One pair consists of one white wire with an orange stripe and an orange wire with a white stripe, and the other pair has a white wire with a green stripe and a green wire with a white stripe.

Here are the proper pin connections:

Pin Number	Proper Connection
Pin 1	White/orange wire
Pin 2	Orange/white wire
Pin 3	White/green wire
Pin 6	Green/white wire

Figure 11-3 shows an RJ-45 plug properly connected.

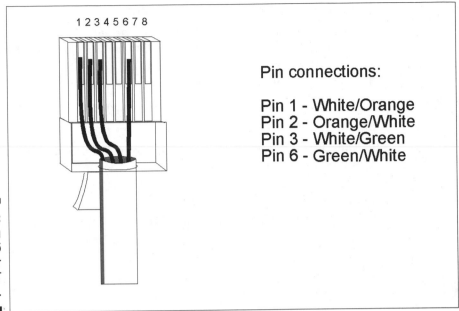

Pin connections:

Pin 1 - White/Orange
Pin 2 - Orange/White
Pin 3 - White/Green
Pin 6 - Green/White

Figure 11-3:
Attaching
an RJ-45
connector
to 10baseT
cable.

Here's the procedure for attaching an RJ-45 connector:

1. **Cut the end of the cable to the desired length.**

   Make sure that you make a square cut, not a diagonal cut.

2. **Insert the cable into the stripper portion of the crimp tool so that the end of the cable is against the stop.**

   Squeeze the handles and slowly pull the cable out, keeping it square. This strips off the correct length of outer insulation without puncturing the insulation on the inner wires.

3. **Arrange the wires so that they lay flat in the following sequence from left to right: white/orange, orange/white, white/green, green/white.**

   Pull the green/white wire a bit to the right and then insert the cable into the back of the plug so that each wire slides into the channel for the correct pin.

4. **Make sure that the wires are in the correct pin channels; especially make sure that the green/white cable is in the channel for pin 6.**

5. **Insert the plug and wire into the crimping portion of the tool and then squeeze the handles to crimp the plug.**

   Remove the plug from the tool and double-check the connection.

Here are a few other points to remember when dealing with RJ-45 connectors and twisted-pair cable:

✔ The pins on the RJ-45 connectors are not numbered, but you can tell which is pin 1 by holding the connector so that the metal conductors are facing up, as shown in Figure 11-3. Pin 1 is on the left.

✔ Some people wire 10baseT cable differently, using the green and white pair for pins 1 and 2 and the orange and white pair for pins 3 and 6. This doesn't affect the operation of the network (the network is color blind), *so long as the RJ-45 connectors on both ends of the cable are wired the same!*

✔ Yes, I know that any normal person would have set up the RJ-45 connectors using pins 1 through 4, not pins 1, 2, 3, and 6. But remember, computer people aren't normal in any particularly relevant sense, so why would you expect the fourth wire to connect to the fourth pin? That's pretty naive, don't you think?

✔ If you're installing cable for a Fast Ethernet system, you should be extra careful to follow the rules of Category-5 cabling. That means, among other things, make sure that you use Category-5 components throughout. The cable and all connectors must be up to Category-5 specs. When you attach the connectors, do not untwist more than ½ inch of cable. And do not try to stretch the cable runs beyond the 100-meter maximum. When in doubt, have cable for a 100MHz Ethernet system professionally installed.

Installing the Network Software

After you install the network cards and cable, all that remains is installing the network software. The procedures for doing this task vary considerably, depending on the network you use, so you need to consult your network software's manual for the details. Here, I describe just some general things to keep in mind.

Installing the server software

Start by setting up your network server. It's the centerpiece of your network, and you won't know whether your workstations are working until you have a working server they can log on to.

If you're using NetWare, installing the server software is the most difficult part of setting up the network. Read the manual carefully, place it ceremoniously on your highest bookshelf, and pick up a copy of *Networking with NetWare For Dummies,* 4th Edition, by Ed Tittel, James E. Gaskin, and Earl Follis (IDG Books Worldwide, Inc.).

Installing the server software for Windows NT Server can be tedious as well. Fortunately, the installation for peer-to-peer networks using Windows 95 or 98 is easier. In fact, for Windows, you have no separate installation process for installing the server software; after you set up Windows, the server is ready to go.

Here are a couple of other tasks that go hand-in-hand with installing the server software:

- ✔ After you install the network software, you must define the server resources to be shared on the network. At this stage, you assign the network names for your shared disk drives and printers. Refer to Chapter 4 for instructions on how to do this using Windows 95 or 98.

- ✔ You also must build the user list. For each user on the system, you supply the user ID, password (if any), and access rights. You can find more information about setting up the user list and managing network security in Chapter 13.

Installing client software

If you're using Windows 95 or 98, setting up the client computer for the network is child's play. For starters, Windows automatically recognizes your network interface card when you start up your computer. All that remains to connect to the network in Windows is to make sure that Windows installed the network protocols and client software properly. To do so, follow these steps:

1. **Choose the Start⇨Settings⇨Control Panel command to summon the Control Panel. Then double-click the Network icon.**

   The Network dialog box appears, as shown in Figure 11-4.

2. **Make sure that the network protocol you're using appears in the list of network resources.**

   If you're creating a Windows-based network using Windows 95 or 98 or Windows NT Server, make sure that you have the NETBEUI protocol listed. For a NetWare network, make sure that the IPX/SPX-compatible Protocol is listed. To enable access to the Internet or an Intranet server, also make sure that TCP/IP is listed.

3. **If a protocol you need isn't listed, click the Add button to add the protocol you need.**

   The dialog box that appears asks if you want to add a network client, adapter, protocol, or service, as shown in Figure 11-5. Click Protocol and then click Add. A list of available protocols appears. Select the one you want to add and then click OK. (You may be asked to insert a disk or the Windows CD-ROM.)

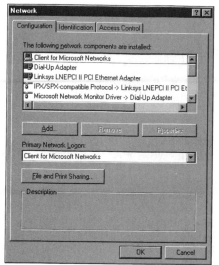

Figure 11-4:
The
Windows 98
Network
dialog box.

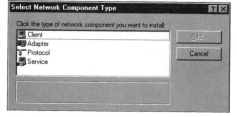

Figure 11-5:
Adding a
network
component.

4. **Make sure that the network client you want to use appears in the list of network resources.**

   For a Windows-based network, make sure that "Client for Microsoft Networks" is listed. For a NetWare network, make sure that "Client for NetWare Networks" appears.

5. **If the client you need isn't listed, click the Add button to add the client you need.**

   The dialog box in Figure 11-5 appears again. This time, click Client and then click Add. Select the network client you want to add and then click OK.

6. **Click OK to dismiss the Network dialog box.**

   You're done! Your computer reboots itself to enable the new network features you just installed.

Testing Your Network Installation

Your network isn't finished until you test it to make sure that it works. Hold your breath as you fire up your computers, starting with the server and then proceeding to the clients. Watch for error messages as each computer starts up. Then log on to the network to see whether it works. If it doesn't, the following paragraphs should help you find the problem:

- ✔ If you have a problem, the first culprit to suspect is your network cable. Check all your connections, especially any connections you crimped yourself. If you're using thinnet, make sure that the terminators are attached properly. If you're using UTP, make sure that the hub is plugged in and turned on.

- ✔ If you're using UTP, you can find a bad cable by checking the light on the back of each network card and each hub connection. The light should be glowing steadily. If it's not glowing at all or if it's glowing intermittently, replace the cable or reattach the connector.

- ✔ Double-check your network card configuration to make sure that you don't have any conflicts with other devices. Also, make sure that your network software configuration agrees with the way your network cards are actually set.

- ✔ If the network doesn't work, you might benefit from running the Windows 98 built-in Networking Troubleshooter, as shown in Figure 11-6. To access the Networking Troubleshooter, click the Start button, and then choose the Help command. When the Help window appears, click Troubleshooting, and then click Windows 98 Troubleshooters and choose the Networking Troubleshooter.

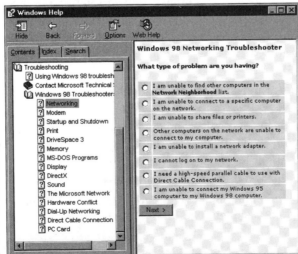

Figure 11-6:
The Windows 98 Networking Trouble-shooter.

Part III
The Dummies Guide to Network Management

The 5th Wave   By Rich Tennant

"This part of the test tells us whether you're personally suited to the job of network administrator."

In this part . . .

You discover that there's more to networking than installing the hardware and software. After you get the network up and running, you have to keep it up and running. That's called network management.

The chapters in this section show you how to set up your network's security system, how to improve its performance, and how to protect your network from disaster. I include a bit of technical stuff here, but no one said life was easy.

Chapter 12

Help Wanted (A Network Manager's Job Description)

*H*elp wanted. Network manager to help small business get control of a network run amok. Must have sound organizational and management skills. Only moderate computer experience required. Part-time only.

Does this sound like an ad that your company should run? Every network needs a network manager, whether the network has two computers or 200. Of course, managing a 200-computer network is a full-time job, whereas managing a two-computer network isn't. At least, it shouldn't be.

This chapter introduces you to the boring job of network management. Oops . . . you're probably reading this chapter because you've been elected to be the network manager, so I'd better rephrase that: This chapter introduces you to the wonderful, exciting world of network management! Oh boy! This is going to be fun!

Identifying the Network Manager: A Closet Computer Geek

Most small companies can't afford and don't need a full-time computer geek. So the network manager is usually just a part-time computer geek. The ideal network manager is a closet computer geek: Someone who has a secret interest in computers but doesn't like to admit it.

The job of managing a network requires some computer skills but isn't entirely a technical job. Much of the work done by the network manager is routine housework. Basically, the network administrator dusts, vacuums, and mops the network periodically to keep it from becoming a mess.

Here are some additional ideas about picking a network administrator:

- The network manager needs to be an organized person. Conduct a surprise office inspection and place the person with the neatest desk in charge of the network. (Don't warn them in advance, or everyone will mess up their desks intentionally the night before the inspection.)

- Allow enough time for network management. For a small network (such as three or four computers), an hour or two each week is enough. More time is needed up-front as the network manager settles into the job and finds out about the ins and outs of the network. But after an initial settling-in period, network management for a small office network doesn't take more than an hour or two per week. (Of course, larger networks take more time to manage.)

- Make sure that everyone knows who the network manager is and that the network manager has authority to make decisions about the network — such as what files can and cannot be stored on the server, how often backups are done, and so on.

- In most cases, the person who installs the network is also the network manager. That's appropriate because no one understands the network better than the person who designs and installs it.

- The network manager needs an understudy, someone who knows almost as much about the network, is eager to make a mark, and smiles when the worst network jobs are "delegated."

- The network manager has some sort of official title, like Network Boss, Network Czar, Vice President in Charge of Network Operations, or Dr. Network. A badge, a personalized pocket protector, or a set of Spock ears helps, too.

Throwing the Book at It

One of the network manager's main jobs is keeping the network book up-to-date. In Chapter 7, I suggest that you keep all the important information about your network in a ½-inch binder. Call this binder your *Network Bible* or *The Good Book*. Here are some things it should include:

✔ Include an up-to-date diagram of the network. This diagram can be a detailed floor plan, showing the actual location of each computer or something more abstract and Picasso-like. Any time you change the network layout, update the diagram. And include a detailed description of the change, the date the change was made, and the reason for the change.

✔ Include a detailed inventory of your computer equipment. Here is a sample form that you can use to keep track of your computer equipment:

Computer Equipment Checklist

Computer location:

User:

Manufacturer:

Model number:

Serial number:

Date purchased:

CPU type & speed:

Memory:

Hard disk size:

Video type:

Printer type:

Other equipment:

Operating system version:

Application software & version:

Network card type:

Connector (BNC/RJ-45):

✔ Include a detailed list of network resources and drive assignments in the binder.

✔ Include copies of any login scripts used by your network.

✔ Include whatever other information you think may be useful, such as details about how you must configure a particular application program to work with the network and copies of every network component's original invoice, in case something breaks and you need to seek warranty service.

✔ Do not put passwords in the binder!

You may want to keep track of the information in your network binder using a spreadsheet or a database program. However, make sure you keep a printed copy of the information on hand.

Managing the Network

The most obvious duty of the network manager is managing the network itself. The network's hardware — the cables, network adapter cards, hubs, and so on — needs oversight, as does the network operating system. On a big network, these responsibilities can become a full-time job. Large networks tend to be volatile: Users come and go, equipment fails, cables break, and life in general seems to be one crisis after another.

Smaller networks are much more stable. After you get your network up and running, you probably won't have to spend much time managing its hardware and software. An occasional problem may pop up, but with only a few computers on the network, problems should be few and far between.

Small network or large, all network administrators must attend to several common chores:

✔ The network manager must put on the pocket protector whenever a new computer is added to the network. The network manager's job includes considering what changes to make to the cabling configuration, what computer name and user ID to assign to the new user, what security rights to grant the user, and so on.

✔ Every once in a while, your trusty network vendor releases a new version of your network operating system. The network manager's job is to read about the new version and decide whether its new features are beneficial enough to warrant an upgrade. Keep in mind that switching to an upgraded network version is often an all-or-nothing proposition: You can't have some computers running version X and others running version Y. Upgrading to a new network version is a bit of a chore, so you need to carefully consider the advantages the new version can bring.

✔ One of the easiest traps to get sucked into is the quest for network speed. The network is never fast enough, and users always blame the hapless network manager. So the manager spends hours and hours tuning and tweaking the network to squeeze out that last 2 percent of performance. You don't want to get caught in this trap, but in case you do, Chapter 14 can help. It clues you in to the basics of tuning your network for best performance.

Doing the Routine Stuff You Hate to Do

Much of the network manager's job is routine stuff, the equivalent of vacuuming, dusting, and mopping. It's boring, but it has to be done.

✔ The network manager has to make sure that the network is properly backed up. If something goes wrong and the network isn't backed up, guess who gets the blame? On the other hand, if disaster strikes but you're able to recover everything from yesterday's backup with only a small amount of work lost, guess who gets the pat on the back, the fat bonus, and the vacation in the Bahamas? Chapter 15 describes the options for network backups. You'd better read it soon.

✔ Chapter 15 also describes another routine network chore: checking for computer viruses. If you don't know what a virus is, read Chapter 15 to find out.

✔ Users think the network server is like the attic: They want to throw files up there and leave them there forever. The network manager gets the fun job of cleaning up the attic once in a while. Oh, joy. The best advice I can offer is to constantly complain about how messy it is up there and warn your users that spring cleaning is coming up.

Managing Network Users

Managing network technology is the easiest part of network management. Computer technology can be confusing at first, but computers are not nearly as confusing as people. The real challenge of managing a network is managing the network's users.

The difference between managing technology and managing users is obvious: You can figure out computers, but you can never really figure out people. The people who use the network are much less predictable than the network itself. Here are some tips for dealing with users:

✔ Training is a key part of the network manager's job. Make sure that everyone who uses the network understands it and knows how to use it. If the network users don't understand the network, they may do all kinds of weird things to it without meaning to.

✔ Never treat your network users like idiots. If they don't understand the network, it's not their fault. Explain it to them. Offer a class. Buy them each a copy of this book and tell them to read the first six chapters. Hold their hands. But don't treat them like idiots.

✔ Make up a network cheat sheet that has everything the users need to know about using the network on one page. Make sure that everyone gets a copy.

✔ Be as responsive as you can when a network user complains of a network problem. If you don't fix the problem soon, the user may try to fix it. You probably don't want that.

Getting the Tools of a Network Manager

Network managers need certain tools to get their jobs done. Managers of big, complicated, and expensive networks need big, complicated, and expensive tools. Managers of small networks need small tools.

Some of the tools the manager needs are hardware tools like screwdrivers, cable crimpers, and hammers. But the tools I'm talking about here are software tools.

✔ Many of the software tools you need to manage a network come with the network itself. As the network manager, you should read through the manuals that come with your network software to see what management tools are available. For example, Windows 95 and 98, as well as Windows NT Server, include a NET DIAG command that you can use to make sure that all the computers on a network can communicate with one another.

✔ The Microsoft System Information program that comes with Windows is a useful utility for network managers.

✔ I suggest that you get one of those 100-in-1 utility programs, such as Symantec's Norton Utilities. Norton Utilities includes invaluable utilities for repairing damaged disk drives, rearranging the directory structure of your disk, gathering information about your computer and its equipment, and so on. These utilities can be useful on NetWare and Windows NT networks, but they're even more useful on peer-to-peer networks, because you can use them on the server computer as well as on the clients. (Symantec also offers a version of Norton Utilities that runs on Windows NT Server 4.0.)

✔ More software tools exist for NetWare and Windows NT networks than for peer-to-peer networks — not only because NetWare and Windows NT are more popular than peer-to-peer networks, but also because NetWare and Windows NT networks tend to be larger and more in need of software management tools than peer-to-peer networks.

Chapter 13

Who Are You? (Or Big Brother's Guide to Network Security)

● ●

In This Chapter

▶ Deciding how much security you need

▶ Setting up user IDs and passwords

▶ Protecting network resources

▶ Simplifying network security by using groups

▶ Understanding user profiles

▶ Dealing with large networks

● ●

*B*efore you had a network, computer security was easy. You just locked your door when you left work for the day. You could rest easy, secure in the knowledge that the bad guys would have to break down the door to get to your computer.

The network changes all of that. Now, anyone with access to any computer on the network can break into the network and steal *your* files. Not only do you have to lock your door, you also have to make sure that everyone else locks their doors, too.

Fortunately, just about every network operating system known to humankind has built-in provisions for network security. This situation makes it difficult for someone to steal your files even if they do break down the door. The networks covered in this book all provide security measures that are more than adequate for all but the most paranoid users.

And when I say *more* than adequate, I mean it. Most networks have security features that would make even Maxwell Smart happy. Using all these security features is kind of like Smart insisting that the Chief lower the "Cone of Silence." The Cone of Silence worked so well that Max and the Chief couldn't hear each other! Don't make your system so secure that even the good guys can't get their work done.

If any of the computers on your network are connected to the Internet, you have a whole new world of security issues to contend with. For more information about Internet security, please refer to Chapter 18.

Do You Need Security?

Most small networks are in small businesses or departments where everyone knows and trusts everyone else. They don't lock up their desks when they take a coffee break, and although everyone knows where the petty cash box is, money never disappears.

Network security isn't necessary in an idyllic setting such as this, is it? You bet it is. Here's why any network should be set up with at least some minimal concern for security:

- ✔ Even in the friendliest office environment, some information is and should be confidential. If this information is stored on the network, you want to store it in a directory that's only available to authorized users.

- ✔ Not all security breaches are malicious. A network user may be routinely scanning through his or her files and discover a filename that isn't familiar. The user then may call up the file, only to discover that it contains confidential personnel information, juicy office gossip, or your resume. Curiosity rather than malice is often the source of security breaches.

- ✔ Sure, everyone at the office is trustworthy now. But what if someone becomes disgruntled, a screw pops loose, and he or she decides to trash the network files before jumping out the window? Or what if that same person decides to print a few $1,000 checks before packing off to Tahiti?

- ✔ Sometimes the mere opportunity for fraud or theft can be too much for some people to resist. Give people free access to the payroll files, and they may decide to vote themselves a raise when no one is looking.

- ✔ Finally, remember that not everyone on the network knows enough about how Windows and the network work to be trusted with full access to your network disks. One careless mouse click can wipe out an entire directory of network files. One of the best reasons for activating your network's security features is to protect the network from mistakes made by users who don't know what they're doing.

User Accounts

The first level of network security is the use of *user accounts* to allow only authorized users access to the network. Without an account, a computer user can't log in and therefore can't use the network.

Every user account is associated with a *user ID,* which the user must enter when logging in to the network. Each account also has other network information associated with it, such as the user's password, the user's full name, user rights that tell the network what the user can and cannot do on the network, and file system rights that determine which drives, folders, and files the user can access.

Besides simply identifying network users, user accounts provide additional controls as well:

✔ Both NetWare and Windows NT Server enable you to specify that certain users can log in only during certain times of the day. This feature enables you to restrict your users to normal working hours, so that they can't sneak in at 2 a.m. to do unauthorized work. The feature also discourages your users from working overtime because they can't access the network after hours, so use it judiciously.

✔ Windows NT Server and NetWare enable you to create *group accounts* that you can use to set up several accounts with identical access rights. When you use a group account, each user still has an individual account with a user ID and password. In addition, the user accounts indicate which group or groups the user belongs to. All user accounts that belong to a particular group "inherit" the group account's access rights.

✔ Group accounts are the key to managing your user accounts. Set up group accounts for each different type of network user your network has. For example, you may create one type of group account for the accounting department and another for the sales department. Then you can easily configure the group accounts so that the accounting users can't mess with the sales users' files and vice versa.

Passwords

One of the most important aspects of network security is the use of passwords. User IDs are not usually considered secret. In fact, network users often need to know one another's user IDs. For example, if you use your network for electronic mail, you have to know your colleagues' user IDs in order to address your e-mail properly.

Passwords, on the other hand, are top secret. Your network password is the one thing that keeps an impostor from logging in to the network using your user ID and therefore receiving the same access rights that you ordinarily do. *Guard your password with your life.*

Here are some tips for creating good passwords:

✔ Don't use obvious passwords, such as your last name, your kid's name, or your dog's name. Don't pick passwords based on your hobbies, either. A friend of mine is into boating, and his password is the name of his boat. Anyone who knows him can guess his password after a few tries. Five lashes for naming your password after your boat.

✔ Store your password in your head, not on paper. Especially bad: writing your password down on a stick-on note and sticking it on your computer's monitor. Ten lashes for that. (If you must write your password down, write it on digestible paper that you can swallow after you've memorized the password.)

✔ Most network operating systems enable you to set an expiration time for passwords. For example, you can specify that passwords expire after 30 days. When a user's password expires, the user must change it. Your users may consider this process a hassle, but it helps limit the risk of someone swiping a password and then trying to break into your computer system later.

✔ Some network managers opt against passwords altogether. Not using passwords is often appropriate on small networks where security is not a major concern, especially when sensitive data isn't kept on a file server or when the main reason for the network is to share access to a printer. (Even if you don't use passwords, imposing basic security precautions such as limiting certain users' access to certain network directories is still possible. Just remember that if passwords aren't used, nothing prevents a user from signing on using someone else's user ID.)

A Password Generator for Dummies

How do you come up with passwords that no one can guess but that you can remember? Most security experts say that the best passwords don't correspond to any words in the English language but consist of a random sequence of letters, numbers, and special characters. But how in the heck are you supposed to memorize a password like *DKS4%DJ2?* Especially when you have to change it three weeks later to something like *3PQ&X(D8.*

Here's a compromise solution that enables you to create passwords that consist of two four-letter words back to back. Take your favorite book (if it's this one, you need to get a life) and turn to any page at random. Find the first four-letter word on the page. Say that it's WHEN. Then repeat the process to find another four-letter word; say you pick MOST the second time. Now combine the words to make your password: WHENMOST. I think you'll agree that WHENMOST is easier to remember than 3PQ&X(D8 and is probably just about as hard to guess. I probably wouldn't want the folks at NORAD using this scheme, but it's good enough for most of us.

Here are some additional thoughts on concocting passwords from your favorite book:

- ✔ If the words end up being the same, pick another word. And pick different words if the combination seems too commonplace, like WESTWIND or FOOTBALL.

- ✔ For an interesting variation, pick one four-letter word and one three-letter word and randomly pick one of the keyboard's special characters (like *, &, or >) to separate the words. You end up with passwords such as INTO#CAT, BALL$AND, or TREE>DIP.

- ✔ If your network allows you to use passwords that are longer than eight characters, use longer words. For example, if your passwords can be ten characters long, use a five-letter word, a four-letter word, and a separator, as in RIGHT)DOOR, HORSE!GONE, or CRIME^MARK.

- ✔ To further confuse your friends and enemies, use medieval passwords by picking words from Chaucer's *Canterbury Tales*. Chaucer is a great source for passwords because he lived before the days of word processors with spelling checkers. He wrote *seyd* instead of said, *gret* instead of great, *welk* instead of walked, *litel* instead of little. And he used lots of seven- and eight-letter words suitable for passwords: *glotenye* (gluttony), *benygne* (benign), and *opynyoun* (opinion).

- ✔ If you use any of these password schemes and someone breaks into your network, don't blame me. You're the one who's too lazy to memorize *D#SC$H4@*.

User Rights

User accounts and passwords are only the front line of defense in the game of network security. After a user gains access to the network by typing a valid user ID and password, the second line of security defense comes into play: rights.

In the harsh realities of network life, all users are created equal, but some are more equal than others. The Preamble to the Declaration of Network Independence contains the statement, "We hold these truths to be self-evident, that *some* users are endowed by the network administrator with certain inalienable rights. . . ."

The specific rights you can assign to users depend on the network operating system you use. Here is a partial list of the user rights that are possible with Windows NT Server:

✔ **Log on locally:** The user can log on to the server computer directly from the server's keyboard.

✔ **Change system time:** The user can change the time and date registered by the server.

✔ **Shut down the system:** The user can perform an orderly shutdown of the server.

✔ **Back up files and directories:** The user can perform a backup of files and directories on the server.

✔ **Restore files and directories:** The user can restore backed up files.

✔ **Take ownership of files and other objects:** The user can take over files and other network resources that belong to other users.

File System Rights (Who Gets What)

User rights control what a user can do on a network-wide basis. File system rights enable you to fine-tune your network security by controlling specific file operations for specific users. For example, you can set up file system rights to allow users into the accounting department to access files in the server's \ACCTG directory. File system rights also can enable some users to read certain files but not modify or delete them.

Each network operating system manages file system rights in a different way. Whatever the details, the effect is that you can give each user permission to access certain files, folders, or drives in certain ways.

Network rights we'd like to see

The network rights allowed by most network operating systems are pretty boring. Here are a few rights I wish were allowed:

✔ **Cheat:** Provides a special option that enables you to see what cards the other players are holding when you're playing Hearts.

✔ **Complain:** Automatically sends e-mail messages to other users that explain how busy, tired, or upset you are.

✔ **Set Pay:** Grants you special access to the payroll system so that you can give yourself a pay raise.

✔ **Sue:** In America, everyone has the right to sue. So, this right should be automatically granted to all users.

Any file system rights that you specify for a folder apply automatically to any of that folder's subfolders, unless you explicitly specify a different set of rights for the subfolder.

In Novell's NetWare, file system rights are referred to as *trustee rights*. NetWare has eight different trustee rights, listed in Table 13-1. For every file or directory on a server, you can assign any combination of these eight rights to any individual user or group.

Table 13-1		NetWare 4.2 Trustee Rights
Trustee Right	*Abbreviation*	*What the User Can Do*
Read	R	The user can open and read the file.
Write	W	The user can open and write to the file.
Create	C	The user can create new files or directories.
Modify	M	The user can change the name or other properties of the file or directory.
File Scan	F	The user can list the contents of the directory.
Erase	E	The user can delete the file or directory.
Access Control	A	The user can set the permissions for the file or directory.
Supervisor	S	The user has all rights to the file.

Windows NT Server refers to file system rights as *permissions*. NT has six basic permissions, listed in Table 13-2. As with NetWare trustee rights, you can assign any combination of NT permissions to a user or group for a given file or folder.

Table 13-2		Windows NT Server 4 Basic Permissions
Permission	*Abbreviation*	*What the User Can Do*
Read	R	The user can open and read the file.
Write	W	The user can open and write to the file.
Execute	X	The user can run the file.

(continued)

Table 13-2 *(continued)*

Permission	Abbreviation	What the User Can Do
Delete	D	The user can delete the file.
Change	P	The user can change the permissions for the file.
Take Ownership	O	The user can take ownership of the file.

Note the last permission listed in Table 13-2: Take ownership. In NT, the concept of file or folder ownership is important. Every file or folder on an NT system has an owner. The owner is usually the user who creates the file or folder. However, ownership can be transferred from one user to another. So why the take ownership permission? To prevent someone from creating a bogus file and giving ownership of it to you without your permission. NT does not allow you to give ownership of a file to another. Instead, you can give another user the right to take ownership of the file. That user must then explicitly take ownership of the file.

You can use NT permissions only for files or folders created on drives formatted as NTFS volumes. If you insist on using FAT for your NT shared drives, you can't protect individual files or folders on the drive. This is one of the main reasons for using NTFS for your NT drives.

God (also known as the Administrator)

It stands to reason that at least one network user must have the authority to use the network without any of the restrictions imposed upon other users. This user is called the *administrator*. The administrator is responsible for setting up the network's security system; that's why the administrator is exempt from all security restrictions.

Many networks automatically create an administrator user account when you install the network software. The user ID and password for this initial administrator are published in the network's documentation and are the same for all networks that use the same network operating system. One of the first things you do after getting your network up and running is change the password for this standard administrator account. Otherwise, all your elaborate security precautions are a farce; anyone who knows the default administrator user ID and password can access your system with full administrator rights and privileges, bypassing the security restrictions that you so carefully set up.

✔ Most network administrators use a boring user ID for the supervisor account, like ADMIN, MANAGER, or SUPRVSOR. Some network administrators like to pretend they're creative by using a cleverer user ID for the supervisor account. Here are some suitable user IDs for your supervisor account:

GOD	R2D2
ALLAH	C3PO
ALADDIN	PICARD
GENIE	DATA
TITAN	BORG
ZEUS	BARNEY
SKIPPER	HAL
GILLIGAN	M5

✔ **Don't forget the password for the supervisor account!** If a network user forgets his or her password, you can log in as the supervisor and change that user's password. But if you forget the supervisor's password, you're stuck.

User Profiles

User Profiles are a Windows 95 and 98 feature that keeps track of an individual user's preferences for their Windows configuration. For a non-networked computer, profiles enable two or more users to use the same computer, each with his or her own desktop settings such as wallpaper, colors, Start menu options, and so on.

The real benefit of user profiles becomes apparent when profiles are used on a network. A user's profile can be stored on a server computer and accessed whenever that user logs on to the network from any Windows computer on the network.

The following are some of the elements of Windows that are governed by settings in the user profile:

✔ Desktop settings from the Display Properties dialog box, including wallpaper, screen savers, and color schemes.

✔ Start menu programs and Windows toolbar options.

✔ Favorites, which provide easy access to the files and folders the user accesses frequently.

> ✔ Network settings, including drive mappings, network printers, and recently visited network locations.
>
> ✔ Application settings, such as option settings for Microsoft Word.
>
> ✔ The My Documents folder.

Too Many Lists! (How to Manage Multiple Servers)

One of the problems you encounter as your network grows is managing the user accounts and other directory information for multiple servers. In the early days of networking, each server kept its own directory of user accounts, access rights, computer names, and so on. That situation meant that if you set up five servers, you had to keep five separate directories up to date. Every time you added a new user to the system, you had to create five different user accounts — one for each server. What a bother.

NetWare 4.2 and 5.0 use NetWare Directory Services to avoid this problem. NDS is a single database of all network directory information. NDS enables you to create a single-user account for every user on the network, no matter how many servers are on the network and no matter how many servers that user needs to access.

Windows NT Server uses a somewhat more complicated approach. NT enables you to create a *domain,* which is a group of network servers and client computers that fall under the umbrella of a single directory. Smaller networks consist of a single domain, but larger networks can be split into two or more domains to simplify the task of administration. That feature is why the login dialog box for a Windows NT network requires that you enter a domain name to access the network.

A company with offices in separate locations is likely to create a separate domain for each location. For example, the San Francisco and Los Angeles offices may have separate domains. Or different departments may have separate domains: The accounting and marketing departments may have their own domains.

Domains can be connected by *trust relationships.* For example, the marketing department domain can be set up so that it trusts the accounting department domain. That means that the marketing domain recognizes users in the accounting domain.

As you can imagine, managing domains and trust relationships for a large network is the stuff of pocket protectors and propeller caps. If your network is large enough to require more than one domain, you need more help than this gentle introduction to network security can offer. I suggest you consult *Windows NT Networking For Dummies,* by Ed Tittel, Mary Madden, and Earl Follis (IDG Books Worldwide, Inc.).

Windows 2000 promises to alleviate the pain of managing large multidomain networks with its new Active Directory. Active Directory is like the Novell NDS in that it provides a single directory database to cover the entire network, no matter how many different servers or users you have and regardless of whether your network is contained within a single room or spread across the entire planet.

Chapter 14

If I Could Save Time in a Bottleneck (Or Optimizing Your Network's Performance)

●●

In This Chapter

▶ Understanding network bottlenecks

▶ Tuning your network

▶ Tuning your server

▶ Making your network server faster

▶ Making your network clients faster

●●

*T*he adage that there's no such thing as a free lunch really is true. When you network your computers, you reap the benefits of being able to share information and resources such as disk drives and printers. But you also have many costs. You have the cost of purchasing network cards, cable, and software, plus the cost of the time required to install the network, find out how to use it, and keep it running.

Another cost of networking exists that you may not have considered yet: the performance cost. No matter how hard you try, you can't hide the ugly truth that putting a computer on a network slows down the computer. Retrieving a word processing document from a network disk takes a bit longer than retrieving the same document from your local disk drive. Sorting that big database file takes a bit longer. And printing a 300-page report also takes a bit longer.

Notice that I use the word *bit* three times in the preceding paragraph. Lest my editor chide me for Overuse of a Three-Letter Word (OTLW), I better point out that I use the word three times to make a point. The network inevitably slows things down, but only a bit. If your network has slowed things down to a snail's pace — so that your users are routinely taking coffee breaks whenever they save a file — you have a performance problem that you can probably solve.

What Exactly Is a Bottleneck?

The term *bottleneck* does not in any way refer to the physique of your typical computer geek. (Well, I guess it *could,* in some cases.) Rather, the phrase was coined by computer geeks when they discovered that the tapered shape of a bottle of Jolt Cola limited the rate at which they could consume the beverage. "Hey," a computer geek said one day, "the narrowness of this bottleneck limits the rate at which I can consume the tasty caffeine-laden beverage contained within. This draws to mind an obvious analogy to the limiting effect that a single slow component of a computer system can have upon the performance of the system as a whole."

"Fascinating," replied all the other computer geeks who were fortunate enough to be present at that historic moment.

The phrase stuck and is used to this day to draw attention to the simple fact that a computer system is only as fast as its slowest component. It's the computer equivalent of the old truism that a chain is only as strong as its weakest link.

For a simple demonstration of this concept, consider what happens when you print a word processing document on a slow printer. Your word processing program reads the data from disk and sends it to the printer. Then you sit and wait while the printer prints the document.

Would buying a faster CPU or adding more memory make the document print faster? No. The CPU is already much faster than the printer, and your computer already has more than enough memory to print the document. The printer itself is the bottleneck, so the only way to print the document faster is to replace the slow printer with a faster one.

Here are some other random thoughts about bottlenecks:

- A computer system always has a bottleneck. Buying a faster printer makes the bottleneck less severe, but the printer may still be a bottleneck. In some extreme cases, a printer can process information faster than the computer can send it. In this case, the printer is not the bottleneck; the parallel port that the printer is attached to has become the bottleneck. The bottleneck still exists, but it has moved. Because you can't eliminate a bottleneck, the best you can do is limit its effect.

✔ One way to limit the effect of a bottleneck is to avoid waiting for the bottleneck. For example, print spooling lets you avoid waiting for the printer. Spooling doesn't speed up the printer, but it does free you up to do other work while the printer chugs along.

✔ One of the reasons computer geeks are switching from Jolt Cola to Snapple is that Snapple bottles have wider necks.

What Are the Eight Most Common Network Bottlenecks?

Funny you should ask. Here they are, in no particular order:

✔ **The CPU in the file server:** If the file server is used extensively, it should have a powerful CPU — Pentium III is best. If you use NetWare or Windows NT Server, look into getting a server computer that can house two or more processors for even better performance.

✔ **The amount of memory in the file server:** You can never have too much memory in the server. With the cost of memory so cheap these days, why not upgrade to 128MB or even 256MB?

✔ **The file server computer's bus:** Oops . . . this is kind of technical, so I put the details in a sidebar that you can skip. The nontechnical version is this: Make sure that your server computer has plenty of PCI slots and use only PCI network cards and disk controllers.

✔ **The network card:** Use 32-bit PCI network cards for the best network performance. Remember that the server computer uses the network a lot more than any of the clients.

✔ **The file server's disk drives:** Get the fastest drives that you can find. And, if possible, use SCSI drives. Sorry! I went technical on you again. Time for another sidebar.

✔ **The file server's disk controller card:** All disks must connect to the computer via a controller card, and sometimes the bottleneck isn't the disk itself but the controller card. A beefed-up controller card can do wonders for performance. PCI cards are best.

✔ **The server's configuration options:** Even simple peer-to-peer networks have options that you can configure. Some of these options can make the difference between a pokey network and a zippy network. Unfortunately, no hard-and-fast rules exist for setting these options. Otherwise, you wouldn't have options.

Warning! Reading this may be hazardous to your sanity

Every computer has a *bus,* which is basically a row of slots into which you can plug expansion cards, such as disk controllers, modems, video controllers, and network adapter cards. New computers today come with two types of buses:

- **ISA:** ISA stands for Industry Standard Architecture. ISA bus is the most common type of expansion bus. It was designed many years ago when IBM introduced its first computers based on the 80286 processor. The ISA bus sends data between the CPU and the expansion cards at 8 or 16 bits at a time, depending on whether you use it with 8- or 16-bit adapter cards. The ISA bus runs at 8MHz.

- **PCI:** Nearly all new computers include a high-speed bus called a PCI bus that overcomes the speed limitation inherent in the ISA bus design. Usually, PCI slots are used for high-speed video, disk controllers, and network cards.

The standard PCI bus works in 32-bit mode and operates at up to 33MHz. For server computers, the faster 64-bit PCI bus operating at up to 100MHz is even better.

If your network server uses disk drives or networking cards that are connected to the ISA bus, don't bother with any other efforts to improve network performance until you upgrade your server to use faster PCI disk controllers and network cards.

- **The network itself:** If you have too many users, the network can become bogged down. The solution is to divide the network into two smaller networks connected with a cool little device called a *bridge.*

The hardest part about improving the performance of a network is determining what the bottlenecks are. With sophisticated test equipment and years of experience, network gurus can make pretty good educated guesses. Without the equipment and experience, you can still make pretty good uneducated guesses.

Tuning Your Network the Compulsive Way

You have two ways to tune your network. The first is to think about it a bit, take a guess at what may improve performance, try it, and see whether the network seems to run faster. This approach is the way most people go about tuning the network.

Just say no to technical stuff about drive interfaces

Disk drives come in several varieties, and not all of them are made equal. Here are the two basic types of drives used today:

✔ **IDE:** IDE, which stands for Integrated Drive Electronics (as if that mattered), is the most common drive type used today. Don't embarrass yourself by trying to pronounce this term in any way other than spelling out the letters. The newest form of IDE, which allows large drives and faster performance, is called by various names, including EIDE, ATA, ATA-2, Fast ATA, Ultra IDE, DMA, and probably others.

✔ **SCSI:** SCSI stands for Small Computer System Interface but is pronounced *Scuzzy*. SCSI drives have several advantages over IDE drives but are also a bit more expensive. SCSI also wins the prize for Best Computer Acronym, hands down. Two newer, faster forms of SCSI are now available. Fast SCSI is twice as fast as basic SCSI, and fast-wide SCSI is twice as fast as fast SCSI, making it four times as fast as basic SCSI.

Performance zealots assure us that SCSI is vastly superior to IDE when it comes to network performance and reliability. Unfortunately, SCSI drives are also more expensive than IDE, which is why IDE remains so popular. In computers, as in everything else, you get what you pay for. If you want top-notch file server performance, use only SCSI drives.

Then you have the compulsive way, suitable for people who organize their sock drawers by color and their food cupboards alphabetically by food groups, or worse, alphabetically within food groups. The compulsive approach to tuning a network goes something like this:

1. **Establish a method for objectively testing the performance of some aspect of the network.**

   This method is called a *benchmark*. For example, if you want to improve the performance of network printing, use a stopwatch to time how long printing a fairly large document takes.

2. **Change one variable of your network configuration and rerun the test.**

   For example, if you think that increasing the size of the disk cache can improve performance, change the cache size, restart the server, and run the benchmark test. Note whether the performance improves, stays the same, or becomes worse.

3. **Repeat Step 2 for each variable you want to test.**

Here are some salient points to keep in mind if you decide to tune your network the compulsive way:

- ✔ If possible, test each variable separately — in other words, reverse the changes you've made to other network variables before proceeding.

- ✔ Write down the results of each test so that you have an accurate record of the impact that each change has on your network's performance.

- ✔ Be sure to change only one aspect of the network each time you run the benchmark. If you make several changes, you won't know which one caused the change. Or one change may improve performance, but the other change may worsen performance so that the changes cancel each other out — kind of like offsetting penalties in a football game.

- ✔ If possible, make sure that no one else uses the network when you conduct the test; otherwise, the unpredictable activities of other network users can spoil the test.

- ✔ To establish your baseline performance, run your benchmark test two or three times to make sure that the results are repeatable. If the print job takes one minute the first time, three minutes the second time, and 22 seconds the third time, something is wrong with the test. A variation of just a few seconds is acceptable, though.

Tuning a Windows 95 or 98 Server

When you use a peer-to-peer network, you have several options available that you can fiddle around with to improve the performance of your server computers. Spending the time is worthwhile, up to a point, because all network users notice the effect of a more efficient server computer.

Setting the File System performance option

Windows has a handy tuning feature that enables you to configure server options with a single click of the mouse. Here's how to tune a Windows server computer:

1. **Choose Settings⇨Control Panel from the Start menu and then double-click the System icon.**

    The System Properties dialog box appears.

2. **Click the Performance tab.**

    The performance settings for your computer appear, as shown in Figure 14-1.

Figure 14-1:
Performance
options for
a Windows
server.

3. **Click the File System button.**

   The dialog box shown in Figure 14-2 appears.

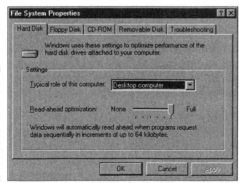

Figure 14-2:
Tuning the
file system
of a
Windows
server.

4. **Set the drop-down list box labeled Typical role of this computer to Network Server.**

   Your computer is now tuned as a network server.

5. **Click OK to dismiss the File System Properties dialog box.**

   You return to the System Properties dialog box.

6. **Click OK to dismiss the System Properties dialog box.**

That's all there is to it.

Using the FAT32 file system

Windows 98 includes an important new feature known as *FAT32,* which can significantly improve network performance. FAT32 is an improved format for hard disks that more efficiently uses the space on drives that are larger than 512MB. With FAT32, you can store more data on your disk drives because less space is wasted.

To convert your hard drive to FAT32, choose Start⇨Programs⇨Accessories⇨ System Tools⇨FAT32 Converter. The conversion takes a long time — perhaps an hour or more. You won't be able to use your computer during the conversion, so just before lunch may be a good time to start.

Unfortunately, FAT32 imposes some limitations on you:

- ✔ If you convert a drive to FAT32, you can't use Microsoft's disk compression program DriveSpace to compress the data on the drive.

- ✔ After you convert a drive to FAT32, you have no easy way to convert it back to the old format.

- ✔ If you set up your computer using a feature called *dual boot,* which enables you to choose between two operating systems when you start your computer, the dual boot feature is disabled by FAT32. So you should not use FAT32 if you also need to use another operating system on the same computer.

- ✔ After you install FAT32, you won't be able to uninstall Windows 98.

In spite of these limitations, I recommend that you use FAT32 for any disk drives that are used primarily as shared drives on a Windows 98 network server.

Although FAT32 is a Windows 98 feature, using FAT32 on a Windows 98 server computer does not mean that all of the client computers on the network must use Windows 98. Pre-Windows 98 client computers and even Macintosh client computers can access shared data that resides on a FAT32 volume.

Tuning up Windows 98

Windows 98 includes another performance-tuning feature called Windows Tune-Up. Windows Tune-Up enables you to run several programs that optimize the performance of Windows, including ScanDisk (which corrects errors on your disk drive), Disk Defragmenter (which juggles your disk data so that it's arranged efficiently on the disk), and a new program called Disk Cleanup (which removes unnecessary files from your computer).

The best thing about Windows Tune-Up is that it enables you to set up a schedule so that the tune-up programs are run automatically on a periodic basis. For example, you can use Windows Tune-Up to specify that Disk Defragmenter and ScanDisk should be run every night at midnight and Disk Cleanup should be run every Friday at noon. This feature can help ensure that you always maintain your Windows 98 server computer at peak efficiency.

You can find Windows Tune-Up buried in the Start menu, under Programs⇨ Accessories⇨System Tools.

Tuning a Windows NT Server

Tuning a Windows NT Server computer is more difficult than tuning a Windows 95 or 98 computer. Windows NT Server includes dozens of options that can affect server performance. You can spend hours tweaking these options to squeeze optimum performance out of NT.

On the other hand, Windows NT Server tends to be somewhat self-tuning. Turn it on and let it run for a few days, and it soon adjusts itself to the pattern of usage it sees on your network. Soon the server is purring like a kitten. You only need to trouble yourself with tuning Windows NT if something appears drastically wrong with the network's performance — for instance, if users complain that opening a two-page document on the network server takes ten minutes or that the print job they sent to the printer last Tuesday still hasn't printed.

To help monitor performance so that you can determine exactly where a performance problem lies, Windows NT Server comes with a program called Performance Monitor. Performance Monitor gathers statistics about all kinds of activity on your server computer, such as disk I/O, program execution, network traffic, and so on. By analyzing these statistics, you can determine the source of a network performance problem. Depending on the problem, you may be able to solve it by adjusting one of NT's configuration settings. Or you may need to purchase additional hardware to correct the problem.

Using Performance Monitor is simple. But interpreting the statistics it gathers isn't. Unless you're really into counting cache hits and average disk seek times, you probably want to steer clear of Performance Monitor if you possibly can.

Tuning a NetWare Server

Like Windows NT Server, NetWare is also a self-tuning system. Let it run for a few days to adjust to the usage patterns of your network, and it runs just fine. If you have a problem, you can always play with the server settings to try to improve performance.

Many NetWare configuration options are controlled with SET commands that you place in the AUTOEXEC.NCF file or the STARTUP.NCF file. For example, SET enables you to specify the amount of memory to use for file caching, the size of each cache buffer, the size of packet receive buffers, and a whole bunch of other stuff that's way too low-level and detailed to go into in a proud book such as this one.

Chapter 15

Things That Go Bump in the Night (How to Protect Your Network Data)

*I*f you're the hapless network manager, the safety of the data on your network is your responsibility. You get paid to lie awake at night worrying about your data. Will it be there tomorrow? If it's not, will *you* be able to get it back? And — most importantly — if you can't get it back, will *you* be there tomorrow?

This chapter covers the ins and outs of being a good, responsible, trustworthy network manager. They don't give out merit badges for this stuff, but they should.

Planning for Disaster

On April Fool's Day about ten years ago, my colleagues and I discovered that some kook had broken into the office the night before and pounded our computer equipment to death with a crowbar. (I'm not making this up.)

Sitting on a shelf right next to the mangled piles of what used to be a Wang minicomputer system was an undisturbed disk pack that contained the only complete backup of all the information that was on the destroyed computer. The vandal didn't realize that one more swing of the crowbar would have escalated this major inconvenience into a complete catastrophe. Sure, we were up a creek until we could get the computer replaced. But after we had a new computer, a simple restore from the backup disk brought us right back to where we were on March 31. Without that backup, getting back on track would have taken months.

I've been paranoid about disaster planning ever since. Before then, I thought that disaster planning meant doing good backups. That's a part of it, but I can never forget the day we came within one swing of the crowbar of losing everything. Vandals are probably much smarter now: They know to smash the backup disks as well as the computers themselves. There's more to being prepared for disasters than doing regular backups.

Don't think that it can happen to you? A few years back, the news was filled with stories of fires in Los Angeles that destroyed 400 homes. How many computers do you think were lost to Hurricane Andrew? To the floods along the Mississippi in 1993? To the San Francisco earthquake in 1989? (Not too many computers were lost in the 1906 earthquake.) And I assume you saw *Armageddon*.

Most disasters are of the less spectacular variety. Make at least a rudimentary plan for how you can get your computer network back up and running should a major or minor disaster strike.

✔ The cornerstone of any disaster/recovery plan is a program of regular backups. I devote much of this chapter to helping you get a backup program started. Keep in mind, though, that your backups are only one swing of the crowbar from being useless. Don't leave your backup disks or tapes sitting on the shelf next to your computer: Store them in a fireproof box or safe and store at least one set at another location.

✔ Your network binder is an irreplaceable source of information about your network. You should have more than one copy. I suggest that you take a copy home so that if the entire office burns to the ground, you still have a copy of your network documentation. Then you can decide quickly what equipment you need to purchase, and how you need to configure it to get your network back up and running again.

✔ After your computers are completely destroyed by fire, vandalism, or theft, how can you prove to your insurance adjuster that you really had all that equipment? A frequently overlooked part of planning for disaster is keeping a detailed record of what computer equipment you own. Keep copies of all invoices for computer equipment and software in a safe place. And consider making a videotape or photographic record of your equipment, too.

✔ Another aspect of disaster planning that's often overlooked is expertise. In many businesses, the one person who takes charge of all the computers is the only one who knows anything more than how to start WordPerfect and print a letter. What if that person becomes ill, decides to go work for the competition, or wins the lottery and retires to the Bahamas? Don't let any one person at the office form a computer dynasty that only he or she can run. As much as possible, spread the computer expertise around.

Backing Up Your Data

The main goal of backups is simple: Make sure that no matter what happens, you never lose more than one day's work. The stock market may crash, and Ross Perot may run for president again, but you never lose more than one day's work if you stay on top of your backups.

Now that we agree on the purpose of backups, we can get to the good stuff: how to do it.

Why you should buy a tape drive

If you plan on backing up the data on your network server's disk drives, you need something to back up the data to. You could copy the data onto diskettes, but your 5GB disk drive would need about 3,500 diskettes to do a full backup. That's a few more diskettes than most of us want to keep in the closet. Instead of diskettes, you want to back up your network data to tape. With an inexpensive tape drive, you can copy as much as 10GB of data onto a single tape.

The beauty of a tape drive is that you can start your backups and leave. You don't have to baby-sit your computer, feeding it disk after disk and reading a bad novel in between disk swaps. A tape drive makes running your backups unattended possible. The labor savings can pay for the cost of the tape drive in the first week.

✔ The most popular style of tape backup for smallish networks is called *QIC*, which stands for "quarter-inch cartridge." QIC drives come in a variety of models with tape capacities ranging from 2GB to 10GB. You can purchase a 2GB drive for about $125 and a 10GB unit for about $300. QIC drives are slow (about 10–20MB per minute), but they get the job done.

✔ For larger networks, you can get high-capacity and high-speed digital audiotape *(DAT)* drives. DAT drives are more expensive than QIC drives, but much faster. You can get an inexpensive DAT drive that can handle up to 8GB and back up about 90MB per minute for about $600. Or you can spend more money to get more speed and tape capacity.

✔ An alternative to tape drives for backups is removable disk drives —
disk drives housed in cartridges that you can insert or remove like a
giant floppy disk. The best known removable disk drives are made by
Iomega. Iomega's Jaz Drive sells for about $350 and can back up 2GB of
data on each cartridge.

Backup programs

Both Windows 95 and 98 come with a built-in backup program. These backup
programs are designed to simplify the task of backing up data on an individual
computer, and they are more than up to the task of backing up a Windows 95
or 98 peer-to-peer server. Figure 15-1 shows the Windows 98 backup program
in action.

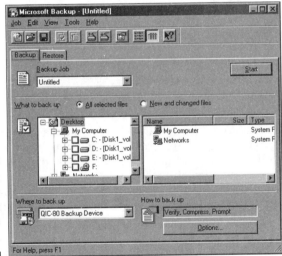

Figure 15-1:
The
Windows 98
backup
program.

Backup programs do more than just copy data from your hard drive to
diskettes or a tape. Backup programs use special compression techniques to
squeeze your data so that you can cram more data onto fewer floppy disks.
Compression factors of 2:1 are common, so you can usually squeeze 4GB of
data onto a tape that would hold only 2GB of data without compression.

You don't have to back up
every file every day

If you have a tape drive and all your network data can fit on one tape, the best
approach to backups is to back up all your data every day. If you have more
data than can fit on one tape, consider using *incremental* backups instead.

Stop me before I get carried away

The Archive Bit is not an old Abbott & Costello routine ("All right, I wanna know who modified the archive bit." "What." "Who?" "No, what." "Wait a minute . . . just tell me what's the name of the guy who modified the archive bit!" "Right.").

The archive bit is a little flag that's tucked into each file's directory entry, right next to the file-name. Any time that a program modifies a file, Windows (or your server operating system) sets the file's archive bit to the ON position. Then

after a backup program backs up the file, it sets the file's archive bit to the OFF position.

Because backup programs reset the archive bit after they back up a file, they can use the archive bit to select just the files that have been modified since the last backup. Clever, eh?

Differential backups work because they don't reset the archive bit. When you use differential backups, each differential backup backs up all the files that have been modified since the last full backup.

An incremental backup backs up only the files that you've modified since the last time you did a backup of any sort. Incremental backups are a lot faster than full backups because you probably only modify a few files each day. And if a full backup takes three tapes, you can probably fit an entire week's worth of incremental backups on a single tape.

Here are some additional tips on using incremental backups:

- The easiest way to use incremental backups is to do a full backup every Monday and then do an incremental backup on Tuesday, Wednesday, Thursday, and Friday.

- When you use incremental backups, the complete backup consists of the full backup tapes and all the incremental backup tapes you've made since you did the full backup.

- A variation of the incremental backup idea is the *differential* backup. A differential backup backs up all the files that have been modified since the last time you did a *full* backup. When you use differential backups, the complete backup consists of the full backup disks plus the disks from your most recent differential backup.

Server versus client backups

When you back up on a peer-to-peer network, you have two basic approaches to running the backup software: You can run the backup software on the file server itself, or you can run the backups from one of the network's clients. If you run the backups from the file server, you probably have to shut down the network in order to run backups. You can run backups from a client without taking down the server.

Even though you can run backups from a client while the network is running, doing backups while the network is being used isn't a good idea. The backup program skips over any files that other users have open, so your backup won't include those files. Ironically, those are the files that need backing up the most because they're the files that are being used and probably modified.

Here are some extra thoughts on client and server backups:

✔ Backing up from a workstation enables you to select network drives from more than one server. If you back up from the server and shut down the network, you can only access the drives on that server.

✔ You may think that backing up directly from the server would be more efficient than backing up from a client because data doesn't have to travel over the network. Actually, this assumption isn't usually the case, because most networks are faster than most tape drives. The network probably won't slow down backups unless you back up during the busiest time of the day, when hordes of network users are storming the network gates.

✔ Setting up a special user ID for the user who does backups is best. This user ID requires access to all the files on the server. If you're worried about security, worry about this user ID. Anyone who knows it — and its password — can log in and bypass any security restrictions that you've placed on that user's normal user ID.

You can counter potential security problems by restricting the backup user ID to a certain client and a certain time of the day. If you're really clever (and paranoid), you can probably set up the backup user's account so that the only program it can run is the backup program.

Windows NT Server provides a special user group that you can use to create backup users.

How many sets of backups should you keep?

Don't try to cut costs by purchasing one backup tape and reusing it every day. What happens if you accidentally delete an important file on Tuesday and don't discover your mistake until Thursday? Because the file didn't exist on Wednesday, it won't be on Wednesday's backup tape. If you have only one tape that's reused every day, you're outta luck.

The safest scheme is to use a new backup tape every day and keep all your old tapes in a vault. Pretty soon, though, your tape vault can start looking like the warehouse where they stored the Ark of the Covenant at the end of *Raiders of the Lost Ark.*

As a compromise between these two extremes, most users purchase several tapes and rotate them. That way, you always have several backup tapes to fall back on in case the file you need isn't on the most recent backup tape. This technique is called *tape rotation,* and several variations are in common use:

- ✔ The simplest approach is to purchase three tapes and label them A, B, and C. You use the tapes on a daily basis in sequence: A, B, C, A, B, C, and so on. On any given day, you have three *generations* of backups: today's, yesterday's, and the day-before-yesterday's. Computer geeks like to call these the *grandfather, father,* and *son* tapes.

- ✔ Another simple approach is to purchase five tapes and use one each day of the week.

- ✔ A variation of this scheme is to buy eight tapes. Take four of them and write *Monday* on one label, *Tuesday* on another, *Wednesday* on the third, and *Thursday* on the fourth label. On the other four tapes, write *Friday 1, Friday 2, Friday 3,* and *Friday 4.* Now, tack a calendar up on the wall near the computer and number all the Fridays in the year: 1, 2, 3, 4, 1, 2, 3, 4, and so on.

  On Monday through Thursday, you use the appropriate daily backup tape. When you do backups on Friday, you consult the calendar to decide which Friday tape to use. With this scheme, you always have four weeks' worth of Friday backup tapes, plus individual backup tapes for the past five days.

- ✔ If bookkeeping data lives on the network, making a backup copy of all your files (or at least all your accounting files) immediately before closing the books each month and retaining those backups for each month of the year is a good idea. Does that mean you should purchase 12 additional tapes? Not necessarily. If you back up just your accounting files, you probably can fit all 12 months on a single tape. Just make sure that you back up with the "append to tape" option rather than the "erase tape" option so that the previous contents of the tape aren't destroyed. And treat this accounting backup as completely separate from your normal daily backup routine.

You should also keep at least one recent full backup at another location. That way, if your office should fall victim to an errant Scud missile or a rogue asteroid, you can re-create your data from the backup copy you stored offsite.

A word about tape reliability

From experience, I've found that although tape drives are very reliable, once in a while they run amok. Problem is, they don't always tell you they're not working. A tape drive — especially the less expensive QIC type drives — can spin along for hours, pretending to back up your data, when in reality your data isn't being written reliably to the tape. In other words, a tape drive can trick you into thinking that your backups are working just fine, but when disaster strikes and you need your backup tapes, you may just discover that the tapes are worthless.

Don't panic! You have a simple way to assure yourself that your tape drive is working. Just activate the "compare after backup" feature of your backup software. Then as soon as your backup program finishes backing up your data, it rewinds the tape, reads each backed-up file, and compares it with the original version on disk. If all files compare, you know your backups are trustworthy.

Here are some additional thoughts about the reliability of tapes:

✔ The compare function doubles the time required to do a backup, but that doesn't matter if your entire backup fits on one tape. You can just run the backup after hours. Whether it takes one hour or ten doesn't matter, as long as it's finished by the time you arrive at work the next morning.

✔ If your backups require more than one tape, you may not want to run the compare-after-backup option every day. But be sure to run it periodically to check that your tape drive is working.

✔ If your backup program reports errors, throw away the tape and use a new tape.

Changing the Oil Every 3,000 Miles

Like cars, disk drives need periodic maintenance. Fortunately, Windows 95 and 98, as well as server operating systems such as Windows NT Server and NetWare, come with programs that can do some of the necessary maintenance for you.

ScanDisk

Bad news: Windows sometimes has trouble keeping track of all the files you heap onto your computer's disk drives. In particular, if your dog steps on your computer's power cord while you're working on a file, Windows may loose track of exactly where the file is located on the disk. The same thing can happen if you simply turn your computer off without first choosing Shut Down from the Start menu and waiting for Windows to tell you it's okay to turn off your computer.

Good news: Windows comes with a program called ScanDisk, which can correct the type of file damage that occurs when your computer is turned off at the wrong moment. In fact, ScanDisk does such a good job of correcting this type of problem that Windows runs it automatically when you turn your computer back on after turning it off without first using the Start⇨Shut Down command.

ScanDisk does more than repair files damaged by premature shutdown. ScanDisk can also check the reliability of your computer's disk drives by trying to write something onto every sector of your disk and then reading it back to see whether it took. (Don't worry — ScanDisk does this without upsetting any of the existing data on your disk.) Figure 15-2 shows the Windows 98 version of ScanDisk.

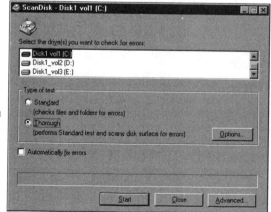

Figure 15-2:
A look at the Windows 98 version of ScanDisk.

ScanDisk can do a thorough check of your disk's recording surface to make sure that it can reliably read and write data. The check takes a while, but it's worth the wait.

If ScanDisk detects a problem, it displays a message that describes the problem and offers to fix it for you. Read the instructions on the screen and select the "More Info" function if you don't understand what's going on.

Windows NT includes its own version of ScanDisk, built into the Disk Administrator program. To activate it, choose Start⇨Programs⇨ Administrative Tools⇨Disk Administrator.

Disk defragmenting

Another routine type of service you should perform on your computer periodically is to defragment its disk drives. Defragmenting a drive rearranges all the data that's stored on the drive so that the data can be accessed efficiently. Because normal use causes the data on most drives to become scattered about, defragment your drives on a regular basis.

Windows includes a program to defragment your hard drives, named appropriately Disk Defragmenter. You can find it on the Start menu under Programs➪Accessories➪System Tools.

Guarding against the Dreaded Computer Virus

Viruses are one of the most misunderstood computer phenomena around these days. What is a virus? How does it work? How does it spread from computer to computer? I'm glad you asked.

What is a virus?

Make no mistake, viruses are real. They're not as widespread as the news media may lead you to believe, but they are very real nonetheless. Every computer user is susceptible to attacks by computer viruses, and using a network increases your vulnerability.

Viruses don't just spontaneously appear out of nowhere. Viruses are computer programs that are created by malicious programmers who've lost a few screws and should be locked up.

What makes a virus a virus is its capability to make copies of itself that can be spread to other computers. These copies, in turn, make still more copies that spread to still more computers, and so on, ad nauseam.

Then on a certain date, or when you type a particular command or press a certain key, the virus strikes, sometimes harmlessly displaying a "gotcha" message, sometimes maliciously wiping out all the data on your hard disk. Ouch.

Viruses move from computer to computer mostly by latching themselves onto floppy disks, which are frequently exchanged between computers. But viruses also can travel over the network cables that connect the computers in your network. That's why networked computers are especially vulnerable to virus attack.

Keep in mind that the network can't be infected by a virus unless the virus enters the network through some other means, typically through an infected floppy disk or a file downloaded from the Internet. But after one computer on the network becomes infected, it's likely that all the computers on the network will soon be infected, as well.

Here are some more tidbits about protecting your network from virus attacks:

- The term *virus* is often used to refer not only to true virus programs (which are able to replicate themselves) but also to any other type of program that's designed to harm your computer. These programs include so-called *Trojan horse* programs that usually look like games but are in reality hard-disk formatters.

- Computer virus experts have identified several thousand "strains" of viruses. Many of them have colorful names, such as the Stoned Virus, the Jerusalem Virus, and the Michelangelo Virus.

- Antivirus programs can recognize known viruses and remove them from your system, and they can spot the telltale signs of unknown viruses. Unfortunately, the idiots who write viruses aren't idiots (in the intellectual sense), so they're constantly developing new techniques to evade detection by antivirus programs. New viruses are frequently discovered, and the antivirus programs are periodically updated to detect and remove them.

The antivirus program

The best way to protect your network from virus infection is to use an antivirus program. These programs have a catalog of several thousand known viruses that they can detect and remove. In addition, they can spot the types of changes viruses typically make to your computer's files, decreasing the likelihood that some previously unknown virus will go undetected.

At one time, Microsoft got into the antivirus program business, bestowing its last and best version of MS-DOS with an antivirus program called MSAV. Unfortunately, neither Windows 95 nor Windows 98 come with antivirus protection, so you have to purchase a program on your own. One of the best-known Windows antivirus programs is McAfee's VirusScan.

The good folks who make antivirus programs periodically issue updates that enable the programs to capture newly discovered viruses. Consult the documentation (ugh!) that came with your antivirus program to find out how you can obtain these updates.

Beware a new kind of virus

A few years ago, a new kind of virus appeared on the virus scene. Once, you could safely assume that viruses were only transmitted via program files. In other words, you couldn't catch a virus from a document file such as a word processing document. Unfortunately, this assumption is no longer absolutely true. Most modern word processing and spreadsheet programs (including Word, WordPerfect, WordPro, Excel, and Lotus 1-2-3) have a feature called *autorun macros,* which enable you to attach small programs called *macros* to document files. These macros then automatically run whenever the document is opened.

Unfortunately, unscrupulous people have figured out how to exploit this seemingly innocent feature to infect document files with viruses. So catching a virus from a document file is now possible.

The best protection against this new virus threat is to make sure that you have the most recent version of a good antivirus program, such as McAfee's VirusScan. The latest versions of these programs should be able to detect document-borne viruses.

Safe computing

Besides using an antivirus program, you have a few additional precautions that you can take to ensure virus-free computing. If you haven't talked to your kids about these safe-computing practices, you had better do so soon.

- Regularly back up your data. If you are hit by a virus, you may need the backup to recover your data.

- If you buy software from a store and discover that the seal has been broken on the disk package, take the software back. Don't try to install it on your computer. You don't hear about tainted software as often as you hear about tainted beef, but if you buy software that's been opened, it may well be laced with a virus infection.

- Use your antivirus software to scan your disk for virus infection after your computer has been to a repair shop or worked on by a consultant. These guys don't intend harm, but they occasionally spread viruses accidentally, simply because they work on so many strange computers.

- Use your antivirus software to scan any floppy disk that doesn't belong to you before you access any of its files.

- And above all, don't leave strange disks in your disk drives overnight. The most common way for computer viruses to spread is by starting a computer with an infected disk in drive A.

Chapter 16

How to Stay on Top of Your Network and Keep the Users Off Your Back

*N*etwork managers really have a rotten deal. Users come to you whenever anything goes wrong, regardless of whether the problem has anything to do with the network. They knock on your door if they can't log in, if they've lost a file, or if they can't remember how to use the microwave. They probably even ask you to show them how to program their VCRs.

This chapter brushes over a few basic things you can do to simplify your life as a network manager.

Training Your Users

After you first get your network up and running, invite all the network users to Network Obedience School, so that you can train them in how to behave on the network. Teach them the basics of accessing the network, make sure that they understand about sharing files, and explain the rules to them.

A great way to prepare your users for this session is to ask them to read the first six chapters of this book. Remember, I wrote those chapters with the network user in mind, so they explain the basic facts of network life. If your users read those chapters first, they are in a much better position to ask good questions during obedience school.

Here are some more ways to make the training process painless for you and your users:

- Write up a summary of what your users need to know about the network, on one page if possible. Include everyone's user ID, the names of the servers, network drive assignments and printers, and the procedure for logging in to the network. Make sure that everyone has a copy of this Network Cheat Sheet.

- Emphasize the etiquette of network life. Make sure that everyone understands that all the free space on the network drive isn't their own personal space. Explain the importance of treating other people's files with respect. Suggest that it may be nice to check with your fellow users before sending a three-hour print job to the network printer.

- Don't bluff your way through your role as network manager. If you're not a computer genius, don't pretend to be one just because you know a little more than everyone else. Be up-front with your users; tell them that you're all in over your collective heads, but that you're in this together, and you're going to do your best to try to solve any problems that may come up.

- If you ask your users to read the first six chapters of this book, place special emphasis on Chapter 6, especially the part about bribes. Subtly suggest which ones are your favorites.

Organizing a Library

One of the biggest bummers about being the network manager is that every network user expects you to be an expert at every computer program he or she uses. That's a manageable enough task when you have only two network users and the only program they use is Microsoft Word. But if you have a gaggle of users who use a bevy of programs, being an expert at all of them is next to impossible.

The only way around this dilemma is to set up a well-stocked computer library that has all the information you may need to solve problems that come up. When a user bugs you with some previously undiscovered bug, you can say with confidence, "I'll get back to you on that one."

Your library should include the following:

- A copy of your network binder, containing all the information you need about the configuration of your network. (Don't put the original copy of the network binder in the library. Keep the original under lock and key in your office.)

✔ A copy of the manuals for every program used on the network. Most users ignore the manuals, so they won't mind if you "borrow" them for the library. If a user won't part with the manual, at least make a note of the manual's location so that you know where to find it.

✔ A copy of the *Windows Resource Kit* for every version of Windows in use on your network. You can get the *Windows Resource Kit* at any bookstore that has a well-stocked section of computer books.

✔ While you're at it, pick up a copy of *Windows 98 Secrets,* by Brian Livingston and Davis Straub (IDG Books Worldwide, Inc.). This book has an excellent section on networking.

✔ A copy of the network software manual or manuals.

✔ At least 20 copies of this book (hey, I have bills to pay). Seriously, your library should contain books appropriate to your level of expertise. Of course, ...*For Dummies* books are available on just about every major computer subject. Devoting an entire shelf to these yellow-and-black books isn't a bad idea.

Keeping Up with the Computer Industry

The computer business changes fast, and one of the things that your users probably expect is for you to be abreast of all the latest trends and developments. "Hey, Ward," they ask, "what do you think about the new version of SkyWriter? Should we upgrade, or should we stick with version 23?"

"Hey, Ward, we want to build an Intranet Web site. What's the best Web page editor for under $200?"

"Hey, Ward, my kid wants me to buy a sound card. Which one is better, the SoundSmacker Pro or the BlabberMouth 9000?"

The only way to give halfway intelligent answers to questions like these is to read about the industry. Visit your local newsstand and pick out a few computer magazines that appeal to you.

✔ Subscribe to at least one general-interest computer magazine and one magazine specifically written for network users. That way, you can keep abreast of general trends plus the specific stuff that applies just to networks.

✔ Look for magazines that have a mix of good how-to articles and reviews of new products.

✔ Don't overlook the value of the advertisements in many of the larger computer magazines. Some people (including me) subscribe to certain magazines because of the number of mail-order advertisements the magazines carry.

✔ Keep in mind that most computer magazines are very technical. Try to find magazines written to your level. You may discover that after a year or two, you outgrow one magazine and are ready to replace it with one that's more technical.

The Guru Needs a Guru, Too

No matter how much you know about computers, plenty of people know more than you do. This rule seems to apply at every rung of the ladder of computer experience. I'm sure that a top rung exists somewhere, occupied by the world's best computer guru. But I'm not sitting on that rung, and neither are you.

As the local computer guru, you have one of your most valuable assets in a knowledgeable friend who's a notch or two above you on the geek scale. That way, when you run into a real stumper, you have a friend you can call for advice. Here are some tips for handling your own guru:

✔ In dealing with your own guru, don't forget the Computer Geek's Golden Rule: "Do unto your guru as you would have your own users do unto you." Don't pester your guru with simple stuff that you just haven't spent the time to think through. But if you have thought it through and can't come up with a solution, give your guru a call. Most computer experts welcome the opportunity to tackle an unusual computer problem. It's a genetic defect.

✔ If you don't already know someone who knows more about computers than you do, consider joining your local PC users' group. The group may even have a subgroup that specializes in your networking software or may be devoted entirely to local folks who use the same networking software you do. Odds are, you're sure to make a friend or two at a users' group meeting. And you can probably convince your boss to pay any fees required to join the group.

✔ If you can't find a real-life guru, try to find an online guru. Check out the various computing newsgroups on the Internet.

✔ Remember that you can use the bribes listed in Chapter 6 on your own guru. The whole point of these bribes is to make your guru feel loved and appreciated.

Network Manager BS

As network manager, you sometimes just won't be able to solve a problem, at least not immediately. You can do two things in this situation. The first is to explain that the problem is particularly difficult and that you'll have a solution as soon as possible. The second is to lie. Here are some of my favorite excuses and phony explanations:

- Blame it on Y2K.
- Blame it on the version of whatever software you're using.
- Blame it on cheap, imported memory chips.
- Blame it on Democrats. Or Republicans. Whatever.
- Hope that the problem wasn't caused by stray static electricity. Those types of problems are very difficult to track down. Did the user discharge him- or herself before using the computer?
- You need more memory.
- You need a bigger disk.
- You need a Pentium III to do that.
- You can't do that in Windows 98.
- You can only do that in Windows 98.
- You're not using disk compression, are you?
- Sounds like a virus.
- Or sunspots.
- Your mind is fuzzy. You'll have to think about it over a round of golf.

Part IV
Webifying Your Network

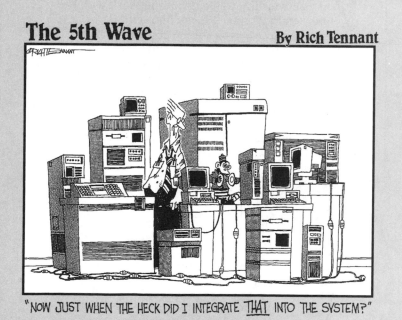

The 5th Wave   By Rich Tennant

"NOW JUST WHEN THE HECK DID I INTEGRATE THAT INTO THE SYSTEM?"

In this part . . .

You discover how to meld your network with the Internet. In Chapter 17, you find out just what the Internet is and why you should connect to it. In Chapter 18, you figure out how to safely and efficiently connect your network users to the Internet. In Chapter 19, you find out how to create your own presence on the Internet by using your network to host your very own Web site. In Chapter 20, you discover how to create an intranet, which is sort of like a Local Area Internet. With an intranet, you can set up a Web server that only users on your own network can access.

Chapter 17

Welcome to the Internet

. . . .

In This Chapter

▶ Getting acquainted with the Internet

▶ Understanding what services are available from the Internet

▶ Figuring out Internet addresses and TCP/IP

. . . .

*T*he Internet is a hot topic among computer users. Thousands of new users are jumping on the Internet every day, and the explosion shows no signs of slowing down. Should you link your computer network up with the Internet? This chapter helps you to decide.

What Is the Internet?

As the Goliath of all computer networks, the Internet links tens of millions of computer users throughout the world. Strictly speaking, the Internet is a network of networks. It consists of tens of thousands of separate computer networks all interlinked so that a user on any of those networks can reach out and touch a user on any of the other networks. This network of networks connects more than 43 million computers to each other.

The Internet consists of several distinct types of networks:

- Government agencies, such as the Library of Congress and the White House

- Military sites (Did you ever see *War Games*?)

- Educational institutions, such as universities and colleges (and their libraries)

- Businesses, such as IBM and Microsoft

- Internet service providers (ISPs), which enable individuals to access the Internet

Just how big is the Internet?

Because no particular organization owns or controls the Internet, no one knows how big the Internet really is. Several organizations do attempt to periodically determine the size of the Internet. One such organization is Network Wizards, which completed its last survey in January 1999. Network Wizards found that more than 43 million host computers were connected to the Internet, compared with fewer than 30 million in January 1998. The Internet continues to grow at a lightning-fast pace.

Unfortunately, no one knows how many actual users are on the Internet. Each domain can support a single user or — in the case of domains such as AOL.COM (America Online), COMPUSERVE.COM (CompuServe), or MSN .COM (The Microsoft Network) — hundreds of thousands or perhaps even millions of users. So, no one really knows. Still, the indisputable point is that the Internet is big, and it's getting bigger every day.

(If you're already on the Net and are interested in checking the latest Internet statistics, you can visit the Network Wizards Web site at www.nw.com.)

✔ Commercial online services, such as CompuServe, America Online, and The Microsoft Network (which is an online service that you can suscribe to, not to be confused with local area networks built using Microsoft networking tools such as Windows NT Server and Windows 98)

What Does the Internet Have to Offer?

In addition to its massive size, the Internet also boasts a great number of different services for its users. The following sections describe the various services available on the Internet.

File Transfer Protocol (FTP)

File Transfer Protocol, or *FTP,* as it's usually called, is the Internet's way of moving files around. Think of FTP as the Internet equivalent to a file server. Hundreds, if not thousands, of computers make their files available for downloading on the Internet. These computers are called FTP sites. You can use FTP to get files from Microsoft and other computer companies, government agencies, and universities. Most of these FTP sites enable anyone to access their treasures, but access to some is restricted to a lucky few.

Boring Internet history you can skip

The Internet has a fascinating history, if such things interest you. You don't have to be interested in such things, of course, except that a superficial understanding of how the Internet began may help you understand and cope with the way this massive computer network exists today. So, here goes the story.

The Internet traces its beginnings back to a small network called ARPANET, built by the U.S. Department of Defense in 1969 to link defense installations. ARPANET soon expanded to include not only defense installations, but universities as well. In the 1970s, ARPANET was split into two networks, one for military use (which was renamed MILNET) and the original ARPANET for nonmilitary use. The two networks were connected using a networking link called IP, the Internet Protocol, so called because it allowed communication between two networks.

The good folks who designed IP had the foresight to realize that soon more than two networks would want to be connected. In fact, they left room for tens of thousands of networks to join the game, which is a good thing, because not long afterward the Internet began to take off.

By the mid-1980s, ARPANET was beginning to reach the limits of what it could do. Enter the National Science Foundation (NSF), which set up a nationwide network designed to provide access to huge supercomputers, those monolithic computers used to discover new prime numbers and calculate the orbits of distant galaxies. The supercomputers themselves were never put to much use, but the network that was put together to support the supercomputers, called NSFNET, did. It replaced ARPANET as the new backbone for the Internet.

Then, out of the blue, the whole world became interested in the Internet. Stories about it appeared in *Time* and *Newsweek*. The Net began to grow so fast that even NSFNET couldn't keep up, so private commercial networks got into the game. The size of the Internet has doubled every year for the past few years, and who knows how long this dizzying rate of growth may continue.

Microsoft Office 97 and the soon-to-be-released Office 2000 enable you to access FTP sites from any Office program by using the standard File Open and Save As dialog boxes. Thus, if you want to retrieve a word processing document that's been archived at an FTP site, you can do so directly from Word. Or, if you want to upload an Excel spreadsheet file to an FTP site, you can do so directly from Excel.

Internet e-mail

E-mail is the main reason most people use the Internet. Internet e-mail is similar to e-mail on your local area network (LAN), except that you aren't limited to exchanging e-mail with users of your own network. With Internet e-mail, you can send messages to and receive messages from anyone anywhere on the Internet.

Internet Relay Chat (IRC)

Internet Relay Chat, or *IRC,* is the Internet's real-time chat feature. It enables Internet users all across the globe to go online at the same time and exchange messages, kind of like a giant conference call. Discussion topics range from politics to lingerie, though IRC conversations tend to be unfocused.

Mailing lists

A *mailing list* is a list of the e-mail addresses of a group of people who are interested in a particular subject, such as flat-tax proposals, *Star Trek* movies, or origami. The mailing list itself has an e-mail address. When you send e-mail to the mailing-list address, your message is automatically distributed to everyone else on the list. To get on a mailing list, you subscribe to it by sending an e-mail message to the list's administrator. (The subscription address is almost always different from the mailing list's normal address, so be careful to send your subscription request to the correct address.)

Telnet

Telnet is a way of connecting to another computer on the Internet and actually running programs on that computer as if your computer were a terminal attached to the other computer. Telnet is one of the many Internet services that is rapidly losing popularity as the World Wide Web (which I describe later in this chapter) becomes more popular. However, many Internet services — such as the ability to scan the card catalogs of many public libraries — are still available only via Telnet.

Usenet newsgroups

Newsgroups are online discussion groups where users with common interests gather to share ideas. Newsgroups exist for just about every topic you can imagine — everything from gardening to car repair.

For technical reasons you don't need or want to know, Internet newsgroups are distributed over what is called *Usenet.* As a result, you sometimes see the terms Usenet and newsgroups used together.

Unlike Internet Relay Chat, which I discuss earlier in this chapter, Usenet newsgroups are not real-time discussions. Newsgroups are more like e-mail: You post a message and then check back a day or two later to see if anyone replied.

What about commercial online services?

The Internet isn't the only, or necessarily the best, source of online information. One of the great strengths of the Internet is also one of its biggest weaknesses: The information on the Internet isn't organized in any official manner, so finding the information you're looking for can be difficult, if not sometimes impossible. If, like a good Presbyterian, you prefer a sense of decency and order, you may try one of the commercial online services, such as America Online, CompuServe, or The Microsoft Network. These services provide an organized approach to online information. You can get discussion forums and download libraries organized logically by topic. You may also find that the commercial online services are a bit friendlier than the Internet, especially to novices. (Many Internet users don't have much patience for the mistakes made by the millions of new users who have recently flooded their once-private turf.)

The main disadvantage of commercial online services is that they're more expensive than the Internet. However, many of the commercial online services also offer access to the Internet, so you can get the best of both worlds and compare them.

World Wide Web

The *World Wide Web,* or *WWW* as it's alliteratively called, is the main method of accessing information on the Internet. Think of it as a graphical interface to Internet information, but with an important twist: The Web is filled with special hypertext links that enable you to jump from one Internet locale to another.

The Web is a vast collection of individual *pages* that you can view one at a time with a program called a *Web browser.* The two most popular Web browsers are Netscape Navigator and Microsoft Internet Explorer. I say more about Web browsers in Chapter 18.

A *home page* is a virtual "page" that serves as the entry point to a company's or individual's collection of Web pages. All the big companies have their own home pages, and many small companies and even some individuals have their own home pages, too. The entire collection of Web pages for a company or an individual is known as a *Web site.*

Basic Web pages are constructed from a simple language known as HTML. You can build more advanced Web pages using various programming languages, the most popular of which are Java, JavaScript, and VBScript. Programmed Web pages can interact with users in much the same way that a Windows program, such as Microsoft Word, does.

Be warned: The Internet is not censored

No censorship exists on the Internet. If you look hard enough, you can find just about anything on the Internet — not all of it wholesome. A few days ago, my youngest daughter needed to research the great sprinter Jackie Joyner Kersee for a school report. A simple search of her name using one of the most popular search services didn't reveal a single Web site devoted to her, but instead the search turned up several pages of links to Web sites featuring pictures of nude celebrities. Sigh.

Unfortunately, you can't do much about the content on the Internet. Congress has tried to legislate Internet decency, but the Supreme Court has ruled such legislation unconstitutional. After all, indecency is a pretty ambiguous concept, and the First Amendment pretty much prohibits Congress from banning any but the most obscene materials from publication on any medium. And even if Congress could define indecency, any law that Congress could pass would apply only to the United States. The Internet is a worldwide network

However, just because Congress can't prevent people from publishing offensive material on the Internet doesn't mean that you have to view it or allow your network users to view it. One of the newest developments on the Internet is a voluntary system of ratings that lets you know whether an Internet site contains offensive material. You can configure Web browsers to prevent such material from being viewed. And you can purchase additional programs, such as NetNanny, that filter out offensive material.

A recent development on the Web is known as *push technology*. Push enables you to subscribe to Web sites that interest you and then automatically receive regular updates whenever the information on the site changes. For example, you can subscribe to a Web site that automatically informs you when an update to your Windows software is available. Or you can get sports scores or stock quotes sent to you automatically every hour, on the hour.

Push technology isn't necessarily a good thing for users who are connected to the Internet via a LAN connection. With push, network users can create an almost constant stream of information flowing to them from the Internet. Unfortunately, this information must travel across the LAN to get from the Internet to the user, taking up valuable bandwidth on the LAN and slowing down the overall speed of the network. If you're a network administrator, you may want to put limits on the use of push subscriptions.

Understanding Internet Addresses

Just as every user of your LAN must have a user ID, everyone who uses the Internet must have an Internet address. Because the Internet has so many computers and so many users, a single user ID would not be sufficient. As a result, Internet addresses are constructed using a method called the *Domain Name System,* or *DNS.*

The term *domain,* when used in discussing Internet addresses, has nothing to do with Windows NT Server domains. Windows NT Server domains are used to segment large networks into smaller groups to simplify the task of managing user IDs and other network directory information. In contrast, Internet domains are a method of naming computers on the Internet.

An Internet address for an individual user follows this format:

```
username@organization.category
```

As you can see, the address consists of these three parts:

- ✔ **User name:** This is the name assigned to the user at his or her computer. It's the Internet's equivalent to Microsoft Network's user ID. If you're an employee of `nasa.gov`, and you log in to NASA's computer as Neil, your full Internet address would be `neil@nasa.gov`.

- ✔ **Organization:** The organization name is, well, the name (or abbreviation of the name) of the organization, institution, or agency. For example, `ibm.com` is a commercial organization named IBM. The educational institution named MIT has the name `mit.edu`. And `nasa.gov` is a government agency named NASA.

- ✔ **Category:** The category is a two- or three-character suffix that indicates the broad category into which the user's computer system falls. The six most commonly used categories are summarized in Table 17-1. The category portion of an Internet address is also known as the *top-level domain.*

Occasionally, some Internet addresses are more complicated. Addresses get complicated when large organizations want to subdivide their networks into two or more groups. For example, a university may break its network down by department. Thus, the address of the history department at a university may be `his.gadolphin.edu`, whereas the track team may be located at `track.gadolphin.edu`.

Table 17-1	Categories Used in Internet Addresses
Category	*Explanation*
edu	Education
mil	Military
gov	Government
com	Commercial
net	Network
org	Organizations that don't fit one of the other categories — usually nonprofit organizations

When pronouncing Internet addresses, the @ symbol is pronounced *at,* and the periods are pronounced *dot.* Thus, the address neil@nasa.gov would be pronounced *Neil at NASA dot gov.*

In addition to e-mail addresses, you also need to know a bit about addresses of places you can visit on the Internet. These addresses are called *URLs,* which stands for *Uniform Resource Locators.* URLs usually consist of three words separated by periods. If the first word is *www,* the site is a page on the World Wide Web. For FTP sites, the first word is usually *ftp.* The second word is typically the name of a company or organization that sponsors the site, and the third word is the sponsor's category name (like the category names used in an e-mail address, which I list in Table 17-1). Thus, www.ibm.com is the URL for IBM's Web page, and www.microsoft.com is the address for Microsoft's Web page.

You sometimes see Web addresses that begin with http://, as in http://www.microsoft.com. All WWW addresses use this prefix, but depending on the software you use to access the Internet, you may be able to omit the http:// prefix when you type in a site's address. The most recent versions of Netscape Navigator and Microsoft Internet Explorer don't require you to enter http://.

You may also see additional information tacked on to the end of a Web address, as in www.nasa.gov/hqpao/nasacenters.html. This Web address displays a page that lists the various centers within NASA. You need to type in the information following www.nasa.gov to reach the page at NASA that outlines its various centers.

Another type of address that you may encounter is the address of an Internet newsgroup. Newsgroup addresses begin with one of the following words:

- ✔ alt
- ✔ comp
- ✔ misc
- ✔ news
- ✔ rec
- ✔ sci
- ✔ soc
- ✔ talk

The rest of the address indicates the topic discussed in the newsgroup. For example, comp.answers is a place to get answers to general computer questions. Try comp.sys.ibm.pc.hardware.networking for answers to questions about network hardware.

Coping with TCP/IP

TCP/IP — which stands for Transmission Control Protocol/Internet Protocol — is the low-level networking protocol that the Internet uses to send data back and forth between computers. Fortunately, you don't need to know many details about TCP/IP to work with the Internet, other than knowing that you have to install TCP/IP on each network computer if you want it to be able to access the Internet.

In network terms, a *protocol* is a set of rules that computers use to communicate with one another over a network. Unfortunately, the Internet uses different protocols than most local area networks use. To use the Internet successfully from a LAN, you have to convince your LAN's protocols and the Internet's protocols to coexist on the same network without stepping on one another's toes. Don't worry . . . you can do it. Windows NT Server, NetWare, and Windows 95 or 98 networks all get along well with Internet protocols.

Here are a few other TCP/IP tidbits you should be aware of:

- ✔ TCP/IP is an open protocol, which means that it isn't tied to any one particular hardware or software vendor. Just about any vendor's hardware or software can work with TCP/IP. In contrast, both NetWare and Windows NT Server like to use their own protocols, which were developed by Novell and Microsoft, respectively.

- ✔ TCP/IP isn't a cabling standard. TCP/IP works with whatever network cabling you already have installed. Thus, you can run TCP/IP on your existing Ethernet network cables.

- ✔ TCP/IP doesn't conflict with NetWare or Windows NT Server protocols. Thus, you can run NetWare, Windows NT Server, and TCP/IP networks together, over the same cables, at the same time.

- ✔ TCP/IP is a software-based protocol. To build a TCP/IP network, all you need to add are software drivers to the computers that you want to participate in the TCP/IP network. You don't have to purchase special network cards or other hardware.

What Is an Intranet?

Okay, enough said about the Internet for now. We know that the Internet has millions and millions of users, that the World Wide Web is the best thing to happen to computers since the invention of the Off switch, and that TCP/IP is the key protocol for the Internet.

Shortly after the Web became popular, companies began to discover that the Web protocols are useful not only for the Internet, with its worldwide reach, but also for a company's local area network. In other words, TCP/IP can be used on a LAN to create a private Internet, a localized version of the World Wide Web that only computers on the LAN can access. Local area Webs became known as *intranets,* because they resemble the Internet but work within a single network rather than across the global network.

Why go to all the trouble to add TCP/IP to an already complicated LAN? Because TCP/IP enables you to create Web applications that run on your LAN. Here are just a few examples of the types of applications that companies build on their Intranets:

- **Company policy manuals.** Any employee can access an up-to-date version of the manual from a Web browser. For large companies, the money saved by not having to print policy manuals is huge.

- **Company bulletin boards, company newsletters, and other forms of internal corporate communications.**

- **Benefits administration, such as medical insurance, retirement plans, and so on.**

- **Support services, such as the computer help desk.** An Intranet is an ideal way to track problem reports through to their resolution.

- **Product information and catalogs.**

- **Executive Information Systems, such as sales trend analysis and production control.**

The list goes on and on. For more information about creating your own Intranet, refer to Chapter 20.

What about IP addresses?

Friendly Internet addresses, such as microsoft.com and idgbooks.com, make surfing the Internet easy for us end users. But as you might imagine, computers don't deal directly with friendly addresses. Instead, TCP/IP uses special addresses called *IP addresses* to uniquely identify every computer in the world that's connected to the Internet.

An IP address is a 32-bit number that is usually written as a series of four decimal numbers separated by periods, like this: 130.32.15.3. Depending on the size of your network, the first two or three numbers in the address are assigned to your entire network. The rest of the address identifies an individual computer on your network.

If you connect your network to the Internet, every computer on your network that attempts to access the Internet needs its own IP address. Fortunately, you don't have to manually assign an IP address to each computer. Instead, Internet addresses can be assigned automatically by a special server computer called a *DHCP Server*. (Don't ask what *DHCP* stands for — you really don't need to know.) If you connect to the Internet via an Internet service provider (ISP), your ISP probably has its own DHCP Server that assigns IP addresses for you. If not, you can configure a Windows NT Server or NetWare server computer to operate as a DHCP server for your network.

Chapter 18

Connecting to the Internet

• •

• •

So you've decided to connect your network to the Internet. All you have to do is run to the local computer discount store, buy a modem, and plug it in, right? Wrong. Unfortunately, there's more to connecting to the Internet than just installing a modem. For starters, you have to make sure that a modem is the right way to connect — other methods are faster but more expensive. Then, you have to select and configure the software you use to access the Internet. And finally, you have to lay awake at night worrying that hackers are breaking into your network via its Internet connection.

Connecting Your Network to the Internet

If you want to enable the users of your network to access the Internet, you have several options. The following sections describe the most commonly used methods of connecting network users to the Internet.

Connecting with modems

A *modem* is a device that enables your computer to connect to another computer via the telephone. Modems are the most common way to connect to the Internet. Modems are inexpensive — you can get cheap ones for as little as $50. Most modems connect to the Internet at a speed of 33.6 Kbps, which means that the modem can send about 33,600 bits of information per second over a standard phone connection. Faster modems, which cost a bit more than 33.6 Kbps modems, operate at 56 Kbps.

To use a modem, you must also have a phone line with a phone jack located near the computer. The modem ties up the phone line whenever you're connected to the Internet, so you can't use the phone for a voice conversation and connect to the Internet at the same time.

The easiest way to connect your network users to the Internet with modems is to give each user who needs Internet access his or her own modem and a dedicated phone line. This system enables each user to access the Internet independently of the LAN. After you install the modems and phone lines, contact a local Internet service provider, and the folks there can help you set up your Internet accounts.

Setting up a separate modem and phone line for each user is probably the easiest way to set up your Internet access. However, this system can get pretty expensive when you start to add up the monthly costs of all those phone lines. To cut costs, you can install a modem on a server computer and use software that enables network users to access the modem as a shared device. This process is a little more complicated because it requires extra work to set up the modem so that it can be shared. Neither NetWare, Windows NT Server, nor Windows 95 or 98 can do this on its own, so you have to purchase additional modem-sharing software to make sharing work.

If you go this route, only one network user can access the Internet at a time. And performance on the server computer is affected whenever the modem is in use. A better way to share modems among your network users is to set up a separate computer to function as a communications server. Then you can install one or more modems in the communications server computer so that your network users can access the modems. Once again, you have to purchase separate modem-sharing software to enable the server to share its modems with the network.

An even better way to share modems is to install a special-purpose device that connects your network to the Internet via modems. For example, Ramp Networks makes a product called the WebRamp, which is a combination of several devices in a single box: A *router* creates a link between your LAN and the Internet, a four-port 10baseT Ethernet hub enables you to connect four computers (or more if you cascade additional hubs), and three serial ports enable you to plug in modems. A basic WebRamp, which enables you to share up to three modems on your network, sells for under $500. (For more information, you can visit the Ramp Networks Web site at www.rampnet.com.)

ISDN, which stands for *Integrated Services Digital Network,* is a digital, rather than analog, phone line. ISDN allows data to be sent much faster than a conventional phone line — up to 128 Kbps rather than 33.6 Kbps or 56 Kbps. As an added plus, a single ISDN line can be split into two separate channels so that you can carry on a voice conversation while your computer is connected to the Internet. Each channel operates at 56 Kbps.

What about the cable guy?

One of the newest methods of connecting to the Internet is to use the same cable that delivers cable TV to homes and businesses. Cable Internet service uses a technology called *broadband* to enable television and data to travel over the cable at the same time. Cable Internet service has many advantages over a dial-up Internet connection:

✔ With cable, the Internet is always immediately available. You don't have to wait for a phone to dial up a service provider.

✔ A cable Internet connection is much faster than any type of dial-up connection. With cable, you can download information from the Internet at a whopping 10 Mbps, which makes it just about the fastest Internet connection you can get. For technical reasons that you don't want to know, uploading information is slower than downloading information. But uploads still run at a brisk 2 Mbps pace.

✔ Cable Internet doesn't tie up a phone line while you're connected to the Internet. It doesn't tie up your television, either: You can watch TV and surf the Web at the same time.

✔ Cable Internet is inexpensive. In fact, a typical TV and Internet subscription costs about $40 per month, which isn't much more than the cost of a basic cable subscription and a dial-up Internet subscription added together. You do have to purchase a special cable modem, but that probably won't cost much more than $100.

✔ Although cable Internet is ideal for home users, most of whom already subscribe to cable TV anyway, it's also great for businesses.

The only drawback to cable Internet access is that it isn't available everywhere yet. In fact, at the time that I write this, only a few select cities have cable Internet service. Cable companies are hard at work getting ready for cable Internet access, however. So cable Internet may well be available in your area soon.

Sounds great. The only catch is that it's expensive. An ISDN connection doesn't require a modem. Instead, you use a special ISDN adapter, and that can set you back at least $200. In addition, an ISDN line is more expensive to install than a normal phone line, and the monthly fee for an ISDN line usually amounts to between $25 and $50, depending on your area. On top of that, you may be billed by the minute for usage. For example, in my area, an ISDN line costs $24.95 per month plus a penny per minute.

An ISDN line can be shared by network users just as a modem can. You can install an ISDN line in a server computer and use special software to share the line with the network, or you can purchase a device called an *ISDN router*, which connects to your network using a standard 10baseT or 10base2 Ethernet connection and connects to the Internet via one or more ISDN connections. ISDN routers cost anywhere from $500 to $2,500 or more.

An alternative to ISDN that may be available in your area is ADSL, which stands for Asymmetric Digital Subscriber Line. This incredibly high-speed modem service lets you access the Internet over ordinary phone lines at speeds up to 8 Mbps for downloads and 1 Mbps for uploads. ADSL is available only in a few areas, but it is worth looking into. If you already have Internet access, you can find out more about ADSL at www.adsl.com.

Connecting with high-speed private lines T1 and T3

If you're really serious about high-speed Internet connections, contact your local phone company (or companies) about installing a dedicated high-speed digital line. These lines can cost you plenty (on the order of hundreds of dollars per month), so they're best suited for large networks in which 20 or more users are accessing the Internet simultaneously.

A T1 line has more than ten times the capacity of an ISDN connection, with speeds up to 1.544 Mbps — that's *million* bits per second. A T1 line can service as many as 24 users simultaneously, each working at 64 Kbps, roughly equivalent to the speed each user can achieve with a dedicated 56 Kbps modem and phone line or an ISDN connection.

A T3 line is even faster than a T1 line. A T3 line transmits data at an amazing 44.184 Mbps. Each T3 line can be divided into 28 T1 lines. Because each T1 line can handle 24 users at 64 Kbps, a T3 line can handle 672 users (24 x 28 = 672). Of course, T3 lines are also considerably more expensive than T1 lines.

If you don't have enough users to justify the expense of an entire T1 or T3 line, you can lease just a portion of the line. With a *fractional T1 line,* you can get connections with speeds of 128 Kbps to 768 Kbps, and with a *fractional T3 line,* you can choose speeds ranging from 4.6 Mbps to 32 Mbps.

Setting up a T1 or T3 connection to the Internet is stuff best left to professionals. Getting this type of connection to work is far more complicated than setting up a basic LAN.

Choosing a Web Browser

When you connect your LAN to the Internet, you must provide software known as a *Web browser* for your network's users to use when accessing the network. Although you have many different Web browsers to choose from, most people use one of two popular programs: Netscape Navigator or

Microsoft Internet Explorer. Navigator has been around longer than Internet Explorer, so it's used by more people. However, Internet Explorer is gaining popularity fast and may eventually match Navigator's success.

The debate about which browser is better — Navigator or Internet Explorer — is one of the hottest holy wars being fought in computerdom these days. Proponents of each program have a nasty tendency to demonize the other, suggesting either that Navigator is a relic of the Stone Age or that Internet Explorer is nothing more than Microsoft chairman Bill Gates's most recent attempt at world domination.

The truth is that both Navigator and Internet Explorer are excellent programs. Both are so good, in fact, that recommending one over the other on any basis, other than personal preference, is difficult. I recommend that you use Internet Explorer, but I base my recommendation solely on the fact that I've written two books about Internet Explorer titled *Internet Explorer 4 For Dummies and Internet Explorer 5 For Dummies* (both published by IDG Books Worldwide, Inc., naturally), and I'd like to retire young. Choose whichever book matches the version of Internet Explorer that you're using.

Both Internet Explorer and Navigator come loaded with features that go beyond simple Web browsing. The complete Internet Explorer package includes a bunch of extra goodies, such as the following:

- Outlook Express, an e-mail program that can also handle Internet newsgroups

- NetMeeting, a conferencing program that enables you to conduct online meetings with other Internet users

- Microsoft Chat, an online chatting program that can display chats in normal text mode or in an interesting (but annoying after a while) comic-strip mode

- Microsoft FrontPage Express, a Web page creation tool

The current version of Microsoft Internet Explorer — Internet Explorer 5 — sports many new features, including offline features that let you view Web pages without connecting to the Internet.

Netscape distributes its Navigator program in a bundle of Internet products called Communicator. Besides Navigator, the Communicator package includes the following:

- Netscape Messenger, an e-mail and news reader program

- Netscape Composer, a tool for creating Web pages

- Netscape Conference, which enables you to conduct online meetings with other users, much like Microsoft's NetMeeting

Internet Explorer's legal problems

At the time that I write this, Microsoft and the U.S. Department of Justice are in court over Microsoft's practice of distributing Internet Explorer 4 along with Windows 98. Microsoft claims that Internet Explorer is an integral part of Windows 98. The Justice Department claims that combining Internet Explorer with Windows 98 is nothing but a clever marketing ploy designed to stifle competition.

Only time will tell how the trial will turn out and what effect, if any, the outcome will have on Microsoft and the computer industry. For now, Microsoft continues to distribute Internet Explorer 4 with Windows 98 and offers Internet Explorer 5 as an add-on.

Microsoft plans to continue its practice of combining Windows and Internet Explorer by bundling Internet Explorer 5 with the next version of Windows, known as Windows 2000. We'll see if the Justice Department will allow Microsoft to do that.

The best news about Internet Explorer and Navigator is that both programs are free. You can download Internet Explorer from Microsoft's Web page at www.microsoft.com/ie, and you can download Communicator from Netscape's Web site at www.netscape.com.

Whichever browser you choose, you should standardize your entire network on one browser or the other. After all, when someone's Internet connection breaks, you're the one who's called in to fix it. If you standardize your Web browser, you become an expert in only one of them. If you don't standardize, you have to be an expert in both Navigator and Internet Explorer.

Internet Explorer 4 is a built-in part of Windows 98, so you don't have to install it separately. However, you can still use Navigator if you prefer. And you can upgrade to Internet Explorer.

Worrying about Security Issues

After any computer on your network connects to the Internet, a whole host of security issues arise. One of the most important security issues to worry about is that, unbeknownst to you, your Internet connection can function as a two-way street. Not only does it enable you to step outside the bounds of your network to access the Internet, it can also allow others to step in and access your network via its Internet connection.

Securing your network

It is absolutely imperative that if any computer on your network is going to connect to the Internet via a modem, you use proper security measures on the entire network. Here are some suggestions:

- ✔ Never allow a computer attached to the Internet via a modem to enable file sharing for TCP/IP on its modem. Doing so practically invites Internet hackers to explore your network. See the next section, "Disabling TCP/IP file sharing on a modem connection," for more information.

- ✔ Make sure that every user must enter a password to access the system. If you're using Windows NT Server or NetWare, require users to change passwords periodically and don't allow short passwords (fewer than seven or eight characters).

- ✔ Make sure that all shared disk drives have restrictions so that only specific users or groups can access them.

- ✔ For Windows NT Server, use only NTFS volumes so that you can provide adequate security.

Disabling TCP/IP file sharing on a modem connection

For a modem connection from a single Windows 95 or 98 computer to the Internet, Windows allows you to enable file and printer sharing for TCP/IP connections over your modem. If you use that modem to connect to the Internet, you are inviting disaster. To make sure that file sharing is not enabled for TCP/IP via the modem, follow these steps:

1. **From the Start menu, choose Settings⇨Control Panel and then double-click the Network icon.**

   This action brings up the Network control panel application, as shown in Figure 18-1.

2. **Click TCP/IP⇨Dial-Up Adapter in the list of network components.**

   You may have to scroll down this list to find it.

3. **Click the Properties button.**

   A dialog box appears, instructing you that this isn't the correct way to change the TCP/IP settings. Ignore it.

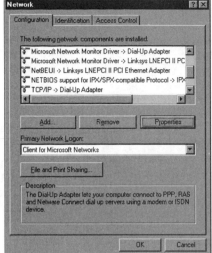

Figure 18-1:
The
Network
control
panel.

4. **Click OK to summon the TCP/IP Properties dialog box and then click the Bindings tab.**

   The dialog box shown in Figure 18-2 appears.

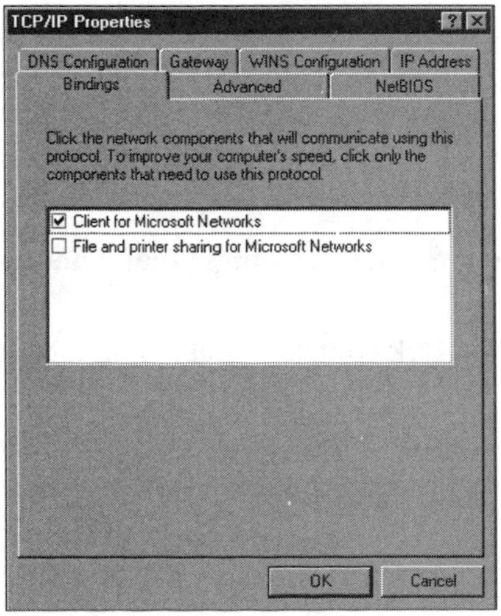

Figure 18-2:
Bindings for
TCP/IP on
the dial-up
adapter.

5. **Make sure that the File and Printer Sharing for Microsoft Networks option is *not* checked.**

   If this option is checked, click it to remove the check mark.

6. **Click OK to dismiss the TCP/IP Properties dialog box and then click OK again to dismiss the Network control panel.**

   Windows may pretend to look busy for a few moments and may even ask you to reboot your computer. If so, be patient.

For the best Internet security, you should install and use a proxy server or firewall, which I describe in Chapter 19.

Considering other Internet security issues

Besides intruders breaking into your network via your Internet connection, you have other security concerns to worry about when your network users have Internet access. Here are some of the more important ones:

- **Sending information over the Internet.** Without the right security measures, sensitive information that users send out over the Internet can be intercepted and stolen. Sensitive information, such as passwords and credit card numbers, should always be transmitted over the Internet in an encrypted form.

- **Downloading programs over the Internet.** Programs that your users download to their computers may contain viruses that can infect your entire network. Virus protection is in order.

- **Viewing Web pages that do more than meets the eye.** Empowered by advanced programming tools, such as Java and ActiveX, and scripting languages, such as JavaScript and VBScript, a Web page can do more than display information: The page itself can act like a computer program. An unscrupulous Web programmer can set up a Web page that displays a smiley face while it secretly erases files on a user's hard disk or plants a virus that infects your network.

To guard against these threats, make sure that your Internet users use the built-in security features of their Web browsers. Fortunately, both Internet Explorer and Navigator have adequate security features to keep the bad guys at bay.

Chapter 19

Hosting Your Own Web Site

• •

• •

Sooner or later, you discover that all your competitors have created their own home pages on the World Wide Web, and you want to do likewise. Take a deep breath. Setting up your LAN so that your users can access the Internet is difficult enough. Creating your own Internet site is another matter altogether. I start by saying outright that this isn't something you should attempt on your own. Seek professional help.

If you choose to ignore my sage advice, read on. (Don't worry, I'm accustomed to being ignored. I have three teenage daughters.)

Serving Up Your Web Page

You have two basic approaches to setting up a server to host your Web page on the Internet. The first and simplest approach is to contact the folks at a local Internet service provider and find out how much setting up shop on their computer costs. Most ISPs allow their users to store a few megabytes of data on the ISP's computers, so you can easily set up a simple home page if you don't want it to be too fancy. A couple of megabytes isn't nearly enough disk space to include complicated graphics, sounds, and video clips — things that make a Web page worth viewing. You probably want to pay for additional space. For the right price, your ISP will probably set up an entire server computer for you.

The second way to create your own home page is to set up your own Web server computer. The Web server computer is connected to the Internet via a high-speed connection, such as an ISDN or a T1 or T3 line. The Internet server computer may run Windows NT Server, NetWare, or UNIX; most Internet servers run UNIX, although Windows NT is growing in popularity. In addition, you need special Internet server software.

Life gets more complicated if you want to connect the Internet server computer to your LAN. In that case, you must take special precautions to ensure that strangers can't use your Internet server as a back door into your LAN. Hackers love to break into computer systems this way, either to trash files, steal information, or just prove they can do it.

Selecting a Web server

To set up a Web site, you need to dedicate a separate computer to act as a Web server. All the information that's available via your Web site resides on this computer's disk, so plenty of disk storage is a must for your Web server. Plenty of RAM is a must also — consider 128MB to be the minimum.

Selecting a Web-friendly operating system

For a Web-friendly network operating system, you have two basic choices: Windows NT Server or UNIX. Because the Internet got its start in the UNIX world, more Web sites run UNIX than Windows NT. However, Windows NT is gaining ground, especially in intranets. If you're familiar with Windows but have never touched a UNIX computer, Windows NT Server is the way to go.

Oh, I know that Novell has recently endowed NetWare with Internet server tools. However, the vast majority of Web sites are hosted on Windows NT Server or UNIX. Stick with one of these options unless you're a NetWare zealot and want to be a renegade.

Selecting Web server software

In addition to a server operating system, you also need Web server software. The following sections briefly describe the most popular Web server software choices.

NCSA HTTPd

By far the most popular Web server software on the Internet is NCSA HTTPd, often called simply NCSA. *NCSA* stands for the National Center for Supercomputing Applications, located at the University of Illinois in Urbana, Illinois. HTTPd is a UNIX-only Web server and requires a certain amount of UNIX expertise to install and operate it.

This Web server is popular for two reasons:

 ✔ NCSA was the first Web server. In fact, NCSA *invented* the Web.
 ✔ NCSA is free. You can download it from `hoohoo.ncsa.uiuc.edu`.

Apache

Apache is another UNIX-only Web server that is free of charge. Apache is essentially an improved version of NCSA and is almost as popular on the Internet. You can obtain Apache from the Internet at `www.apache.org`.

Netscape Web servers

Netscape, one of the most successful Internet companies, markets several Web servers. Unlike NCSA or Apache, the Netscape servers run on UNIX or Windows NT Server. The bad news is that these servers aren't free: You must pay a one-time fee of $295–$995, depending on which server you choose.

Netscape offers the following server products:

 ✔ **Netscape Enterprise Server.** The latest and greatest version of Netscape's Web server, which includes support for Java, the Web scripting language that everyone's talking about. This server is also available as a part of a suite of server products called SuiteSpot.
 ✔ **Netscape FastTrack Server.** A user-friendly Web server that includes setup wizards to make installation easier, as well as point-and-click tools for creating Web pages. Netscape's FastTrack Server is included with Novell's Network 5 network operating system.

Microsoft Internet Information Server

Internet Information Server, or IIS, is Microsoft's answer to Netscape's servers. Unlike the Netscape servers, IIS runs only on Windows NT Server (after all, IIS is from Microsoft). But also unlike Netscape, IIS is free — you can download it from `www.microsoft.com`. Or you can get it by purchasing Windows NT Server 4.0.

Protecting Your LAN from the Internet

A *firewall* is a security-conscious router that sits between the outside world and your network, in an effort to prevent *them* from getting to *us*. The firewall acts as a security guard between the Internet and your LAN. All network traffic into and out of the LAN must pass through the firewall, which runs special software that prevents unauthorized users from accessing the LAN.

Some type of firewall is a must if you host a Web site on a server computer that's connected to your LAN. Without a firewall, anyone who visits your Web site can potentially break into your LAN and steal your top-secret files, read your private e-mail, or worse yet, reformat your hard drive.

Firewalls can also work the other way, preventing your network users from accessing Internet sites that you designate as off-limits.

Choosing Tools for Creating Web Pages

Back when the Web was young, the easiest way to crank out Web pages was to fire up your trusty text editor and start typing. Your text had to include complicated formatting commands, called *HTML tags,* which resembled a rudimentary programming language and therefore required a graduate degree in computer science to comprehend.

Those days are gone. Now, point-and-click tools are available to help you create Web pages without worrying about the details of HTML tags. Here are the four basic categories of development tools for creating the pages that make up your Web site:

- ✔ **Web site development tools.** For most Web developers, the best type of program to use is one dedicated to the task of creating sophisticated Web sites. Such programs have excellent HTML page editors, plus tools that help you coordinate all the pages of a complete site. One of the best Web site development tools is Microsoft's FrontPage, which you can see in Figure 19-1.

- ✔ **Simple Web page editors.** These programs enable individuals or small businesses to create simple Web pages. Internet Explorer comes with a free program of this type called FrontPage Express (it's a scaled-back version of FrontPage), and Netscape Communicator comes with a similar program called Composer. Although these programs are easy to use, their HTML capabilities are limited.

- ✔ **Hard-core development tools.** Serious Web developers should look into a comprehensive Java development tool, such as Symantec's Visual Café and Microsoft's Visual J++.

- ✔ **Web-enhanced office suites.** All three major office suites — Microsoft Office, Lotus SmartSuite, and Corel Office — are now Internet enabled. That means, for example, that you can create a document in Microsoft Word and save it in HTML format, suitable for publishing on the Web. These applications are ideal when your Intranet exists primarily as a means of making corporate publications (policy manuals, for example) available.

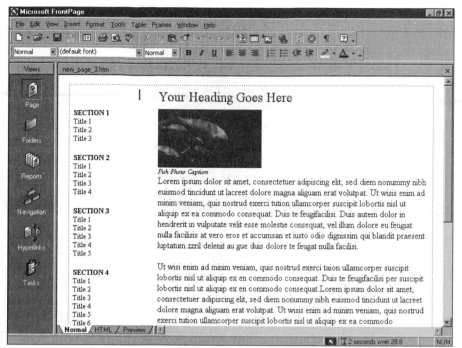

Figure 19-1:
Microsoft's
FrontPage in
action.

Dealing with CGI

The earliest forms of HTML allowed only static information to appear on Web pages. Users could request the display of certain pages, but the flow of information was in one direction only: from the server to the client.

Then along came an HTML feature called *forms,* which enables Web developers to put simple data entry fields on their Web pages. Form fields were limited to simple text boxes, radio buttons, check boxes, and just two types of command buttons: one to send data to the server, the other to clear data entered on the form. This limited repertoire of controls allowed only simple interactions, but forms took off. The best Web sites used forms to create simple interactive applications.

Probably the best-known examples of Web sites that use forms are the search sites like Yahoo! and AltaVista. In a search site, you type a keyword into a text box and then click a command button. The search site then displays a list of Web sites that are related to the keyword you entered.

To use HTML forms, you have to contend with a feature called *CGI,* which stands for *Common Gateway Interface.* Here's how a form-based interaction using CGI works:

1. **The client (that is, the Web browser) requests a page that contains a form. The server sends the requested page to the client, which displays the page along with its form fields.**

2. **The user types information into the form fields and then clicks the Submit button. The Web browser gathers the information entered by the user and sends it back to the server.**

3. **The server receives the information sent from the client, realizes that it's data from a form, and runs a program that's specially designed to handle the data from the form.**

   This program is called a *CGI program.* You have to create the CGI program yourself, which means you have to understand the CGI scripting language if you want to use forms in your Web site.

4. **The CGI program examines the data and does something worthwhile with it.**

   In most cases, the CGI program retrieves information from a database.

5. **The CGI program generates an HTML document that contains the results of the processing done in Step 4.**

   For example, if the CGI program performed a database query, the HTML document contains the results of the query.

6. **The server sends the HTML document generated by the CGI program to the client.**

7. **The client displays the HTML document.**

The key thing to note about CGI is that the CGI program itself always runs on the server. So although CGI enables you to create interactive applications on the Web, it isn't very flexible or efficient.

Wake Up and Smell the Java

The latest rage in the Web world is to use slick new products that are named after various types of coffee. The whole thing started when Sun Microsystems released a revolutionary programming language for Web pages called *Java.* Everyone soon jumped on the bandwagon. Now you have JavaScript, Visual Café, Latte, Mocha, Hot Java (as if you want your Java cold), Star Buck, and JavaBeans. It all sounds like a scene from *L.A. Story.* ("I'll have a double decaf JavaBean Latte with a twist.")

So what exactly is Java? Java is a programming language that's used to create programs that run on an Internet user's computer rather than on the server computer. Java Web programs are called *applets* because they're not stand-alone programs. An applet must run within a Java-enabled Web browser, such as Navigator or Internet Explorer.

Java solves many of the problems inherent in the form-based CGI approach to building interactive Web applications. For starters, form-based applications can use only a limited range of controls: text boxes, radio buttons, check boxes, and Submit and Reset buttons. In contrast, you can build a Java applet to display any type of custom control that you want on a Web page. With Java, you can build interactive Web applications that sport fancy slider boxes, spin buttons, draggable objects, and any other type of control that you can imagine.

But even better than the ability to use fancy controls is the simple fact that Java programs run within the Internet user's Web browser. In contrast, CGI programs run on the Web server computer. This difference results in huge improvements in performance.

Scripts

Java is good, but its main drawback is that it's a complicated programming language that requires special tools to use. Enter scripts, which are simple programs that you can place directly into HTML documents without the need for any special type of programming tool. Scripts run much slower than Java applets but are much easier to create and use.

You have two competing scripting languages to choose from:

- **JavaScript,** which was developed by Netscape and is the main scripting language for Navigator. Don't be fooled by the clever name: JavaScript bears little resemblance to Java. In fact, when Netscape first started developing JavaScript, this language was called LiveScript. Netscape changed the name to JavaScript in an attempt to capitalize on Java's popularity, even though JavaScript is not related in any way to Java.

- **VBScript,** which is Microsoft's scripting language for Internet Explorer. VBScript is based on Microsoft's popular Visual Basic programming language and is a tad bit easier to learn than JavaScript.

Note that Microsoft also ships Internet Explorer with its own version of JavaScript, called JScript. So with Internet Explorer, you have two scripting languages to choose from: JScript and VBScript. With Navigator, JavaScript is the only choice.

JavaBeans and ActiveX

Warning: The following information requires full pocket protectors and beanie caps to understand.

One of the latest developments in Web page design is the ability to create *objects* using programming languages such as Java or Visual Basic, embed those objects in a Web page, and allow the Web page and the object to communicate with one another via a script written in JavaScript or VBScript.

For example, you may create a stock ticker object that displays stock market information on a Web page. The Web page may include buttons or other controls that set options for the stock ticker, such as which stocks to track or how often to refresh the display. When the user activates one of these controls, the Web page runs a script, which in turn communicates with the stock ticker object to tell it which stocks to track or how often to refresh its display.

Two competing styles of Web objects exist: Microsoft and non-Microsoft. The Microsoft style is called *ActiveX;* the non-Microsoft style is called *JavaBeans.* The main difference between the two is that Microsoft controls ActiveX and practically every other computer company thinks you should use JavaBeans instead, just to get back at Bill Gates for being such a meanie.

Active Server Pages (ASP)

One more recent development in the world of programmable Web pages is Microsoft's Active Server Pages, also known as ASP. ASP lets you create Web pages that include VBScript scripts that run at the Web server, before the page is sent to the Internet user's computer. This development allows the script to customize the page before it is delivered. With ASP, you no longer have to use the clunky CGI method of customizing Web pages at the server before sending them over the Internet.

Chapter 20

Creating an Intranet

● ●

In This Chapter

▶ Getting acquainted with intranets

▶ Finding good uses for intranets

▶ Setting up an intranet with Personal Web Server

● ●

*N*o, I'm not mispronouncing the word *Internet. Intranet* is a term that's gained popularity in recent years. It's similar to the Internet, but with a twist: Instead of connecting your computer to millions of other computers around the world, an intranet connects your computer to other computers in your company or organization. How is an intranet different from your ordinary, run-of-the-mill network? Read on and I'll explain.

What Is an Intranet?

Everyone knows that the Internet, and especially the World Wide Web, has become a phenomenon. Millions of computer users worldwide surf the Web, and thousands join the bandwagon every day.

Recently, ingenious network managers at large companies figured out that although the Web is interesting for distributing public information to the world, the Web is even better for distributing private information within a company. Thus, the idea of intranets was born. An intranet is a network that's built using the same tools and protocols that are used by the global Internet but applied to an organization's internal network.

You can think of an intranet as a small, private version of the World Wide Web. Anyone who connects to your local area network (LAN) can access your intranet. The intranet is accessed via a Web browser, such as Netscape Navigator or Microsoft Internet Explorer. However, users don't need a dial-up connection or Internet service provider because the information on the intranet is stored on the company's server computers rather than on a computer that must be accessed via the Internet.

The intranet is analogous to a closed-circuit television system, which can only be viewed by those within the organization that owns the system. In contrast, the Internet is more like cable television in that anyone who's willing to pay $20 or so per month can watch.

Here are two interesting but contradictory points of view about the significance of intranets:

- According to some computer industry pundits, the intranet is actually more popular than the Internet. For example, Netscape, one of the biggest and best-known Internet browser companies, actually makes more money selling software used for intranets than for the Internet.

- On the other hand, some industry pundits think the intranet phenomenon is merely a fad that some other promising new technology, such as pet rocks or hula hoops, will replace in a few years. Only time will tell.

What Do You Use an Intranet For?

Intranets can distribute just about any type of information within a company. You have two basic types of intranet applications:

- **Publishing applications:** Information is posted in the form of pages that you can view from any computer with access to the intranet. This type of intranet application is commonly used for company newsletters, policy manuals, price lists, and so on.

- **Transaction applications:** Information is gathered from users of the intranet. Examples include filing online expense reports, reporting problems to the help-desk, enrolling in employee-benefit programs, and so on.

The key difference between these two types of intranet applications is that in a publishing application, the flow of information is one way: from the intranet to the user. The user requests some information, and the intranet system delivers it. In a transaction application, information flows in both directions — not only does the user request information from the intranet system, but the intranet system itself requests information from the user.

Publishing applications are simple to set up. In fact, you may be able to set one up yourself without a lot of outside help from highly paid computer consultants. Transaction applications are much more complicated, however. Expect to spend big bucks on computer consulting to get an intranet transaction application set up.

What You Need to Set Up an Intranet

An intranet is fairly simple to set up. Here's a list of the various requirements:

- ✔ **A LAN.** An intranet doesn't require its own cabling; it can operate on an existing Ethernet LAN using twisted-pair or coax wiring.

- ✔ **A server computer that's dedicated to the intranet.** Make sure that this computer has plenty of RAM (at least 64MB) and gigabytes (at least 10GB) of disk space. Of course, the more users your network has and the more information you intend to place on the server, the more RAM and disk storage you need.

- ✔ **Windows NT Server or a UNIX operating system.** Web server software requires one or the other.

- ✔ **Web server software for the server computer.** You can find more information about Web server software in Chapter 19.

- ✔ **Programs to help you create Web pages.** If you're the type who dreams in binary, you can create Web pages by typing HTML codes directly into text files. In that case, the only program you need is Notepad. Alternatively, you can use a Web-authoring program, such as Microsoft FrontPage. For more information, refer to Chapter 19.

- ✔ **Client computers with at least the minimum system requirements.** Make sure that each client computer that accesses the Intranet has a 486 or better processor, at least 8MB of RAM, 20MB or more of free disk space, and a connection to the LAN.

- ✔ **A Web browser such as Navigator or Internet Explorer on each client computer.**

How You Create a Small Intranet with Personal Web Server

If you have a small, peer-to-peer network based on Windows 95 or 98, you can create a basic intranet using a free Microsoft program called Personal Web Server (PWS). This program comes with Microsoft Internet Explorer 4.0, and you can also find it buried on the Microsoft Office 97 CD-ROM or included on the Windows 98 CD-ROM.

Personal Web Server works only with Windows 95 or 98 and isn't nearly as slick as a real Web server, such as Microsoft Internet Information Server or Netscape Enterprise Server. But Personal Web Server is an ideal way to set up an intranet on a small LAN that has just a few users.

Although Personal Web Server is distributed with Internet Explorer 4.0 and designed to work with it, Personal Web Server also works with other Web browsers including Navigator.

With Internet Explorer 5.0 and Windows 2000, Microsoft includes a new, improved version of PWS called Personal Web Server 5.0. The following sections show you step-by-step how to set up and use PWS 5. The procedures for using previous versions of Personal Web Server are similar.

Starting Personal Web Server

To start Personal Web Server, choose Programs⇨Internet Explorer⇨ Personal Web Server⇨Personal Web Manager from the Windows Start menu. Personal Web Manager enables you to control how Personal Web Server operates. Figure 20-1 shows the main Personal Web Manager dialog box.

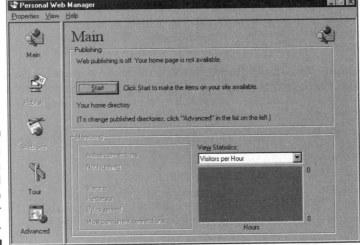

Figure 20-1:
The main
Personal
Web
Manager
dialog box.

Notice in Figure 20-1 that Personal Web Manager indicates the status of the Web server; in this case, the message Web publishing is off shows that PWS is inactive. To activate Web publishing and make your Web site available to others on your network, click the Start button. The PWS Manager dialog box changes, as shown in Figure 20-2.

You can disable the server by clicking the Stop button. When you do, the Personal Web Manager dialog box changes back to the way it was before you activated Web publishing.

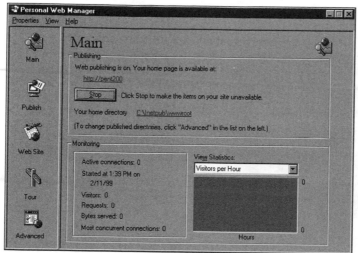

Figure 20-2:
Web
publishing
is on!

 After Personal Web Server starts, the icon shown in the margin appears in the Windows taskbar. You can double-click this icon at any time to summon the Personal Web Manager.

 Personal Web Server comes with a set of Web pages that serve as Help files to give you an overview of how PWS works and how to manage it. To access these help files, start up Personal Web Manager and then choose Help⇨ Personal Web Server Topics.

Publishing a Web page to Personal Web Server

Publishing your HTML files to Personal Web Server so that you or other network users can view them is easy. PWS uses a folder named C:\Inetpub\wwwroot as the root directory for your Web pages. To post an HTML file to Personal Web Server, all you have to do is save the file in the C:\Inetpub\wwwroot folder.

 Alternatively, you can use Personal Web Server's built-in Publishing Wizard to publish Web files to your PWS folder. To do so, start Personal Web Manager and click the Publish icon (shown in the margin). This action brings up the Publishing Wizard, as shown in Figure 20-3. Fill in the blanks to publish your HTML files to your PWS folder.

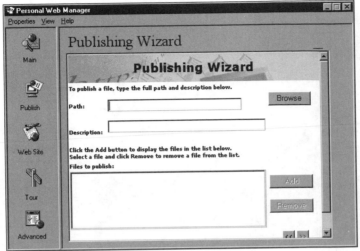

Figure 20-3:
The
Publishing
Wizard.

If you haven't already created Web pages that you want to publish and if you don't have a sophisticated Web-development program such as Microsoft FrontPage, you can use Personal Web Server's built-in Home Page Wizard to create a simple Web site. For more information, see the section "Using the Home Page Wizard," later in this chapter.

Accessing a Web page on Personal Web Server

To access a page stored in Personal Web Server, you need to know the Internet address for your Personal Web Server root directory. To find out what that address is, start Personal Web Manager. The Internet address of your PWS site appears in the Personal Web Manager dialog box. For example, back in Figure 20-2, the address for the PWS site is `http://pent200`.

The default Web page for Personal Web Server is default.html. Thus, if you create a file named default.html in C:\Inetpub\wwwroot, you can display that page by entering your Personal Web Server address in the Internet Explorer Address box. For example, if your Web server address is Pent200, just type `Pent200` in the Address box to display your home page.

To display a different HTML file, type the filename after the Internet address, separated by a slash. For example, to display a page named softball.html, you type `Pent200/softball.html`.

The Internet address used by Personal Web Server is based on your Windows computer name, which you create when you first install Windows on your computer. If you want to change this name, open Control Panel and double-click the Network icon, which reveals the Network dialog box. Click the Identification tab, and then type a new computer name in the Computer Name field. After you click OK, your computer restarts, and then you can use the new name for your Personal Web Server Internet address.

Using the Home Page Wizard

Personal Web Server includes a Home Page Wizard that helps you create a Web site without requiring that you work directly with HTML. To use the Home Page Wizard, start Personal Web Manager and click the Web Site icon (shown in the margin). A Wizard appears and asks you a few questions about what features you want to include on your home page. Then, the Wizard generates the page for you. Figure 20-4 shows an example of a home page created by the Home Page Wizard.

Figure 20-4: A simple home page created by the Home Page Wizard.

After you create a home page, clicking the Web Site icon enables you to manage your home page by using the options shown in Figure 20-5. Click Edit your home page to make changes to your home page, click View your guest book to see a list of users who have visited your Web site and signed your guest book, or click Open your drop box to see private messages users have left for you.

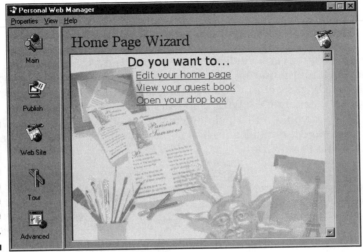

Figure 20-5: Using the Home Page Wizard to manage your home page.

Part V
More Ways to Network

The 5th Wave   By Rich Tennant

"You the guy having trouble staying connected to the network?"

In this part . . .

After you've got the basics down, this part helps you do some of the more advanced stuff, which includes setting up a network at your home, creating a dial-up connection so that you can access your network while you're at home or on the road, using the network features of Microsoft Office, and building a network that includes older MS-DOS and Windows computers as well as Macintosh computers.

Chapter 21

Networking Your Home

- -

In This Chapter

▶ Setting up a simple home network in seven steps

▶ Addressing some home network concerns

- -

*T*hese days, more and more people have more than one computer in the home. Some families have several generations of hand-me-down computers: an old clunker 386, a workable 486, a Pentium (or maybe even two), and perhaps a notebook computer that one of the kids got through a school program.

In this chapter, I show you a simple, step-by-step procedure that you can follow to network two computers in your home so that you can share a printer, disk drive, or CD-ROM drive. Nothing fancy here, just the bare necessities you need to get a network up and running.

To keep things simple, this chapter assumes that all the computers you want to network are already running Windows 95 or 98. If you want to add Macintosh computers to your network, refer to Chapter 25. If you have an older computer that can't run Windows 95 or 98, see Chapter 24.

For more complete information about creating a network in your home, refer to *Networking Home PCs For Dummies,* by Kathy Ivens (IDG Books Worldwide, Inc.).

Step 1: Go Shopping

First, make a shopping list of things you need to buy when you go to your local computer warehouse store. Here's what to include on your shopping list:

> ✔ **A 10baseT Ethernet network card for each computer.** You have no need to spend big money on the networking cards. If you can find them for $25 each, buy them.

Make sure that the cards say "Plug and Play" on the box. If they don't, you have to fuss around with configuring the cards' IRQ settings and port addresses. With Plug and Play cards, all the configuration settings are made automatically, so you don't have to worry about such details.

Also, make sure that you get a card that fits one of the available expansion slots inside your computer. You need to know what type of available expansion slots your computer has. Most newer computers have two types of slots: ISA and PCI. If you have an older computer, you may have a different type of slot, most likely VESA or EISA. Check the manual that came with your computer to find out for sure.

✔ **A 10baseT hub with enough ports for all of your computers.** You can get four- or five-port hubs for about $50.

✔ **A twisted-pair cable with RJ-45 connectors on both ends for each computer.** A 25-foot cable costs about $10.

Do *not* buy phone cable. The twisted-pair cable used for 10baseT networks looks like phone cable, but it isn't the same.

You can probably find an inexpensive starter kit that includes everything you need to network two computers together: two twisted-pair network cards, a hub, and two cables. If you have more than two computers, you can buy an add-on kit for each additional computer.

Step 2: Install the Cards

Follow the instructions that come with the cards to install them into your computers. The only tools that you need are a flathead and a Phillips screwdriver.

Make sure that you shut down Windows, turn off your computer, and unplug the power cord before you remove the computer's case and start working inside.

Step 3: Connect the Cable

Plug one end of each cable into a connector on the hub, then plug the other end into the connector on the back of the network cards that you installed in the computers.

Step 4: Restart the Computers

After you restart each computer, Windows notices that you installed a new card into your computer and automatically configures it. If for some reason Windows doesn't notice the card, double-click the Add New Hardware icon in the Control panel. Then instruct the Add Hardware Wizard to automatically sniff out your new networking cards and install them for you.

Step 5: Check the Network Settings

Double-click the Network icon in the Control Panel to summon the Network dialog box, shown in Figure 21-1. Then check to make sure that the following items appear in the list of installed network components:

- ✔ "Client for Microsoft Networks."

- ✔ Your network card, which may appear as "NE2000 Compatible" or may be specific to the brand of network card you purchased.

- ✔ "NetBEUI –> NE2000 Compatible." (If your network card is other than "NE2000 Compatible," the name of your network card appears here instead.)

- ✔ "File and printer sharing for Microsoft Networks."

If any of these items are missing, click the Add button to add them.

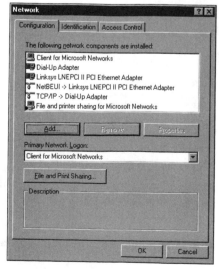

Figure 21-1:
Checking
the network
settings.

Now click the Identification tab in the Network dialog box. This brings up the computer identification settings shown in Figure 21-2. Type a different name and description for each computer but make sure that both computers use the same Workgroup name.

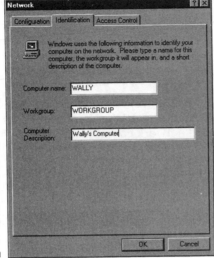

Figure 21-2:
Eliminating
your
computer's
identity
crisis.

Step 6: Share Your Disk Drives

The next step is to set up each computer's disk drive so that the other computer can access it. To do so, follow these steps:

1. **Double-click My Computer.**

   The My Computer window appears.

2. **Click the disk drive that you want to share.**

   Ordinarily, this is the C drive.

3. **Choose the File⇨Sharing command.**

   The Sharing properties dialog box appears, as shown in Figure 21-3. (The figure shows how the dialog box appears after the settings in Steps 4 and 5 are made.)

4. **Click Shared As.**

   If you want, you can change the Share Name and Comment fields.

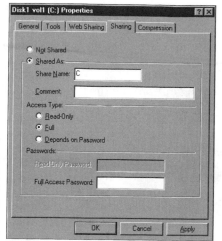

Figure 21-3:
The Sharing
tab of the
Properties
dialog box.

5. **Click Full for the Access Type.**

   This action enables you to do anything you want to the shared drive
   from the other computer — including creating, deleting, or renaming
   files or folders.

6. **Click OK.**

   The Properties dialog box disappears.

Be sure to perform the procedure on both computers.

To access another computer's shared disk drive, double-click the Network
Neighborhood icon. The Network Neighborhood window lists the name of the
workgroup you specified for both computers. Double-click the workgroup
name to see a list of all the computers that belong to that workgroup. Then
double-click the computer whose disk you want to access to see a list of
shared disks and folders for that computer.

Step 7: Share Your Printers

If you have a printer that you want to share on the network, you can do so by
following these steps:

1. **On the computer with the printer that you want to share, double-click
   My Computer.**

2. **Double-click Printers in the My Computer window.**

   The Printers folder appears, listing all the printers available on your
   computer.

3. **Click the printer that you want to share and then choose the File⇨Sharing command.**

   The Sharing tab of the Properties dialog box for the printer appears.

4. **Click Share As.**

   This action enables the sharing options, so the Properties dialog box now resembles Figure 21-4.

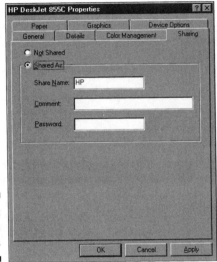

Figure 21-4:
Sharing a
printer.

5. **Type a name for the printer if you want.**

6. **Click OK.**

7. **On the other computer, double-click My Computer and then double-click Printers.**

   The Printers folder appears.

8. **Double-click the Add Printer icon.**

   The Add Printer Wizard appears, as shown in Figure 21-5.

9. **Follow the Add Printer Wizard steps to add the printer you shared in Steps 1 through 6.**

   The Add Printer Wizard asks if you're installing a local or network printer and enables you to browse the network to locate the printer you want to access. You also have to indicate to the Wizard the make and model of the printer that you're adding. If the exact make and model of the printer doesn't appear in the list provided by the Wizard, you have to insert the disk that came with the printer to complete the installation.

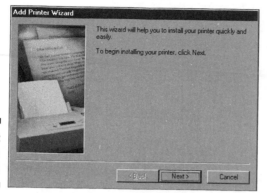

Figure 21-5:
Adding a
printer.

10. **You're done!**

You can now print to the network printer by choosing the network printer from the normal File⇨Print command in any Windows program.

Managing Your Home Network

After you network the computers in your home, you — or whoever has the most computer savvy in your household — must become the home network manager. Unfortunately, all the concerns that arise when using a network in a business situation apply to home networks as well. In particular, the following list highlights some of the things to stay on top of with your home network:

✔ **Make sure that everyone knows how to access the network and use the shared drives and printers.** Hold a family meeting to go over the do's and don'ts of the network.

✔ **Think about whether or not you really want to grant full access to the C drive over the network.** What if your teenager gets mad at you because you won't let him borrow the car, so he decides to delete a bunch of your important files from the privacy of his bedroom? Maybe you should think about security, giving each user a user ID and password, sharing only certain folders on each drive rather than the entire drive, and password-protecting folders that contain private information.

✔ **Make sure that everyone knows that backing up is his or her own responsibility.** Don't let your kid blame you when he or she loses a 30-page term paper because of the "stupid network." The epitome of parenting for the new millennium may be to add backing up the network to the kids' list of Saturday chores, right after mowing the lawn and cleaning the bathrooms.

✔ **Keep an eye on disk space.** With the whole family using the network, you may be amazed at how quickly the gigabytes fill up.

Chapter 22

Dialing In to Your Network

- -

- -

*W*ith portable computers and home computers becoming more and more popular, many computer users take work home with them to work on in the evening or over the weekend and bring back to the office the following weekday. This arrangement works reasonably well, except that exchanging information between a portable or home computer and your office computer is far from easy.

One way to exchange files is to copy them from one computer to a diskette and then copy the files from the diskette to the other computer. However, this approach has its drawbacks. What if the files you want to exchange won't fit on a single diskette? And what if, in the rush to get out of the house the following morning, you forget to put the diskette in your pocket or bag?

If you use a portable laptop or notebook computer, you can use a software program such as LapLink to connect the portable computer to your office computer by using a cable connected to both computers' serial or parallel ports. After you connect the computers, you can then transfer files over the cable. This process is much more efficient than copying the files using diskettes but still has drawbacks. What if you get home and discover that you forgot to copy one important file?

If you must work from home, the best way to access your work at the office is to create a dial-up connection that uses modems to connect your home computer directly to your office network. Using this setup, you can access from your home computer any shared disk drives available on the office network, just as if your home computer were a part of the office network.

This chapter shows you how to create a remote connection using a feature of Windows called Dial-Up Networking. This feature provides a simple but limited modem link between a remote computer and a networked computer. I also point out some advantages of using a more sophisticated approach to remote access, such as Windows NT Remote Access Service or NetWare Connect.

Security is a major concern whenever you enable dial-up networking. If you can dial in to your office computer and access your files, so can anybody else. Passwords offer some measure of protection, but serious computer hackers can get past simple password protection as easy as experienced car thieves can hotwire a car. If security is a concern, use Windows NT Server or NetWare Connect access rather than Windows Dial-Up Networking. Both programs provide tighter security controls than Windows does.

Throughout this chapter, I assume that you're using remote access to call in to your work computer from a home computer. Of course, this isn't the only way to use dial-up connections. You can do it the other way around, call up your home computer from the office. Or you can call your office or home computer from a hotel room using a laptop computer. The point is that I refer to the computer that you use to call in to another computer as the *home computer,* and I refer to the other computer — the one that you're calling in to — as the *office computer.*

Dial-Up Networking

If both your computer at work and your computer at home use Windows 95 or 98, you can easily set up a dial-up connection between the two that enables you to connect to your office computer while you're at home. After you're connected to your office computer, you can use its disk drives and printers. In addition, you can use any network disks or printers that are accessible to your office computer. In short, any resource — disk drive or printer — that's available to your office computer becomes available to your home computer when you establish the dial-up connection.

The Windows feature that enables you to create a dial-up connection is called *Dial-Up Networking,* sometimes known as *DUN* because computer geeks love to confuse us with three-letter acronyms. I promise not to use the term *DUN* again in this chapter.

To use DUN — oops, I mean Dial-Up Networking — to connect from home to office, both your home and office computers must have a modem, and they must both be connected to a phone line.

In Dial-Up Networking terminology, the computer that you dial in to — that is, your office computer — is referred to as a *dial-up server.* Likewise, the computer you dial in from — your home computer — is called a *dial-up client.* Note that the dial-up server computer doesn't have to be a server computer on a network.

Installing the dial-up server feature

Dial-Up Networking is a standard part of Windows, but the capability to configure a dial-up server is not. You must install this feature separately before you can designate your office computer as a dial-up server.

Windows 98 comes with the necessary dial-up server programs on the Windows 98 CD. To install the programs, follow these steps:

1. **Choose Start➪Settings➪Control Panel.**

   The Control Panel comes to life.

2. **Double-click Add/Remove Programs.**

   The Add/Remove Programs Properties dialog box appears.

3. **Click the Windows Setup tab.**

   The Windows Setup options appear, as shown in Figure 22-1.

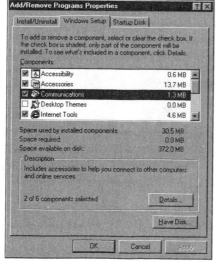

Figure 22-1: The Windows Setup options in the Add/Remove Programs Properties dialog box.

4. **Click Communications and then click the Details button.**

   This brings up the Communications dialog box, shown in Figure 22-2.

5. **Click the Dial-Up Server check box.**

   A check mark appears in the check box. (If the check mark does not appear, click again until the check mark appears.)

0** **Part V: More Ways to Network**

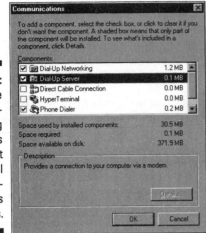

Figure 22-2:
The
Communica-
tions dialog
box lets
you select
optional
communica-
tions
features.

6. **Click OK to return to the Windows Setup options.**

7. **Click OK again to install the Dial-Up Server feature.**

   The Add/Remove Programs Properties dialog box disappears, and Windows installs the Dial-Up Server feature.

   If Windows asks you to insert the Windows 98 CD-ROM, do it.

8. **That's all!**

You're ready to use Dial-Up Networking.

If the computer at your office runs Windows 95, you must first add a program called Microsoft Plus! or upgrade to Windows 98. You can purchase Microsoft Plus! for about $50, but the cost of upgrading to Windows 98 isn't much more, so I recommend upgrading instead.

You can tell whether you already have Microsoft Plus! on your computer by watching the *splash screen* display whenever you start up Windows 95. If the words *Microsoft Plus!* appear beneath the Windows 95 logo, Microsoft Plus! is installed. Another way to tell is to go to the Control Panel and double-click the Add/Remove Programs icon. If "Microsoft Plus! for Windows 95" appears in the list of programs, Microsoft Plus! is installed.

Before you can use a dial-up connection, you must configure both your home and office computers for Dial-Up Networking. First, you must configure your office computer to work as a dial-up server. Then you must configure your home computer to function as a dial-up client. After you configure both computers, you can use the dial-up client computer at home to call in to the dial-up server computer at work. I describe how to configure the dial-up server and client in the following sections.

Configuring a dial-up server

After you install Dial-Up Networking in Windows 95 or 98, you can configure
your office computer so that it can function as a dial-up server:

1. **Double-click the My Computer icon on your desktop and then double-click the Dial-Up Networking icon.**

   The Dial-Up Networking window appears, as shown in Figure 22-3. Note
   that if you previously used Dial-Up Networking to create a connection to
   an Internet service provider or some other dial-up network, other icons
   besides the Make New Connection icon appear in the Dial-Up
   Networking window.

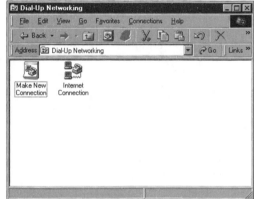

Figure 22-3:
The Dial-Up
Networking
window.

2. **Choose the Connections⇨Dial-Up Server command.**

   The Dial-Up Server dialog box appears, as shown in Figure 22-4.

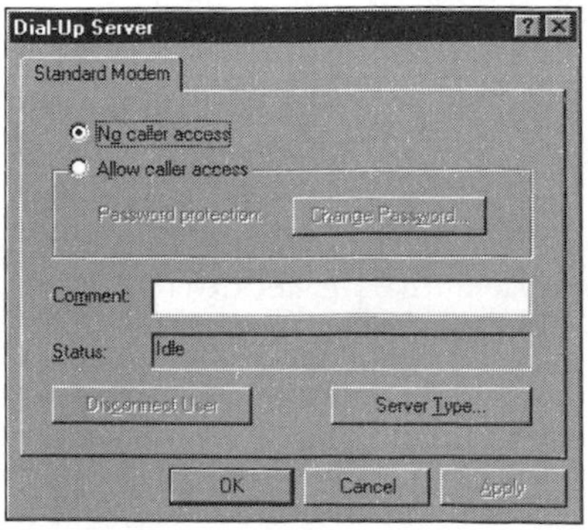

Figure 22-4:
The Dial-Up
Server
dialog box.

3. **Click Allow caller access.**

   Doing so allows other computers to call in to the office computer. After you click Allow caller access, the Change Password button is enabled.

4. **Click the Change Password button.**

   A dialog box appears asking you to enter a password.

5. **Type a password and then click OK.**

   Choose a password to use when you call in to your office computer. Write it down somewhere so that you won't forget it.

   Creating a password when you set up a dial-up server is very important. If you don't create a password, anyone who knows the phone number can call up your computer and access not only your computer but also your entire network.

6. **Click OK.**

   The computer is now set up as a dial-up server. All that remains is to share any disk drives or printers you want to be able to access from home.

7. **To share a disk drive so that you can access it from home, double-click My Computer. Then click the drive you want to share and choose the File⇨Sharing command. Click Share As and then click OK.**

8. **To share a printer, double-click the Printers icon in the My Computer window, select the printer in the My Computer window, choose File⇨Sharing, click Share As, and then click OK.**

You're all set.

Here are a few additional points to ponder when you use a dial-up server:

- ✔ After you click OK in Step 6, the Dial-Up Server icon shown in the margin appears in your taskbar. This icon indicates that the computer is monitoring the phone line, waiting to pick up an incoming call to establish a dial-up connection.

- ✔ To disable the dial-up server, double-click the Dial-Up Server icon in the taskbar. This summons the Dial-Up Server dialog box. Click No Caller Access and then click OK. The Dial-Up Server dialog box disappears, and the Dial-Up Server icon vanishes from the taskbar. To reinstate the Dial-Up Server, you have to repeat the entire procedure to configure the dial-up server.

- ✔ If you shut down your computer while it's in Dial-Up Server mode, the Dial-Up Server is automatically restarted after you restart your computer.

▶ If the Dial-Up Networking window doesn't have a Connections⇨Dial-Up Server command, you must first install dial-up server support. See the section "Installing the dial-up server feature," earlier in this chapter. (For Windows 95, you must purchase either Microsoft Plus! or upgrade to Windows 98 to get the dial-up server feature.)

▶ Don't, under any circumstances, set up a Dial-Up Server without a password! Yes, I know I already warned you about this, but it's worth a second warning.

▶ If you're a network administrator, the thought of users creating Dial-Up Servers to gain remote access to your network may give you the willies. If so, you can ban the Dial-Up Server function by using a Windows program called the System Policy Editor.

Configuring your home computer for Dial-Up Networking

To configure your home computer to act as a dial-up client, you must create a new dial-up connection by following these steps:

1. **Double-click the My Computer icon on your desktop and then double-click the Dial-Up Networking icon.**

   The Dial-Up Networking window appears (refer to Figure 22-3).

2. **Double-click the Make New Connection icon.**

   The Make New Connection Wizard comes to life. This Wizard asks you a few simple questions. Then it creates an icon for the connection to your office computer.

3. **Type a name for the connection to your office computer.**

   Use a simple name, such as *Office*.

4. **Click Next.**

   The Wizard asks for your office computer's phone number.

5. **Type the phone number for the phone line that's connected to your office computer's modem and then click Next.**

   The Wizard displays a confirmation dialog box saying that it's ready to create the connection.

6. **Click Finish.**

   The Wizard creates the new connection, which appears as an icon in the Dial-Up Networking window.

Here are a few tidbits to consider when setting up your home computer for Dial-Up Networking:

- The Make New Connection Wizard may ask for additional information if it discovers that your modem hasn't yet been configured for Dial-Up Networking. If this happens, just follow the bouncing ball and answer whatever questions it asks as best you can. If you become confused, just act like you know what you're doing, and the Wizard won't notice.

- If you can't find Dial-Up Networking anywhere on your computer, you may not have installed it. Find your Windows 95 CD and then double-click the Add/Remove Programs icon in the Control Panel. Click the Windows Setup tab in the Add/Remove Programs dialog box and then double-click the Communications icon and make sure that Dial-Up Networking is selected. Click OK and then insert your Windows 95 or 98 CD in your CD-ROM drive to install Dial-Up Networking.

- If you plan on calling your office computer often, drag the office computer connection icon from the Dial-Up Networking window onto your desktop. Then you won't have to wade through My Computer every time you want to connect.

Making the connection

After you configure your office and home computers for Dial-Up Networking, you undoubtedly want to call your office computer and put Dial-Up Networking to work. Here's how:

1. **On your home computer, choose the Start⇨Programs⇨Accessories⇨ Dial-Up Networking and then double-click the icon for the office computer's connection.**

   Or if you dragged a copy of the icon to your desktop, just double-click the icon on your desktop. Either way, the Connect To dialog box appears, as shown in Figure 22-5.

Figure 22-5: The Connect To dialog box.

2. **Make sure that the phone number, user name, and password are correct. Then click Connect.**

   Windows calls in to your office computer and establishes a connection. This process may take a minute or so, so be patient. You see various messages on the screen while the connection is being made, such as "Dialing," "Verifying User Name and Password," "Waiting for Godot," "Twiddling Thumbs," and so on. Eventually, the message says "Connected," at which point you're officially connected to your office computer.

After you're connected, you can access your office computer's disk drives and printers. However, you can't use the Network Neighborhood icon to access your office computer's resources. Windows automatically disables Network Neighborhood for dial-up connections because the dial-up connection is so slow compared to a normal Ethernet connection. Instead, follow these steps to access your office computer's resources when connected over the phone:

1. **Choose the Start⇨Run command.**

2. **Type two backward slashes followed by the name of your office computer.**

   For example, type **Office**.

3. **Click OK.**

   Your home computer takes a while to access your office computer over the phone. Eventually, though, a window, such as the one shown in Figure 22-6, appears. You can now access your office computer's shared disk drives and printers.

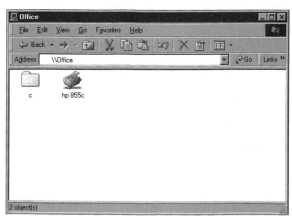

Figure 22-6:
Accessing another computer's resources using Dial-Up Networking.

To disconnect from the office computer, double-click the modem icon that appears in the taskbar and then click Disconnect. Or if you prefer, righ-click the modem icon and choose Disconnect from the pop-up menu that appears.

Other Ways to Let Users Dial In

If you're concerned about the security of your remote network connection, or if you want to enable several network users to dial in from home, abandon Windows Dial-Up Server altogether and use a more sophisticated program to enable users to dial in to your network. You have two basic approaches to doing this. One is to use software such as Windows NT Server's Remote Access Service or Novell's NetWare Connect. The other way is to add special remote-access hardware to your network.

Using software for remote access

Windows NT Server includes built-in support for remote access, using a program called Remote Access Service, also known as RAS. With RAS, you equip a server computer with one or more modems (standard modems or ISDN modems) and dedicate it as a remote access server. Remote users can then dial in to the network and, once connected, use the network as if they were connected with an Ethernet cable. Of course, the connection is much slower because it operates over phone lines rather than real Ethernet cable.

The advantage of Remote Access Service over a simple dial-up server using Windows is that you have more control over security when you use RAS. RAS enables you to use all the basic security features of Windows NT Server, plus its own few extra security features designed just for dial-up users.

Figure 22-7 shows the Remote Access Permissions dialog box, which allows a Windows NT Server administrator to specify the access privileges for a remote user. In this dialog box, you can tell Windows NT Server to use call-back security, which works like this:

1. **A user dials in to the RAS server from a home computer.**

2. **The RAS server verifies the user's name and password.**

3. **The RAS server hangs up on the user.**

4. **The RAS server then calls the user back, using either a prearranged phone number or a phone number entered by the user.**

5. **The user's computer answers the phone and reverifies the connection.**

6. **The user can then use the network.**

For the tightest security, use a preset call-back number. That way, you can ensure that the remote user can access Windows NT Server only from a designated phone number.

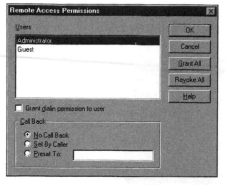

Figure 22-7:
Setting
remote
access
permissions
for
Windows
NT Server.

Novell offers a similar remote access program called NetWare Connect.
Connect also enables you to create a modem pool so that network users can
share modems for outbound calls (for example, to connect to the Internet or
send a fax) as well as for remote access.

Using hardware for remote access

An alternative to creating a dedicated communication server running
Windows NT Server or NetWare is to use specialized remote access hardware. That way, you don't have to contend with setting up and maintaining
Windows NT Server or NetWare, and you don't have to dedicate an entire PC
to the task of sharing modems for remote access.

The best known remote access hardware is LanRover, made by Shiva.
LanRover is a self-contained remote access server that includes an Ethernet
port so that you can connect LanRover to your network and either four or
eight serial ports for plug-in modems. Or you can get LanRover Plus, which
includes built-in modems. LanRover can use normal modem connections or
high-speed ISDN connections for faster connections.

For more information about LanRover, check out Shiva's home page on the
Internet at www.shiva.com.

Chapter 23

Using Microsoft Office on a Network

In This Chapter

▶ Installing Office on a network

▶ Opening files over the network

▶ Using workgroup templates

▶ Using Office's collaboration features

▶ Sharing an Access database on a network

*M*icrosoft Office is far and away the most popular suite of application programs used on personal computers, and it includes the most common types of application programs used in an office: a word processing program (Word), a spreadsheet program (Excel), a presentation program (PowerPoint), a database program (Access), and an excellent e-mail program (Outlook). Depending on the version of Office you purchase, you may also get a Web site development program (FrontPage), a desktop publishing program (Publisher), a set of Ginsu knives (KnifePoint), and a slicer and dicer (Salsa).

This chapter describes the networking features of Microsoft Office 2000, the latest and greatest version of Office. Some of these features also work with previous versions of Office as well.

To get the most from using Office on a network, you should purchase the Microsoft Office Resource Kit. The Office Resource Kit (also known as *ORK*) contains information about installing and using Office on a network and comes with a CD that has valuable tools. If you don't want to purchase the ORK, you can view it online and download the ORK tools from Microsoft's TechNet Web site (technet.microsoft.com). Nanu-nanu.

Installing Office on a Network — Some Options

You need to make two basic decisions when you prepare to install Microsoft Office on a network. The first is whether you want to copy the Office program files onto each computer's local hard disk or place some or all of the Office program files on a shared server disk. Here are the pros and cons of each option:

- ✓ Installing the Office program files onto each computer's hard disk is usually the best choice. However, this option requires that each computer have enough free disk space to hold the Office program files. Office 97 can require close to 200MB of free space. Office 2000 will probably need even more.

- ✓ Placing Office program files on the server frees up disk space on the client computers' hard drives. However, network users will notice that Office runs slower because network files are slower to access than local files. To alleviate this, you can install the most frequently needed Office program files on each computer's local disk and the less frequently used files on the network server.

The second choice to make when installing Office on a network is which of several alternative installation methods to use. Here are the options:

- ✓ Ignore the fact that you have a network, purchase a separate copy of Office for each user on the network, and install Office from the CD on each computer. This option works well if your network is small, if each computer has ample disk space to hold the necessary Office files, and if each computer has its own CD-ROM drive.

- ✓ Buy a separate copy of Office for each computer but install Office onto each computer from a shared CD-ROM drive located on a server computer. This option works well when you have network client computers that do not have their own CD-ROM drives.

- ✓ Copy the entire Office CD into a shared folder on a network server. Then from each network computer, connect to the shared folder and run the Office Setup program to install Office onto each computer on the network.

- ✓ Use the Office Setup program in Administrative Setup mode. This option lets you create a special type of setup on a network server disk, from which you can install Office onto network computers. Administrative Setup enables you to control the custom features selected for each network computer and reduce the amount of user interaction required to install Office onto each computer.

If you choose to use Administrative Setup, you can use the Network Installation Wizard that comes with the Office Resource Kit. The Network Installation Wizard lets you customize settings for installing Office onto client computers. For example, you can choose which Office components to install, provide default answers to yes/no questions that Setup asks the user while installing Office, and select the amount of interaction you want the Setup program to have with the user while installing Office.

No matter which option you choose for installing Office on your network, you must purchase either a copy of Office or a license to install Office for every computer that uses Office. Purchasing a single copy of Office and installing it on more than one computer is illegal.

Accessing Network Files

Opening a file that resides on a network drive is almost as easy as opening a file on a local drive. All Office programs use the File⇨Open command to summon the Open dialog box, as shown in its Excel incarnation in Figure 23-1. (The Open dialog box is nearly identical in other Office programs.)

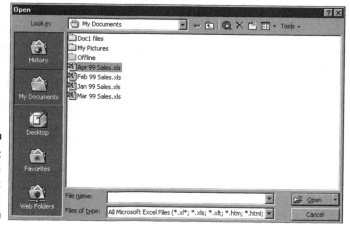

Figure 23-1:
The Open dialog box in Excel.

To access a file that resides on a network volume that has been mapped to a drive letter, all you have to do is use the Look in drop-down list to select the network drive. If the network volume has not been mapped to a drive, use the Look in drop-down list to select Network Neighborhood and then browse through the network to find the file.

You can map a network drive directly from the Open dialog box by following these steps:

1. **Choose the File⇨Open command.**

   This summons the Open dialog box.

2. **Click Tools in the Open dialog box and then choose Map Network Drive.**

   The Map Network Drive dialog box appears, as shown in Figure 23-2.

Figure 23-2:
Mapping a
network
drive.

3. **If you don't like the drive letter suggested in the Drive field, change it.**

   Map Network Drive defaults to the next available drive letter — in the case of Figure 23-2, drive G:. If you prefer to use a different drive letter, you can choose any of the drive letters available in the Drive drop-down list.

4. **In the Path field, type the complete network path for the shared drive you want to map.**

   In most cases, the network path is two back slashes, the server name, another back slash, and the shared volume's share name. For example, to map a shared volume named MYDOCS on a server named WALLY, type the following in the Path field:

   ```
   \\WALLY\MYDOCS
   ```

5. **If you want this drive to be mapped automatically each time you log on to the network, check the Reconnect at logon option.**

   If you leave this option unchecked, the drive mapping vanishes when you log off the network.

6. **Click OK.**

   You return to the Open dialog box. The Look in field automatically shows the newly mapped network drive, so the Open dialog box lists the files and folders in the network drive.

Using Workgroup Templates

A *template* is not a place of worship, though an occasional sacrifice to the Office gods may make your computing life a bit easier. Rather, a template is a special type of document file that holds formatting information, boilerplate text, and other customized settings that you can use as the basis for new documents.

Three Office programs — Word, Excel, and PowerPoint — enable you to specify a template whenever you create a new document. When you create a new document in Word, Excel, or PowerPoint by choosing the File⇨New command, you see a dialog box that lets you choose a template for the new document. For example, Figure 23-3 shows the dialog box that appears when you create a new document in Word 2000.

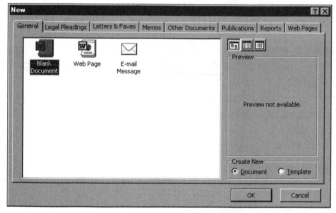

Figure 23-3:
The New
dialog box
(Word 2000).

Office comes with a set of templates for the most common types of documents. These templates are grouped under the various tabs that appear across the top of the New dialog box.

In addition to the templates that come with Office, you can create your own templates in Word, Excel, and PowerPoint. Creating your own templates is especially useful if you want to establish a consistent look for documents prepared by your network users. For example, you can create a Letter template that includes your company's letterhead or a Proposal template that includes a company logo.

Office enables you to store templates in two locations. The first location, referred to as the User Templates folder, usually resides on the user's local disk drive. The second location, called the Workgroup Templates folder, is usually a folder on a shared network drive. This arrangement lets you store templates that you want to make available to all network users on a network server, but still allows each user to create his or her own templates that are not available to other network users.

When you use both a User Templates folder and a Workgroup Templates folder, Office combines the templates from both folders and lists them in alphabetical order in the New dialog box. For example, suppose that the User Templates folder contains templates called Blank Document and Web Page, and the Workgroup Templates folder contains a template called Company Letterhead. In this case, three templates appear in the New dialog box, in this order: Blank Document, Company Letterhead, and Web Page.

To set the User Templates and Workgroup Templates folders, choose Tools➪Options in Word to summon the Options dialog box and then click the File Locations tab to display the file location options, such as those shown in Figure 23-4.

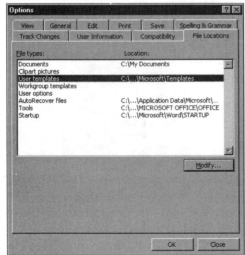

Figure 23-4:
The Options
dialog box.

Although the User Templates and Workgroup Templates settings affect Word, Excel, and PowerPoint, you can change these settings only from Word. The Options dialog boxes in Excel and PowerPoint don't show the User Templates or Workgroup Templates options.

When you install Office, the standard templates that come with Office are copied into a folder on the computer's local disk drive, and the User Templates option is set to this folder. The Workgroup Templates option is left blank. You can set the Workgroup Templates folder to a shared network folder by clicking Network Templates, clicking the Modify button, and speci-fying a shared network folder that contains your workgroup templates.

Working with Collaboration Features

According to my high school English teacher, Benjamin Franklin turned down an invitation to write the Declaration of Independence because he did not want to write a document that others would edit. Old Ben would have hated the network collaboration features built into Office. Office comes with several features that make it easy for a group of people to work together to create a document. The following sections describe these features.

Routing documents

All the main Office programs — Word, Excel, PowerPoint, and Access — include a document-routing feature that lets you send a document to a list of e-mail recipients. Document routing enables you to choose one of two methods for sending a document to multiple users:

- ✔ You can send the document to the users on the list one at a time. When the first user receives the document, that person can review it, modify it, and add annotations. Then, the first user forwards the document to the next user in the list. When the last user in the list receives and acts upon the document, that person forwards the document back to you. You can then view all the users' revisions and annotations together.

- ✔ You can send a separate copy of the document to all the users on the list at once. Then, each user reviews, revises, and annotates the document and sends it back to you. You wind up with multiple versions of the document that you can review independently.

Here's how to route a document to several users:

1. **Create or open the document you want to route.**

2. **Choose the File⇨Send To⇨Routing Recipient command.**

   This summons the Routing Slip dialog box, shown in Figure 23-5.

3. **Click the Address button to summon the Address Book.**

4. **For each person you want to route the document to, click the person's name in your Address Book and then click the To button.**

   Keep adding names until the list is complete.

5. **Click OK to dismiss the Address Book.**

   You return to the Routing Slip dialog box. The names you selected in the Address Book appear in the Routing Slip dialog box.

6. **Type a message in the Message text field.**

   For example, you can say "Please review this by Thursday!" or some other friendly message.

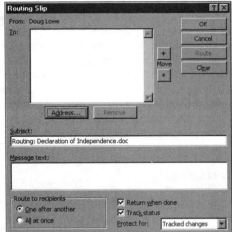

Figure 23-5:
The Routing
Slip dialog
box.

7. **Select One after another or All at once as the routing method.**

8. **Check the Return when done option if you want the document to be returned to you after everyone has reviewed it.**

9. **Check the Track status option if you want to follow the progress of the document.**

   If you choose the Track status option, you get an e-mail message each time a user forwards the document to the next person on the list.

10. **Click Route to send the document on its way.**

Tracking changes

Both Word and Excel have a Track Changes feature that lets you keep track of the revisions made to a document or worksheet. This feature enables you to see what changes other users have made to your document and accept or reject the changes based on your own whimsical judgements.

In Word, the Track Changes feature highlights changes to a document by drawing a line through any deleted text and underlining any inserted text. In addition, any text that contains a change — either an insertion or a deletion — is marked with a vertical line in the margin so that you can quickly scan through a document to find changes.

In Excel, each changed cell is marked with a special symbol. Excel allows you to flag all the changes to the worksheet, just those changes made since the worksheet was last saved or since a particular date, or just those changes that you have not yet reviewed.

Both Word and Excel indicate who made each change. As a result, the revision-tracking feature works together with the routing feature. As each routing recipient makes changes to the document, those changes are tracked so that when the document returns to you, you can see the changes that each user proposes.

When a document with changes returns to you, open the document and choose Tools⇨Track Changes⇨Accept or Reject Changes. Word or Excel displays the changes in the document one at a time, along with the name of the person who made the change and the time and date the change was made. You can then accept or reject each change.

Word, Excel, and PowerPoint enable users to insert comments into the document by using the Insert⇨Comment command. In Excel and PowerPoint, the Insert⇨Comment command places a yellow sticky-note comment into the worksheet or presentation. Comments in Word are a little more complicated; they appear in a separate pane at the bottom of the screen rather than right in the document.

Replying with discussions

Office 2000 takes the Comments feature a step further with a new feature called *Discussions*. The features are similar, but the Discussions feature enables users to reply to remarks made by other users. For example, one user may post a discussion remark about a particular paragraph in a Word document. Another user may post a reply to the first remark, stating that he or she disagrees with the original remark. When you review the discussion, you can see the original remarks along with the various replies.

Networking an Access Database

If you want to share a Microsoft Access database among several network users, you should be aware of a few special considerations. Here are the more important ones:

✔ When you share a database, more than one user may try to access the same record at the same time. This situation can lead to problems if two or more users try to update the record. To handle this, Access locks the record so that only one user at a time can update it. Access uses one of three methods to lock records:

• **Edited Record,** which locks a record whenever a user begins to edit a record. For example, if a user retrieves a record in a form that allows the record to be updated, Access locks the record while the user edits it so that other users can't edit the record until the first record is finished.

- **No Locks,** which doesn't really mean that the record isn't locked. Instead, No Locks means that the record is not locked until a user actually writes a change to the database. This method can be confusing to users because it enables one user to overwrite changes made by another user.

- **All Records,** which locks an entire table whenever a user edits any record in the table.

✔ Access lets you split a database so that the forms, queries, and reports are stored on each user's local disk drive, but the data itself is stored on a network drive. This feature can make the database run more efficiently on a network but is a little more difficult to set up. To split a database, use the Tools⇨Database Utilities⇨Database Splitter command.

✔ Access includes built-in security features that you should use if you store an Access database on a Windows 95 or 98 server or on a FAT drive on a Windows NT server. If you store the database on an NTFS volume on an NT server or on a NetWare server, you can use the server's security features to protect the database.

✔ Access automatically refreshes forms and datasheets every 60 seconds. That way, if one user opens a form or datasheet and another user changes the data a few seconds later, the first user sees the changes within one minute. If 60 seconds is too long (or too short), you can change the refresh from the Advanced tab of the Options dialog box.

Chapter 24

Networking Older Computers

● ●

● ●

*W*ouldn't it be great if every computer on your network had a shiny new Pentium III processor, 64MB of RAM, and a 10GB disk drive? Managing a network like this would be a breeze. Everyone could take advantage of the latest networking features of Windows 98, you wouldn't have to worry about incompatible network cards or software conflicts, and the users would never complain about lousy performance (except for the real nerds, who want Pentium *IV* processors).

Unfortunately, few networks in the real world have the luxury of working with only the most current computers. Most networks consist of a hodgepodge of computers, ranging from brand-new Pentium III computers with plenty of RAM and disk space, to older Pentium computers with adequate RAM and disk space, to still older 486 computers with barely enough RAM and disk space, to ancient 386 computers with not enough RAM or disk space. Getting all these computers to work on your network is the topic of this chapter.

Networking Old Computers Presents Challenges

Accommodating older computers on your network presents you with a plethora of challenges to overcome. The following list highlights the major areas of difficulty you face when networking computers that are less than state-of-the-art:

✔ Your client computers may run several different versions of Windows. You probably have to figure out how to incorporate Windows 98, Windows 95, Windows 3.1, and Windows for Workgroup computers into your network. Windows 95 and 98 have built-in networking support, but configuring older versions of Windows for networking can be a challenge.

✔ Some of the client computers may not even run Windows. You may have to figure out how to incorporate computers running DOS without Windows into your network.

✔ Older computers are probably very tight on disk space. Not long ago, 400MB of disk space seemed like a lot. Now it's barely enough to hold Windows and a few applications. Users of these computers will crave disk space on your network servers.

✔ Older computers have hardware limitations that make installing and configuring network cards difficult. (For more info, see the section "Configuring a Network Card in an Older Computer," later in this chapter.)

✔ When you mix old computers with new computers on the network, software incompatibilities are bound to arise. For example, some users may use Microsoft Office 97, while others use DOS versions of WordPerfect and Lotus 1-2-3.

Dealing with Older Computers in Three Ways

The following paragraphs summarize three basic approaches to handling the challenges of networking older computers.

Option 1: Don't include older computers in the network

One option is to simply state a minimum configuration that you will support on your network and refuse even to attempt to network any computer that doesn't meet that minimum. For example, you may say that you won't network any computer that doesn't already run Windows 95. Anyone who is still using Windows 3.1 or plain old DOS is out of luck.

Of course, this approach can make a lot of people mad — especially the ones with older computers. To make these people happy, you have two options: upgrade their old computers so that they can run Windows 98, or throw the old computers away and replace them with new computers.

If the computer isn't too old, you may be able to upgrade it to Windows 98 or 95 without much trouble. According to Microsoft, the minimum system requirements for Windows 98 are as follows:

- ✔ A 486 or better processor running at 66 MHz or faster
- ✔ 16MB of RAM
- ✔ 120MB of available disk space

The minimum requirements for Windows 95 are:

- ✔ A 486 or better processor running at 25 MHz or faster
- ✔ 4MB of RAM (8MB recommended)
- ✔ 40 to 45MB of free disk space

Most 486-based computers meet the requirements for Windows 95 and can be upgraded easily to meet the Windows 98 requirements by adding more RAM and, if necessary, installing a second disk drive. The computer remains slow, but it works.

The biggest trick is installing and configuring a network card to work in a 486-based computer. For tips on how to do this, see the section "Configuring a Network Card in an Older Computer," later in this chapter.

A computer with a 386 processor (or older) requires a more substantial overhaul to bring it up to Windows 95 or 98 standards. In fact, to upgrade a 386 computer to run Windows 95 or 98, you probably need to replace almost every major component of the computer: the motherboard, disk drive, video card, and maybe even the monitor. By the time you finish, you have spent as much or actually more than a new computer costs. Better to just discard these computers and replace them with new ones.

Option 2: Use your network's DOS support

If you have computers that run MS-DOS, with or without old-fashioned Windows 3.1, you can include them in your network by using your network operating system's built-in support for MS-DOS client computers. Both Windows NT Server and NetWare support MS-DOS client computers. An MS-DOS client computer can access shared network disk drives and printers, but cannot share its own drives or printers with other network users.

For more information about using a DOS computer on a network, see the section "Using a DOS Client Computer," later in this chapter.

Option 3: Use Artisoft's LANtastic

A third option for networking older computers is to use Artisoft's LANtastic as your network operating system. In the days of MS-DOS and Windows 3.1, LANtastic was one of the most popular NOS choices for small networks. Now that Windows 95 and 98 come with built-in networking, LANtastic has lost ground. However, LANtastic still has one advantage over both Windows 95 and 98: LANtastic still supports DOS. LANtastic even lets a DOS computer operate as a server, sharing its disk drives and printers.

If your network has a mixture of DOS and Windows 95 or 98 computers, LANtastic may be the way to go.

Using a DOS Client Computer

Both Windows NT Server and NetWare enable you to use DOS computers as clients on the network. A DOS client computer cannot share its own disk drives or printers with other network users, but it can access network drives and printers. The following sections describe the basics of using a DOS computer on a network.

Logging on to the network

To use network resources, a DOS client computer must first log on to the network. Usually, the logon process is started automatically by the computer's AUTOEXEC.BAT file when you start up your computer. You see a prompt similar to the following:

```
Enter your login name:
```

Type your user ID and press Enter. Then a prompt similar to this one appears:

```
Enter your password:
```

When you type your password, the password doesn't appear on the screen, which prevents someone looking over your shoulder from learning your password, unless of course they watch your fingers while you type.

After the network verifies your user ID and password, a special *login script* runs. The login script sets up your computer so that you can use network drives and printers.

Using a network drive

After you log on to the network, you have access to one or more network drives. Just like local drives, network drives are accessed using drive letters that are assigned to the network drives by the login script.

Every network is set up differently, so I can't tell you what your network drive letters are or what restrictions are in place for accessing your network drives. But you can find out easily enough. If you work on a Windows NT Server network, just type the following command at an MS-DOS prompt:

```
NET USE
```

This command displays a list of the network drives that are available to you. To see a similar list for a NetWare network, use this command:

```
MAP
```

This displays a list of all mapped network drives.

Network printing with NetWare

If your network is Novell NetWare and you're using NetWare's DOS client software, you set up redirection for a network printer by using the CAPTURE command. This command tells the NetWare software to capture everything sent to a particular printer port and redirect it to a network print queue.

Here's a typical CAPTURE command:

```
CAPTURE Q=LJET TI=10
```

This command redirects any printer output you send to LPT1 to a print queue named LJET. TI=10 sets the time-out value to ten seconds. If your program stops sending output to the printer for ten seconds, NetWare assumes the print job is finished.

If you have a local printer attached to your LPT1 port, you set up LPT2 as a network printer. Here's a CAPTURE command that does that:

```
CAPTURE L=2 Q=LJET TI=10
```

The L=2 tells CAPTURE to redirect LPT2.

Here are some additional important points regarding network printing with NetWare:

- Hopefully, a CAPTURE command is set up in your AUTOEXEC.BAT file, after the LOGIN command. That way, your network printer is set up for you automatically when you start your computer.

- Sometimes, ten seconds isn't long enough for the time-out value. If your reports are being broken apart into several print jobs, try a higher time-out value. If you omit TI altogether, time-out checking is turned off. Then your programs can take as long as they want to create the output.

- To cancel printer redirection, use the ENDCAP command. Good news! ENDCAP doesn't have any parameters, switches, or other adornments! Just say ENDCAP.

- CAPTURE has an AUTOENDCAP option that automatically releases output to the network printer whenever you exit an application. Don't confuse this option with the ENDCAP command, which not only releases any pending printer output to the network, but cancels printer redirection as well.

- Suppose that you have a local printer and two network printers: A laser printer named LASER and an inkjet printer named INKY. To easily switch between these printers, create three batch files named LOCAL.BAT, LASER.BAT, and INKY.BAT. The LOCAL.BAT file should contain this command:

```
ENDCAP
```

LASER.BAT should contain this command:

```
CAPTURE Q=LASER TI=10
```

And INKY.BAT should contain this command:

```
CAPTURE Q=INKY TI=10
```

To switch to the local printer, just type LOCAL at the DOS prompt. To switch to a network printer, type LASER or INKY.

Network printing with Windows NT

If your network is Windows NT and you use Microsoft MS-DOS client software, you set up printer redirection by using the NET USE command. This command tells the MS-DOS client software to use a particular network printer whenever you send output to a printer.

Here's a typical NET USE command to set up a network printer:

```
NET USE LPT1: \\WARD\LASER
```

This command redirects any printer output that you send to LPT1 to a printer named LASER on the server named WARD.

Here are some additional tips concerning network printing with Windows NT:

- ✔ A NET USE command should be set up in your AUTOEXEC.BAT file. That way, your network printer is set up for you automatically after you start your computer.

- ✔ To cancel printer redirection, use the NET USE /DELETE command, like this:

```
NET USE LPT1: /DELETE
```

- ✔ Suppose that you have a local printer and two network printers: a laser printer named LASER and an inkjet printer named INKY. To easily switch between these printers, create three batch files named LOCAL.BAT, LASER.BAT, and INKY.BAT. The LOCAL.BAT file should contain this command:

```
NET USE LPT1: /DELETE
```

This command disables any network connection for LPT1, so LPT1 reverts to your local printer. LASER.BAT should contain this command:

```
NET USE LPT1: \\WARD\LASER
```

And INKY.BAT should contain this command:

```
NET USE LPT1: \\WARD\INKY
```

To switch to the local printer, just type LOCAL at the DOS prompt. To switch to a network printer, type LASER or INKY.

Logging off the network

When you have finished using the network, you should log off. Logging off the network makes the network drives and printers unavailable, so strangers can't walk up to your computer and access the network.

If you just turn off your computer, you are automatically logged off the network. If you want to log off the network but keep your computer on so that you can continue using it, type the command LOGOUT if you use a NetWare network or NET LOGOFF if your network uses Windows NT Server.

Configuring a Network Card in an Older Computer

One of the best features about Windows 95 and 98 is *Plug and Play,* which makes installing new devices, such as a network interface card, a snap. Plug and Play automatically recognizes your network card, configures it, and installs any special device drivers that the card needs to operate.

To install a network card in a computer that doesn't run Windows 95 or 98, you have to configure the card manually. You may have to fiddle with confusing software configuration settings, or, worse yet, you may actually have to make changes on the card itself before you install it into your computer. If that's the case, the following tips should prove helpful:

✔ On some cards, configuration settings are made by changing special switches called *DIP switches* or moving a *jumper block.* Figure 24-1 shows what a DIP switch and jumper block look like. The switch or block must be set *before* you install the card into your computer.

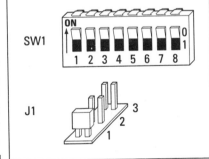

Figure 24-1:
A DIP
switch and
a jumper
block.

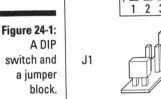

✔ A straightened-out paper clip is the ideal tool for setting DIP switches.

✔ To change a jumper block, you move the *plug* from one set of pins to another. You need fingernails to do it properly. Or a good set of tweezers.

✔ If you're lucky, your network cards have been preconfigured for you with the most likely settings. You need to double-check, though, because (1) the factory settings are not always appropriate, and (2) sometimes they make mistakes at the factory and configure the cards incorrectly.

✔ If you're even luckier, your cards don't use DIP switches or jumper blocks at all. These cards still have to be configured, but the configuration is done with software rather than with a paper clip or your fingernails.

✔ Most network cards have two configuration settings: IRQ number and I/O port address. Some cards also enable you to configure a DMA channel. These settings are described under separate headings in the next few pages. The information is technical and boring, so make sure that you're wide awake.

✔ Network cards that support more than one type of cable connector also have to be configured for the proper cable type. For example, if your card supports both 10baseT and coax connectors, you have to configure the card depending on the type of cable you use.

✔ When you configure a network card, write down the settings you select. You need these settings later when you install the client software. Store your list of network card settings in your network binder.

✔ Adding a joke about DIP switches here would be too easy. Insert your own joke if you're so inclined.

Configuring those irksome IRQ numbers

IRQ stands for *Interrupt ReQuest*. You don't need to know that; I tell you only because I think it's funny that the Q is capitalized in the middle of the word. Each computer has 16 different IRQ numbers, and each I/O device — such as a printer port, modem, mouse, and so on — must be assigned a separate IRQ number. Finding an IRQ number that's not already used isn't always easy. (On old XT computers, only eight IRQ numbers exist. That makes avoiding IRQ conflicts even harder.)

The trick to setting the IRQ number is knowing what IRQ numbers the computer is already using. Table 24-1 shows the usual IRQ settings.

Table 24-1	**Typical IRQ Assignments**
IRQ Number	*What It's Used For*
IRQ0	The computer's internal timer
IRQ1	The keyboard
IRQ2	Not usable
IRQ3	Serial port COM2, often a mouse or modem
IRQ4	Serial port COM1, often a mouse or modem
IRQ5	Parallel port LPT2
IRQ6	Floppy disk
IRQ7	Parallel port LPT1

(continued)

Table 24-1 *(continued)*

IRQ Number	What It's Used For
IRQ8	Internal clock
IRQ9–13	Usually available
IRQ14	Hard disk
IRQ15	Usually available

Here is some additional information about IRQ settings:

- Some network interface cards support only a few IRQ numbers, such as IRQ3, IRQ4, or IRQ5. IRQ5 is usually a safe choice unless the computer has two printers. However, if you installed a device such as a CD-ROM drive or a scanner, make sure that IRQ5 isn't already in use.

- IRQ3 and IRQ4 are used by the serial ports COM1 and COM2. If you have a modem and a serial-port mouse, don't use IRQ3 or IRQ4 for the network card.

- If your computer is loaded up with extra devices, check which IRQs are available *before* you buy your network cards. Make sure that the cards you buy can be configured to an IRQ number you can use.

- If you're not sure what IRQ numbers are in use and you have DOS Version 6.0 or 6.2 or Windows 3.1, run the MSD program from a DOS prompt. Press Q to display the IRQs that are in use.

Configuring the I/O port address

The I/O port address is a doorway that the network card uses to transfer information to and from the network. The address is usually set to a number such as 300, 310, 320, and so on. The only trick to setting the I/O port is making sure that it doesn't conflict with the port setting used by another device.

Here are some other things you should know about I/O port addresses:

- Unlike IRQ lines, I/O port conflicts are less common. You have lots of I/O port addresses to choose from, so avoiding conflicts is easier. The factory I/O port address setting is likely acceptable.

- The factory certainly won't ship out a network card with an I/O port setting that conflicts with your printer port, mouse, disk drive, or other common components. You're likely to see a conflict only if you have other stuff attached to your computer, such as a sound card, CD-ROM drive, or scanner. When you configure a network card, just make sure that the I/O port setting isn't the same as the setting you use for some other device.

✔ I/O port addresses are hexadecimal numbers that include the letters A–F along with the digits 0–9. For example, 37C is a valid I/O port address number. Be thankful that you don't have to understand hexadecimal numbering to set the port address correctly; just follow the instructions that come with the card, and the hex monsters won't bite you.

✔ The *h* that's sometimes added to the end of the I/O address — like 300h or 37Ch — is just to remind you that the number is hexadecimal, as if that mattered.

Configuring the DMA channel

Some network cards use DMA channels for faster performance. (DMA stands for Direct Memory Access, but that's not important now.) If your card uses a DMA channel, you may have to change the default setting to avoid conflicting with some other add-on card that also may use DMA, such as a CD-ROM adapter or a scanner. Check the manual that came with your card to find out if the card uses DMA.

Chapter 25

Networking Macintosh Computers

- -

In This Chapter

▶ Hooking up a Macintosh network

▶ Using a Macintosh network

▶ Mixing Macs and PCs

- -

*T*his book dwells on networking PCs as if IBM were the only game in town. To be politically correct, I should at least acknowledge the existence of an altogether different breed of computer: the Apple Macintosh.

Apple prides itself on its ability to include stuff in its Macintosh operating system that Windows users have to purchase separately. Network support is an example. Every Macintosh comes with built-in networking support. All you have to do to network your Macintosh is buy network cable.

Well, you actually discover that networking your Macintosh involves a lot more than that. This chapter presents what you need to know to hook up a Macintosh network, use a Macintosh network, and mix Macintoshes and PCs on the same network. This chapter is not a comprehensive tome on networking Macintoshes, but if you want more information, you can pick up the humongoid book, *Macworld Networking Bible,* 2nd Edition, by Dave Kosiur, Ph.D., and Joel M. Snyder, Ph.D. (IDG Books Worldwide, Inc.).

What You Need to Know to Hook Up a Macintosh Network

Hooking up a small Macintosh network is easy: All you really have to do is buy cables and plug them in.

AppleTalk and Open Transport

As I said, every Macintosh ever built includes networking support. The built-in networking features are similar to those of Windows — not as powerful as NetWare or Windows NT Server, but more than adequate to set up a basic network so that several users can share files and printers.

The Macintosh built-in network feature is called AppleTalk. One of the advantages of having AppleTalk built in is that it has become an inarguable networking standard among Macintosh users. You don't have to worry about the differences between different network operating systems, because all Macintosh networking is based on AppleTalk.

In 1996, with the release of MacOS System 7.5.3, Apple folded AppleTalk into a grander networking scheme known as Open Transport. The idea behind Open Transport is to bring all the different communications software used on Macintoshes under a common umbrella and make them easy to configure and use. Currently, two types of networking are handled by Open Transport.

- Open Transport/AppleTalk handles local area networks based on the AppleTalk protocols. Open Transport/AppleTalk is a beefed-up version of AppleTalk that's more efficient and flexible.
- OpenTransport/TCP handles TCP/IP communications, such as Internet connections.

Open Transport is standard fare on all new Macintosh computers, and old Macintosh computers can be upgraded to Open Transport, provided that they're powerful enough. (The minimum system requirements for Open Transport are a 68030 processor, 5MB RAM, and MacOS System 7.5.3.)

AppleTalk enables you to subdivide a network into *zones,* which are similar to workgroups in Windows for Workgroups. Each zone consists of the network users who regularly share information.

Although basic support for networking is built into every Macintosh, you still have to purchase cables to connect the computers to one another. You have several types of cables to choose from. You can use AppleTalk with two different cabling schemes that connect to the Macintosh printer port, or you can use it with faster Ethernet interface cards.

LocalTalk: The cheap way to network

LocalTalk is an older method of connecting Macintosh computers that don't have built-in network adapters. LocalTalk connects Macintosh computers together using special cables that attach to each computer's printer port.

Who's winning in the AFP West?

AFP is not a division of the NFL, but an abbreviation for AppleTalk Filing Protocol. It's the part of AppleTalk that governs how files are stored and accessed on the network. AFP allows files to be shared with non-Macintosh computers. You can integrate Macintoshes into any network operating system that recognizes AFP. NetWare, Windows NT, and Windows 95 and 98 use AFP to support Macintoshes in their networks.

Unfortunately, Windows for Workgroups doesn't support AFP, so you can't use Macintoshes in a Windows for Workgroups network.

In case you're interested (and you shouldn't be), AFP is a presentation-layer protocol. See Chapter 30 if you don't have a clue what I'm talking about.

Here are the details:

- ✔ LocalTalk connectors are self-terminating, which means that separate terminators are not required on both ends of the cable segment.

- ✔ Each LocalTalk connector comes with a 2-meter-long LocalTalk cable (that's about 6 ½ feet). You can also purchase 10-meter cables if your computers aren't that close together.

- ✔ LocalTalk uses shielded twisted-pair cable. The shielding protects the cable from electrical interference but limits the total length of cable used in a network segment to 300 feet.

- ✔ No more than 32 computers and printers can be connected to a single segment.

- ✔ A popular alternative to LocalTalk is PhoneNET, made by Farallon Computing. PhoneNET uses inexpensive telephone cable rather than the shielded twisted-pair cable used by LocalTalk.

Ethernet with Macintosh computers

LocalTalk is popular because it's cheap. But LocalTalk has one major problem: It's unbearably slow. LocalTalk uses the Macintosh serial printer ports and so transmits data over the network at a paltry 230,400 bits per second. This transmission rate is acceptable for casual use of a network printer and for occasionally copying a small file to or from another computer but not for serious networking.

Fortunately, AppleTalk also supports Ethernet network adapters and cables. With Ethernet, data travels at 10 million bits per second. Much more suitable for real-life networking.

When you use Ethernet, you have access to all the cabling options described elsewhere in this book: 10base5 (yellow cable), 10base2 (thinnet), and 10baseT (twisted pair). Fast (100 Mbps) Ethernet works as well.

Here are some additional points to ponder when you use Ethernet to network your Macintosh computers:

✔ An AppleTalk network that uses Ethernet is sometimes called an *EtherTalk network.*

✔ Ethernet interface cards for Macintoshes are a bit more expensive than their PC counterparts, mostly because they aren't as widely used. However, most Macs built within the last few years have Ethernet built in, so if your Macs are new, you probably don't need cards.

✔ All of the current Apple Macintosh computers come with either 10MHz Ethernet or combination 10/100MHz Ethernet adapters built in, so you don't have to purchase and install separate network cards for new computers.

✔ Most newer Macintosh computers have PCI expansion slots, the same expansion slots that PCs have. That means you can use any PCI Ethernet card in a PCI-equipped Macintosh. (Well, almost any. The manufacturer of the card must supply a Macintosh driver for the card, and some manufacturers don't.)

✔ When you opt for an Ethernet network, you have to contend with a device driver to support the network card. You use the Installer program to set up the driver.

✔ Some older Macintosh computers used a special interface for Ethernet cards called the Ethernet cabling system. When the Ethernet cabling system is used, the network cards themselves don't have coax or 10baseT connectors. Instead, they have a special type of connector called an Apple Attachment Unit Interface (AAUI). You must plug a device called a transceiver into the AAUI connector so that you can attach the computer to a coax or twisted-pair cable. Newer Macintosh computers with built-in Ethernet adapters use standard RJ-45 connectors.

✔ You can use a router to connect a LocalTalk network to an Ethernet network. This arrangement often connects a small group of Macintosh users to a larger network or connects an existing LocalTalk network to an Ethernet network.

AppleShare

AppleShare turns a Macintosh computer into a dedicated file server. It's the Macintosh equivalent of Windows NT Server or NetWare. It can support up to 250 users connected to the server simultaneously using AppleTalk or 500 users with TCP/IP.

The current version of AppleShare, called AppleShare IP 6.1, offers the following features:

✔ File server using AppleTalk's standard file protocol, ATP

✔ Print server

✔ Mail server

✔ Web server

✔ FTP server

✔ Support for both AppleTalk and TCP/IP protocols

You need to purchase AppleShare only if you want to set up a Macintosh computer to act as a dedicated file server. All Macintosh computers come with the ability to connect to a network, access network printers and drives, and share their own printers and disk drives with other network users.

What You Need to Know to Use a Macintosh Network

Here are some of the most common questions that come up after you install the network cable. Note that the following sections assume that you're working with AppleTalk networking. The procedures may vary somewhat if you're using Open Transport networking.

How to configure a Mac for networking

Before you can access the network from your Mac, you must configure it for networking by activating AppleTalk and assigning your network name and password.

Activating AppleTalk

After all the cables are in place, you have to activate AppleTalk. Here's how:

1. **Choose the Chooser desk accessory from the Apple menu.**

2. **Click the Active button.**

3. **Close the Chooser.**

That's all there is to it.

Assigning your name and password

Next, assign an owner name, a password, and a name for your computer. This process allows other network users to access your Mac. Here's how:

1. **Choose the File Sharing control panel from the Apple menu (Apple menu➪Control Panels➪File Sharing).**

2. **Type your name in the Owner Name field.**

3. **Type a password in the Owner Password field. Don't forget what the password is.**

4. **Type a descriptive name for your computer in the Computer Name field. Other network users will know your computer by this name.**

5. **Close File Sharing.**

Piece of cake, eh?

How to access a network printer

Accessing a network printer with AppleTalk is no different than accessing a printer when you don't have a network. If more than one printer is available on the network, you use the Chooser to select the printer you want to use. Chooser displays all the available network printers; just pick the one you want to use. And keep the following points in mind:

✔ Be sure to enable Background Printing for the network printer. If you don't, your Mac is tied up until the printer finishes your job — that can be a long time if someone else sent a 500-page report to the printer just before you. When you enable Background Printing, your printer output is captured to a disk file and then sent to the printer later while you continue with other work.

To enable Background Printing, choose the printer you want to use from the Chooser and click the Background Printing On button.

✔ Rescind that last order if a dedicated print server has been set up. In that case, print data is automatically spooled to the print server's disk so that your Mac doesn't have to wait for the printer to become available.

How to share files with other users

To share files on your Mac with other network users, you must set up a shared resource. You can share an entire disk, or you can share just individual folders. And you can restrict access to certain users, if you want.

Before you can share files with other users, you must activate the AppleTalk file-sharing feature. Here's how:

1. **Choose the File Sharing control panel from the Apple Menu.**
2. **Click the Start button in the File Sharing section of the control panel.**
3. **Close File Sharing.**

To share a file or folder, click the file or folder once. Then open the File menu, choose Get Info, and then choose Sharing from the submenu that appears. You can also use the Sharing section of the Info window to set access privileges to restrict access to the file or folder.

How to access shared files

To access files on another Macintosh, follow this procedure:

1. **Choose the Chooser from the Apple menu.**
2. **Click the AppleShare icon from the Chooser window.**
3. **Click the name of the computer you want to access. (If your network has zones, you must first click the zone you want to access.)**
4. **Click OK.**
5. **A login screen appears. If you're a registered user on the computer, click the Registered User button and enter your user name and password. Otherwise, click the Guest button and then click OK.**
6. **A list of shared folders and disks appears. Click the ones you want to access and then click OK.**

    A check box appears next to each item on this list. If you check this box, you connect to the folder or disk automatically each time you start your computer.

With Mac OS 8.5, you can also use the Network Browser, found in the Apple menu, to access network drives or folders. Just open the Network Browser from the Apple menu, double-click the server that contains the shared disk or folder, and then double-click the drive or folder you want to use.

What You Need to Know to Network Macintoshes with PCs

Life would be too boring if Macs lived on one side of the tracks and PCs lived on the other. If your organization has a mix of both Macs and PCs, odds are you eventually want to network them together. Fortunately, you have several ways to do so:

- ✔ If your network has an AppleShare server, you can use the Windows client software that comes with AppleShare to connect any version of Windows to the AppleShare server. Doing so enables Windows users to access the files and printers on the AppleShare server.

- ✔ If you have Windows NT Server, you can use a feature called Services for Macintosh to allow Macintosh computers to access files and printers managed by the Windows NT Server using the AppleTalk protocol. This feature doesn't require that you install special client software on the Macintosh computers.

- ✔ If you use NetWare, you must purchase separate NetWare client software for your Macintosh computers. After you install this client software, the Macs can access files and printers managed by your NetWare servers.

The biggest complication that occurs when you mix Macintosh and Windows computers on the same network is that the Mac OS and Windows have slightly different rules for naming files. For example, Macintosh filenames are limited to 31 characters, but Windows filenames can be up to 255 characters. And while a Macintosh filename can include any characters other than a colon, Windows filenames can't include backslashes, greater than or less than signs, and a few other oddball characters.

These filename conflicts are resolved by translating any filenames that violate the rules of the system being used into a form that is acceptable to both Windows and the Macintosh. Unfortunately, doing so sometimes leads to cryptic or ambiguous filenames. To avoid filename problems, try to stick with short names (under 31 characters) and limit your filenames to letters, numbers, and common symbols such as the hyphen or pound sign.

Part VI

The Part of Tens

The 5th Wave — By Rich Tennant

"I DON'T THINK OUR NEWEST NETWORK CONFIGURATION IS GOING TO WORK. ALL OF OUR TRANSMISSIONS FROM OHIO SEEM TO BE COMING IN OVER MY ELECTRIC PENCIL SHARPENER."

In this part . . .

1f you keep this book in the bathroom, the chapters in this section are the ones that you'll read most. Each chapter consists of ten (more or less) things that are worth knowing about various aspects of networking. Without further ado, here they are, direct from the home office in Fresno, California.

Chapter 26

Ten (Or Fewer) Big Network Mistakes

*J*ust about the time you figure out how to avoid the most embarrassing computer mistakes, such as folding a 5 ¼-inch disk in half to make it fit in a 3 ½-inch drive, the network lands on your computer. Now you have a whole new list of dumb things you can do, mistakes that can give your average computer geek a belly laugh because they seem so basic to him. Well, that's because he's a computer geek. Nobody had to tell him not to fold the disk — he was born with an extra gene that gave him an instinctive knowledge of such things.

Here's a list of some of the most common mistakes made by network novices. Avoid these mistakes and you deprive your local computer geek of the pleasure of a good laugh at your expense.

Turning Off or Restarting a Server Computer While Users Are Logged On

The fastest way to blow your network users to kingdom come is to turn off a server computer while users are logged on. Restarting it by pressing its reset button can have the same disastrous effect.

If your network is set up with a dedicated file server, you probably won't be tempted to turn it off or restart it. But if your network is set up as a true peer-to-peer network, where each of the workstation computers — including your own — also doubles as a server computer, be careful about the impulsive urge to turn your computer off or restart it. Someone may be accessing a file or printer on your computer at that very moment.

Before turning off or restarting a server computer, find out whether anyone is logged on. If so, politely ask him or her to log off.

Deleting Important Files on the Server

Without a network, you can do anything you want to your computer, and the only person you can hurt is yourself. Kind of like the old "victimless crime" debate. Put your computer on a network, though, and you take on a certain amount of responsibility. You must find out how to live like a responsible member of the network society.

That means you can't capriciously delete files from a network server just because you don't need them. They may not be yours. You wouldn't want someone deleting your files, would you?

Be especially careful about files that are required to keep the network running. For example, Windows e-mail uses a folder named wgpo0000 as a workgroup post office. Delete this folder and your e-mail is history.

Copying a File from the Server, Changing It, and Then Copying It Back

Sometimes working on a network file is easier if you first copy the file to your local disk. Then you can access it from your application program more efficiently because you don't have to use the network. This is especially true for large database files that have to be sorted to print reports.

You're asking for trouble, though, if you copy the file to your PC's local hard disk, make changes to the file, and then copy the updated version of the file back to the server. Why? Because somebody else may be trying the same thing at the same time. If that happens, the updates made by one of you — the one who copies the file back to the server first — are lost.

Copying a file to a local drive is an okay thing to do, but not if you plan on updating the file and copying it back.

Sending Something to the Printer Again Just Because It Didn't Print the First Time

What do you do if you send something to the printer and nothing happens? Right answer: Find out why nothing happened and fix it. Wrong answer: Send it again and see whether it works this time. Some users keep sending it over and over again, hoping that one of these days, it'll take. The result is rather embarrassing when someone finally clears the paper jam and then watches 30 copies of the same letter print.

Unplugging a Cable While the Computer Is On

Bad idea! If for any reason you need to unplug a cable from behind your computer, turn your computer off first. You don't want to fry any of the delicate electronic parts inside your computer, do you?

If you need to unplug the network cable, you should wait until all the computers on the network are off. This is especially true if your network is wired with thinnet coax cable; it's not such a big deal with twisted-pair cable.

Note: With thinnet cable, you can disconnect the T connector from your computer as long as you don't disconnect the cable itself from the T connector.

Assuming That the Server Is Safely Backed Up

Some users make the unfortunate assumption that the network somehow represents an efficient and organized bureaucracy worthy of their trust. Far from the truth. Never assume that the network jocks are doing their jobs backing up the network data every day. Check up on them. Conduct a surprise inspection one day: Burst into the computer room wearing white gloves and demand to see the backup tapes. Check the tape rotation to make sure that more than one day's worth of backups are available.

If you're not impressed with your network's backup procedures, take it upon yourself to make sure that you never lose any of your data. Back up your most valued files to floppy disks frequently.

Thinking You Can't Work Just Because the Network Is Down

A few years back, I realized that I can't do my job without electricity. Should a power failure occur and I find myself without electricity, I can't even light a candle and work with pencil and paper because the only pencil sharpener I have is electric.

Some people have the same attitude about the network: They figure that if the network goes down, they may as well go home. That's not always the case. Just because your computer is attached to a network doesn't mean that it won't work when the network is down. True — if the wind flies out of the network sails, you can't access any network devices. You can't get files from network drives, and you can't print on network printers. But you can still use your computer for local work: accessing files and programs on your local hard disk and printing on your local printer (if you're lucky enough to have one).

Always Blaming the Network

Some people treat the network kind of like the village idiot who can be blamed whenever anything goes wrong. Networks do cause problems of their own, but they aren't the root of all evil.

If your monitor displays only capital letters, it's probably because you pressed the Caps Lock key. Don't blame the network.

If you spill coffee on the keyboard, well, that's your fault. Don't blame the network.

Your toddler sticks Play-Doh in the floppy drive — hey, kids will be kids. Don't blame the network.

Get the point?

Chapter 27
Ten Networking Commandments

In This Chapter

▶ Thou shalt back up thy hard disk religiously

▶ Thou shalt protect thy network from infidels

▶ Thou shalt remember thy network disk, to keep it clean of old files

▶ Thou shalt not tinker with thine network configuration files unless thou knowest what thou art doing

▶ Thou shalt not covet thy neighbor's network

▶ Thou shalt schedule downtime before working upon thy network

▶ Thou shalt keep an adequate supply of spare parts

▶ Thou shalt not steal thy neighbor's program without license

▶ Thou shalt train thy users in the way in which they should go

▶ Thou shalt write down thy network configuration upon tablets of stone

"Blessed is the network manager who walks not in the council of the ignorant, nor stands in the way of the oblivious, nor sits in the seat of the greenhorn, but delights in the Law of the Network and meditates on this Law day and night."

— Networks 1:1

And so it came to pass that these Ten Networking Commandments were passed down from generation to generation, to be worn as frontlets between the computer geeks' eyes and written upon their doorposts. Obey these commandments and it shall go well with you, with your children, and with your children's children.

I. Thou Shalt Back Up Thy Hard Disk Religiously

Prayer is a wonderful thing, but when it comes to protecting the data on your network, nothing beats a well-thought-out schedule of backups followed religiously.

II. Thou Shalt Protect Thy Network from Infidels

Remember Colonel Flagg from *M*A*S*H*, who hid in trashcans looking for Commies? You don't exactly want to become him, but on the other hand, you don't want to ignore the possibility of getting zapped by a virus or your network being invaded by hackers. Make sure that your Internet connection is properly secured, and do not allow the use of modems to access the Internet unless you have provided adequate security.

As for virus threats, start by making sure that every user realizes that any floppy disk from the outside can be infected, and after one computer on the network is infected, the entire network is in trouble. Then show the users how easily they can scan suspicious disks before using them.

III. Thou Shalt Remember Thy Network Disk, to Keep It Clean of Old Files

Don't wait until your 10GB network drive is down to just one cluster of free space before thinking about cleaning it up. Set up a routine schedule for disk housekeeping, where you wade through the files and directories on the network disk to remove old junk.

IV. Thou Shalt Not Tinker with Thine Network Configuration Files Unless Thou Knowest What Thou Art Doing

Networks are finicky things. After yours is up and running, don't mess around with it unless you know what you're doing. And be especially careful if you think you know what you're doing. It's people who think they know what they're doing who get themselves into trouble!

V. Thou Shalt Not Covet Thy Neighbor's Network

Network envy is a common malady among network managers. If your network uses plain old Windows 98 and it works, nothing can be gained by coveting someone else's network. If you run NetWare 3.2, resist the urge to upgrade to 4.2 unless you have a really good reason. And if you run NetWare 4.2, fantasizing about Windows NT Server is a venial sin.

You're especially susceptible to network envy if you're a gadget freak. There's always a better hub to be had or some fancy network protocol gizmo to lust after. Don't give in to these base urges! Resist the devil, and he will flee!

VI. Thou Shalt Schedule Downtime Before Working upon Thy Network

As a courtesy, try to give your users plenty of advance notice before you take down the network to work on it. Obviously, you can't predict when random problems strike. But if you know you're going to add a new computer to the network on Thursday morning, you earn points if you tell everyone about the inconvenience two days before rather than two minutes before.

VII. Thou Shalt Keep an Adequate Supply of Spare Parts

There's no reason that your network should be down for two days just because a cable breaks. Always make sure that you have at least a minimal supply of network spare parts on hand. As luck would have it, Chapter 28 suggests ten things you should keep in your closet.

VIII. Thou Shalt Not Steal Thy Neighbor's Program without License

How would you like it if Inspector Clouseau barged into your office, looked over your shoulder as you ran Lotus 1-2-3 from a network server, and asked, "Do you have a liesaunce?"

"A liesaunce?" you reply, puzzled.

"Yes of course, a liesaunce, that is what I said. The law specifically prohibits the playing of a computer program on a network without a proper liesaunce."

You don't want to go against the law, do you?

IX. Thou Shalt Train Thy Users in the Way in Which They Should Go

Don't blame the users if they don't know how to use the network. It's not their fault. If you're the network administrator, your job is to provide training so that the network users know how to use the network.

X. Thou Shalt Write Down Thy Network Configuration upon Tablets of Stone

If you cross the river Jordan, who else will know diddly-squat about the network if you don't write it down somewhere? The back of a napkin won't cut it. Write down everything and put it in an official binder labeled *Network Bible* and protect the binder as if it were sacred.

Your hope should be that 2,000 years from now, when archaeologists are exploring caves in your area, they find your network documentation hidden in a jar and marvel at how meticulously the people of our time recorded their network configurations.

They'll probably draw ridiculous conclusions such as we offered sacrifices of burnt data packets to a deity named NOS, but that makes it all the more fun.

Chapter 28

Ten (Or Fewer) Things You Should Keep in the Closet

- -

- -

*W*hen you first networkize your office computers, you need to find a closet where you can stash some network goodies. If you can't find a whole closet, shoot for a shelf, a drawer, or at least a sturdy cardboard box.

Here's a list of what stuff to keep on hand.

Tools

Make sure that you have at least a basic computer toolkit, the kind you can pick up for $15 from just about any office supply store. You also should have wire cutters, wire strippers, and cable crimpers that work for your network cable type.

Extra Cable

When you buy network cable, never buy exactly the amount you need. In fact, buying at least twice as much cable as you need isn't a bad idea, because half the cable is left over in case you need it later. You will. Something will go wrong, and you'll suspect a cable problem, so you'll need extra cable to replace the bad cable. Or you may add a computer or two to the network and need extra cable.

If you glue your entire network together with preassembled 25-foot lengths of thinnet coax cable, having at least one 25-foot segment lying around in the closet is a good idea.

Extra Connectors

Don't run out of connectors, either. If you use twisted-pair cabling, you'll find that connectors go bad more often than you'd like. Buy the connectors 25, 50, or 100 at a time so that you have plenty of spares lying around.

If you use thinnet cable, keep a few spare BNC connectors handy, plus a few T connectors and a few terminators. Terminators have been known to mysteriously disappear. Rumor has it that they are sucked through some kind of time vortex into the distant future, where they're refabricated and returned to our time in the form of Arnold Schwarzenegger.

Preassembled Patch Cables

If you wired your network the professional way, with wall jacks in each office, keep a few preassembled patch cables of various lengths in the closet. That way, you won't have to pull out the cable crimpers every time you need to change a patch cable.

Twinkies

If left sealed in their little individually wrapped packages, Twinkies keep for years. In fact, they'll probably outlast the network itself. You can give 'em to future network geeks, ensuring continued network support for generations to come.

An Extra Network Card

Ideally, you want to use identical network cards in all your computers. But if the boss's computer is down, you'd probably settle for whatever network card the corner network street vendor is selling today. That's why you should always keep at least one spare network card in the closet. You can rest easy knowing that if a network card fails, you have an identical replacement card sitting on the shelf, just waiting to be installed — and you won't have to buy one from someone who also sells imitation Persian rugs.

Obviously, if you have only two computers on your network, justifying spending the money for a spare network adapter card is hard. With larger networks, it's easier to justify.

Complete Documentation of the Network on Tablets of Stone

I've mentioned several times in this book the importance of documenting your network. Don't spend hours documenting your network and then hide the documentation under a pile of old magazines behind your desk. Put the binder in the closet with the other network supplies so that you and everyone else always know where to find it. And keep backup copies of the Word, Excel, or other documents that make up the network binder in a fire-proof safe or at another site.

Don't you dare chisel passwords into the network documentation, though. Shame on you for even thinking about it!

If you do decide to chisel the network documentation in stone tablets, consider using sandstone. It's attractive, inexpensive, and easy to update (just rub out the old info and chisel in the new). Keep in mind, however, that sandstone is subject to erosion from spilled Jolt Cola or Snapple. Oh, and make sure that you store it on a reinforced shelf.

The Network Manuals and Disks

In the land of Oz, a common lament of the Network Scarecrow is "If I only had the manual." True, the manual probably isn't a Pulitzer-prize candidate, but that doesn't mean you should toss it in a landfill, either. Put the manual where it belongs: in the closet with all the other network tools and artifacts.

Likewise the disks. You may need them someday, so keep them with the other network stuff.

Ten Copies of This Book

Obviously, you want to keep an adequate supply of this book on hand to distribute to all your network users. The more they know, the more they stay off your back. Sheesh, 10 copies may not be enough — 20 may be closer to what you need.

Chapter 29

Ten (Or Fewer) Network Gizmos Only Big Networks Need

● ●

In This Chapter

▶ Repeaters

▶ Bridges

▶ Switches

▶ Routers

▶ Gateways

▶ Superservers

▶ RAIDs

▶ Firewalls

▶ Fast Ethernets

● ●

*P*eople who compile statistics on things, such as the ratio of chickens to humans in Arkansas and the likelihood of the Mets losing when the other team shows up, report that more than 40 percent of all networks have fewer than ten computers and that this percentage is expected to increase in coming years. A Ross Perot-style pie chart would be good here, but my editor tells me I'm running long, so I have to pass on that.

The point is that if you're one of the lucky 40 percent with fewer than ten computers on your network, you can skip this chapter altogether. Here, I briefly describe various network gizmos that you may need if your network is really big. How big is big? There's no hard-and-fast rule, but the soft-and-slow rule is that you should look into this stuff when your network grows to about 25 computers.

The exceptions to the soft-and-slow rule are as follows: (1) Your company has two or more networks that you want to hook together, and these networks were designed by different people who refused to talk to each other until it was too late; (2) your network needs to connect computers that are more than a few hundred yards apart, perhaps in different buildings.

Repeaters

A *repeater* is a gizmo that gives your network signals a boost so that they can travel farther. It's kind of like the Gatorade stations in a marathon. As they travel past the repeater, the network signals pick up a cup of Gatorade, take a sip, splash the rest of it on their heads, toss the cup, and hop in a cab when they're sure that no one is looking.

You need a repeater when the total length of a single span of network cable is larger than the maximum allowed for your cable type:

Cable	Maximum Length
Thick coax (yellow stuff)	500 meters or 1,640 feet
Thin coax (cheaper net)	185 meters or 606 feet
10baseT (twisted sister)	100 meters or 328 feet

For coax cable (thick and thin), the preceding cable lengths apply to cable segments, not individual lengths of cable. A *segment* is the entire run of cable from one terminator to another and may include more than one computer. In other words, if you have ten computers and you connect them all with 25-foot lengths of thin coax cable, the total length of the segment is 225 feet. (Made you look! Only nine cables are required to connect ten computers — that's why it's not 250 feet.)

For 10baseT cable, the 100-meter length limit applies to the cable that connects a computer to the hub or the cable that connects hubs to each other when hubs are daisy-chained with twisted-pair cable. In other words, you can connect each computer to the hub with no more than 100 meters of cable, and you can connect hubs to each other with no more than 100 meters of cable.

Figure 29-1 shows how you can use a repeater to connect two groups of computers that are too far apart to be strung on a single segment. When you use a repeater like this, the repeater divides the cable into two segments. The cable length limit still applies to the cable on each side of the repeater.

Here are some points to ponder when you lie awake tonight wondering about repeaters:

✔ Repeaters are used only with Ethernet networks wired with coax cable. 10baseT networks don't use repeaters.

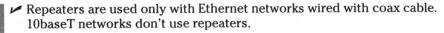

Actually, that's not quite true: 10baseT does use repeaters. It's just that the repeater isn't a separate device. In a 10baseT network, the hub is actually a multiport repeater. That's why the cable used to attach each computer to the hub is considered a separate segment.

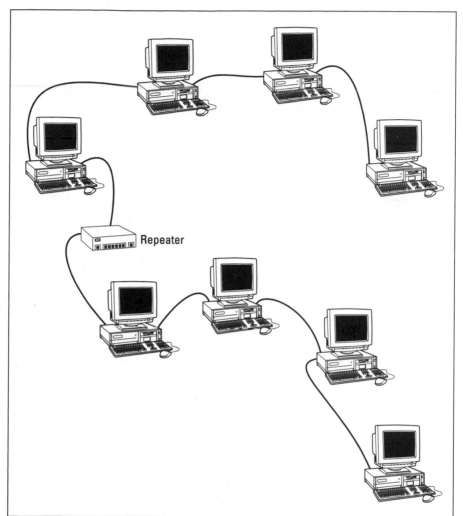

Figure 29-1:
Using a
repeater.

✔ Most 10baseT hubs have a BNC connector on the back. This BNC connector is a thinnet repeater that enables you to attach a full 185-meter thinnet segment. The segment can attach other computers, 10baseT hubs, or a combination of both. (Some cheaper 10baseT hubs don't have this extra connector, which means that you can't connect them to a thinnet segment.)

✔ A basic rule of Ethernet life is that a signal cannot pass through more than three repeaters on its way from one node to another. That doesn't mean you can't have more than three repeaters or hubs, but if you do, you have to carefully plan the network cabling so that the three-repeater rule isn't violated.

✔ You can get two-port thinnet repeaters for about $200 from mail-order suppliers.

✔ Repeaters are legitimate components of a by-the-book Ethernet network. They don't extend the maximum length of a single segment; they just enable you to tie two segments together. Beware of the little black boxes that claim to extend the segment limit beyond the standard 185-meter limit for thinnet or 500-meter limit for the yellow stuff. These products usually work, but playing by the rules is better.

Bridges

A *bridge* is a device that connects two networks so that they act as if they're one network. Bridges are used to partition one large network into two smaller networks for performance reasons. You can think of a bridge as a kind of smart repeater. Repeaters listen to signals coming down one network cable, amplify them, and send them down the other cable. They do this blindly, paying no attention to the content of the messages they repeat.

In contrast, a bridge is a little smarter about the messages that come down the pike. For starters, most bridges have the capability to listen to the network and automatically figure out the address of each computer on both sides of the bridge. Then the bridge can inspect each message that comes from one side of the bridge and broadcast it on the other side of the bridge only if the message is intended for a computer that's on the other side.

This key feature enables bridges to partition a large network into two smaller, more efficient networks. Bridges work best in networks that are highly segregated. For example (humor me here — I'm a Dr. Seuss fan), suppose that the Sneetches networked all their computers and discovered that, although the Star-Bellied Sneetches' computers talked to each other frequently and the Plain-Bellied Sneetches' computers also talked to each other frequently, rarely did a Star-Bellied Sneetch computer talk to a Plain-Bellied Sneetch computer.

A bridge can partition the Sneetchnet into two networks: the Star-Bellied network and the Plain-Bellied network. The bridge automatically learns which computers are on the Star-Bellied network and which are on the Plain-Bellied network. The bridge forwards messages from the Star-Bellied side to the Plain-Bellied side (and vice versa) only when necessary. The overall performance of both networks improves, although the performance of any network operation that has to travel over the bridge slows down a bit.

Here are a few additional things to consider about bridges:

- As I mentioned, some bridges also have the capability to translate the messages from one format to another. For example, if the Star-Bellied Sneetches build their network with Ethernet and the Plain-Bellied Sneetches use Token Ring, a bridge can tie the two together.

- You can get a basic bridge to partition two Ethernet networks for about $500 from mail-order suppliers. More sophisticated bridges can cost as much as $5,000 or more.

- If you've never read Dr. Seuss's classic story of the Sneetches, you should.

- If you're not confused yet, don't worry. Read on.

Switches

A *switch* is similar to a bridge but provides much better performance. The difference between a switch and a bridge is that a switch can create a separate internal connection (called a *segment*) between any two of the switch's ports. Each of these connections operates at a full 10 MHz, or in the case of a 100 MHz switch, at 100 MHz.

The best switches constantly monitor the traffic that comes across them and reroute its internal connections automatically to provide the most efficient operation for the network. This technique is called *load balancing*.

Switches have become so popular that they have all but replaced bridges except for unusual applications. You can get an inexpensive two-port switch for under $300 and 16-port switches for about $1,500. Switches with all the bells and whistles are naturally more expensive.

Routers

A *router* is like a bridge or a switch, but with a key difference. Bridges and switches can tell the address of the network node to which each message is sent, and can forward the message to the appropriate segment. But *routers* have the extra ability to actually peek inside the message to see what type of information is being sent. In contrast, bridges and switches are completely ignorant of the content of network messages.

You can think of a router as a super-intelligent bridge. Bridges know the addresses of all the computers on each side of the bridge and can forward messages accordingly. But routers know even more about the network. A router knows not only the addresses of all the computers but also other routers on the network and can decide the most efficient path to send each network message. In fact, the router knows everything about you and your little network.

One key difference between a bridge and a router is that a bridge is essentially transparent to the network. In contrast, a router is itself a node on the network, with its own address. That means that messages can be directed to a router, which can then examine the contents of the message to determine how it should handle the message.

You can configure a network with several routers that can work cooperatively together. For example, some routers are able to monitor the network to determine the most efficient path for sending a message to its ultimate destination. If a part of the network is extremely busy, a router can automatically route messages along a less-busy route. In this respect, the router is kind of like a traffic reporter up in a helicopter. The router knows that 101 is bumper-to-bumper all the way through Sunnyvale, so it sends the message on 280 instead.

Here is some additional information about routers:

- ✔ Routers aren't cheap. But for big networks, they're worth it.

- ✔ The functional distinctions between bridges, switches, and routers get blurrier all the time. As bridges and switches become more sophisticated, they're able to take on some of the chores that used to require a router, thus putting many routers out of work.

- ✔ Some routers are nothing more than computers with several network interface cards and special software to perform the router functions. In fact, NetWare comes with a router program that lets a NetWare server act as a router, and Windows NT Server has a similar feature.

- ✔ Routers can also connect networks that are geographically distant from one another via a phone line (using modems) or ISDN. You can't do that with a bridge.

- ✔ If you're confused about the distinction between bridges, switches, and routers, join the club. The technical distinction has to do with the OSI Reference Model network layer where the devices operate. Bridges operate at the MAC layer (MAC stands for Media Access Control), whereas routers operate at the next level up: the network layer.

Gateways

No, not the Bill Gates way. This kind of gateway is a super-intelligent router, which is a super-intelligent bridge, which is a super-intelligent repeater. Notice a pattern here?

Gateways are designed to connect radically different types of networks together. They do this by translating messages from one network's format to another's format, much like the Universal Translator that got Kirk and Spock out of so many jams. (Ever notice how all those planets with gorgeous females never seem to have a word for *kiss,* so Kirk has to demonstrate?)

Gateways usually connect a network to a mainframe or minicomputer. If you don't have a mainframe or minicomputer, you probably don't need a gateway.

Keep the following points in mind:

- Gateways are necessary only because of the mess that computer manufacturers got us into by insisting on using their own proprietary designs for networks. If computer manufacturers had talked to each other 20 years ago, we wouldn't have to use gates to make their networks talk to each other today.
- Gateways come in several varieties. My favorite is ornamental wrought iron.

Superservers

A funny thing happened to personal computers when networks became popular. They turned into mainframe computers.

As networks grew and grew, some organizations found that they had to have dozens of PCs functioning as dedicated file servers. Some networks had 50 or 100 dedicated servers! You can imagine the network management nightmares you'd have to contend with on a network that large.

To ease the burdens of managing a gaggle of file servers, some network managers are turning to superservers, unbelievably high-powered computers that can single-handedly take on the duties of half a dozen or more mere mortal computers. These superservers have huge cabinets that can hold stacks of disk drives, specialized high-speed disk controllers, room for more memory than Colonel Hathi, and — get this — more than one CPU.

Superservers aren't cheap — they sell for tens of thousands of dollars. But they're often less expensive than an equivalent number of ordinary computers, they're more efficient, and they're easier to manage.

One common argument against the use of superservers is the old "don't put all your eggs in one basket" line. What if the superserver breaks? The counter to this argument is that superservers are loaded with state-of-the-art fault-tolerance gizmos that make it unlikely that they'll ever break. In contrast, if you use ten separate file servers, you actually increase the likelihood that one of them will fail, probably sooner than you'd like.

It's a RAID!

In most small networks, it's a hassle if a disk drive goes south and has to be sent to the shop for repairs. In some large networks, a failed disk drive is more than a hassle: It's an outright disaster. Big companies don't know how to do anything when the computer goes down. Everyone just sits around, looking at the floor, silently keeping vigil 'til the computers come back up.

A *RAID system* is a fancy type of disk storage that hardly ever fails. It works by lumping several disk drives together and treating them as if they were one humongous drive. RAID uses some fancy techniques devised by computer nerds at Berkeley. These computer nerds guarantee that if one of the disk drives in the RAID system fails, no data is lost. The disk drive that failed can be removed and repaired, and the data that was on it can be reconstructed from the other drives.

Here are a few additional thoughts on RAID:

- ✔ RAID stands for Redundant Array of Inexpensive Disks, but that doesn't matter. You don't have to remember that for the test.

- ✔ A RAID system is usually housed in a separate cabinet that includes its own RAID disk controller. It's sometimes called a disk subsystem.

- ✔ In the coolest RAID systems, the disk drives themselves are *hot swappable*. That means that you can shut down and remove one of the disk drives while the RAID system continues to operate. Network users won't even know that one of the disks has been removed because the RAID system reconstructs the data that was on the removed disk using data from the other disks. After the failed disk has been replaced, the new disk is brought online without a hitch.

Firewalls

A *firewall* is a security-conscious router that sits between your network and the rest of the world in an effort to prevent "them" from getting to "us."

It's also Pat Buchanan's favorite computer component.

Firewalls are often used when you're providing Internet access to your network, and they're a must if you create a World Wide Web (WWW) site, which enables Internet users all around the world to access files on your network. Naturally, you want to limit the files that Internet users can access. A firewall is the best way to do that.

If your network isn't connected to the Internet, it doesn't need a firewall. If your network needs a firewall, hire a firewall consultant.

Fast Ethernet

Most small networks operate just fine with standard Ethernet connections. However, if your network is large enough to merit a high-speed backbone connection, or if your users are constantly sharing huge amounts of data such as video files, you may want to look into Fast Ethernet. Fast Ethernet is a relatively new version of Ethernet, which is ten times as fast: 100 Mbps instead of 10 Mbps.

Fast Ethernet is also called 100baseT. As its name suggests, 100baseT uses twisted-pair cable like 10baseT. In some cases, you can use existing 10baseT cable, but only if you use top-quality Category 5 cable and keep the cable lengths under 100 meters. Unfortunately, Fast Ethernet cannot operate on coax cable.

Fast Ethernet used to be a bit pricey but is becoming more affordable. You can get basic 100 Mbps Fast Ethernet adapter cards for about $50, and you can get an eight-port Fast Ethernet hub for about $150. For a few bucks more, you can get hubs that speak both 10 Mbps and 100 Mbps, so you can buy the hub and use it with a 10 Mbps Ethernet network now, and then upgrade the network to Fast Ethernet later without having to replace the hub.

Chapter 30

Ten (Or Fewer) Layers of the OSI Model

● ●

In This Chapter

▶ The physical layer

▶ The data link layer

▶ The network layer

▶ The transport layer

▶ The lemon-pudding layer

▶ The session layer

▶ The presentation layer

▶ The application layer

● ●

*O*SI sounds like the name of a top-secret government agency you hear about only in Tom Clancy novels. What it really stands for, as far as this book is concerned, is Open System Interconnection, as in the Open System Interconnection Reference Model, affectionately known as the OSI model.

The OSI model breaks the various aspects of a computer network into seven distinct layers. These layers are kind of like the layers of an onion: Each successive layer envelopes the layer beneath it, hiding its details from the levels above. The OSI model is also like an onion in that if you start to peel it apart to have a look inside, you're bound to shed a few tears.

The OSI model is not itself a networking standard in the same sense that Ethernet and Token Ring are. Rather, the OSI model is a framework into which the various networking standards can fit. The OSI model specifies what aspects of a network's operation can be addressed by various network standards. So, in a sense, the OSI model is sort of a standard's standard.

Although the OSI model contains seven layers, the bottom two are the layers that have the most practical impact on smaller networks. Networking standards like Ethernet and Token Ring are layer-1 and layer-2 standards. The higher layers of the OSI model haven't resulted in widespread standards.

Don't read this if you're dyslexic

The OSI standard was developed by a group known as ISO, for International Standards Organization. So technically, it can be called the ISO OSI standard. Hold that up to a mirror and see what happens.

ISO develops standards for all sorts of stuff, like the size of sprinkler pipes and machine screws. Other ISO standards include SOI, SIO, OIS, and IOS.

Layer 1: The Physical Layer

The bottom layer of the OSI model is the physical layer. It addresses the physical characteristics of the network: the types of cables used to connect devices, the types of connectors used, how long the cables can be, and so on. For example, the Ethernet standard for 10baseT cable specifies the electrical characteristics of the twisted-pair cables, the size and shape of the connectors, the maximum length of the cables, and so on.

Another aspect of the physical layer is the electrical characteristics of the signals used to transmit data over the cables from one network node to another. The physical layer doesn't define any meaning to those signals other than the basic binary values 0 and 1. The higher levels of the OSI model must assign meanings to the bits that are transmitted at the physical layer.

Layer 2: The Data Link Layer

The data link layer is the layer at which meaning is assigned to the bits that are transmitted over the network. A standard for the data link layer must address things such as the size of each packet of data to be sent, a means of addressing each packet so that it's delivered to the intended recipient, and a way to ensure that two or more nodes don't try to transmit data on the network at the same time.

The data link layer also provides basic error detection and correction to ensure that the data sent is the same as the data received. If an uncorrectable error occurs, the data link standard must specify how the node is to be informed of the error so that it can retransmit the data.

You don't really care how Ethernet fits into the OSI model, do you?

Ethernet is a standard published by the IEEE (if you pronounce this term eye-triple-ee, people will think you know what you're talking about). It's official title is 802.3, pronounced eight-oh-two-dot-three. The 802.3 standard addresses both the physical layer of the OSI model and the data link layer.

You can blame the portion of the 802.3 that addresses the physical layer for the need to attach terminators to each end of a segment of thinnet coax, for the fact that BNC connectors are a pain in the rumpus to attach, and for the limit on the number of hubs that you can daisy-chain together when you use twisted-pair cabling. The physical-layer portion of the 802.3 standard is also responsible for the colorful terms 10base5, 10base2, and 10baseT.

The portion of 802.3 that deals with the data link layer actually deals only with one portion of the

data link layer, called the Media Access Control Sublayer, or MAC sublayer. The MAC portion of 802.3 spells out how the CSMA/CD operation of Ethernet works — how Ethernet listens for network traffic, sends data if the network appears to be free of traffic, and then listens for collisions and resends the information if necessary.

The other portion of the data link layer of the OSI model is called the Logical Link Control Sublayer, or (you guessed it) the LLC sublayer. The LLC sublayer spells out the basics of sending and receiving packets of information over the network and correcting errors. The LLC standard used by Ethernet is called 802.2.

None of this stuff really matters unless you plan on building network interface cards in your garage.

Layer 3: The Network Layer

The network layer addresses the interconnection of networks by routing packets from one network to another. The network layer is most important when you use a router to link two different types of networks, such as an Ethernet network and a Token Ring network. Because the network layer is one step above the data link layer, whether the two networks use different standards at the data link and physical layers doesn't matter.

Layer 4: The Transport Layer

The transport layer is the basic layer at which one network computer communicates with another network computer. The transport layer identifies each node on the computer with a unique address and manages connections between nodes. The transport layer also breaks large messages into smaller messages and reassembles the messages at the receiving node.

The transport layer and the OSI layers above it are implemented differently by various network operating systems. You can thank the OSI model for the capability to run NetWare, LANtastic, Windows for Workgroups, or just about any other network operating system on a standard Ethernet network. Ethernet addresses the lower layers of the OSI model. As long as the network operating system's transport layer is able to interface with Ethernet, you're in business.

Layer 4a: The Lemon-Pudding Layer

The lemon-pudding layer is squeezed in between the rather dry and tasteless transport and session layers to add flavor and moisture.

Layer 5: The Session Layer

The session layer establishes *sessions* between network nodes. A session must be established before data can be transmitted over the network. The session layer makes sure that these sessions are properly established and maintained.

Layer 6: The Presentation Layer

The presentation layer is responsible for converting the data sent over the network from one type of representation to another. For example, the presentation layer can apply sophisticated compression techniques so that fewer bytes of data are required to represent the information when it's sent over the network. At the other end of the transmission, the transport layer then uncompresses the data.

The presentation layer also can scramble the data before it's transmitted and unscramble it at the other end, using a sophisticated encryption technique that even Sherlock Holmes would have trouble breaking.

Layer 7: The Application Layer

The highest layer of the OSI model, the application layer deals with the techniques that application programs use to communicate with the network. The name of this layer is a little confusing. Application programs like Lotus 1-2-3 and WordPerfect aren't a part of the application layer. Rather, the network operating system itself works within the application layer.

Chapter 31

Ten Windows 2000 Server Features to Look Forward To

*T*he soon-expected release of the next major version of Windows NT, now known as Windows 2000 Server, promises many new features that may tip the balance of the network sever scale in Microsoft's favor. This chapter briefly describes ten new Windows 2000 Server features that will have a major impact on network users and administrators.

Active Directory

Active Directory is a single directory that replaces multiple directories used in Windows NT Server 4.0. Active Directory keeps track of all network resources, including users, servers, client computers, printers, disk files, and so on.

Active Directory uses names that look like Internet names instead of the traditional eight-character names used in NT 4.0. For example, an Active Directory domain may have a name such as accounting.cleaver.com.

A user on that domain named `Wally` would have an e-mail address such as `Wally@accounting.cleaver.com`.

An Active Directory contains entries for hundreds of different types of network resources, and it can hold millions of objects. Because of its complexity, the biggest benefits of Active Directory are for large networks, in which keeping dozens of separate NT 4.0 domains up-to-date is a nightmare. However, Active Directory is not difficult to administer for smaller networks.

Microsoft Management Console

Windows NT Server has too many different programs that you must use to administer a network: User Manager for Domains, Disk Administrator, Network Client Administrator, Control Panel applets such as Network and System, file and folder Properties dialog box that you use to set share options, and various Wizards are just a few. Between Windows NT Server and Microsoft BackOffice, you can use more than 50 administration programs.

Microsoft Management Console (MMC) brings all the NT administration tools under the control of a single program. You can customize MMC to include specific combinations of administration tools. And you can easily create your own MMC console pages using HTML. These custom pages, called *taskpads,* can contain links to specific administration tools.

IntelliMirror

IntelliMirror is a feature that enables a user's complete environment to follow him or her around from computer to computer. No matter which computer the user uses to log on to the Windows 2000 network, IntelliMirror recreates that user's computing environment, including custom operating system options such as desktop settings, Favorites, recently used documents, network drive mappings, and even installed applications along with the user's custom application settings.

Encrypted File System

Windows 2000 Server enables you to designate specific files or entire folders to be stored on disk in an encrypted form. That prevents even advanced hackers from defeating existing security features to access sensitive data stored on your network server disks.

Encrypted files are available only for NTFS drives.

Remote Storage Server

Remote Storage Server (RSS) is a feature that monitors the amount of free space available on a disk drive and keeps tabs on which files are used frequently and which are seldom used. When a disk drive runs low on free space, Remote Storage Server automatically copies seldom-used files to backup media, such as a tape drive. Then RSS removes the backed-up files from the disk to free up additional space.

The cool thing about RSS is that when it removes a file that has been backed up, it doesn't remove the file's directory entry. Instead, it updates the directory to indicate the file's new location. When a user attempts to access the file, RSS automatically retrieves the file from its backup tape and copies it to its original location.

Distributed File System

Distributed File System (DFS) enables you to combine file shares from one or more server volumes to create a single shared network volume. The file shares can be physically located on a single drive in a server computer, on two or more drives in a server, or on drives that are located on separate servers within the same domain. DFS lets you create shared volumes that include all the data you want to access from the network without regard to which drives or servers the data is located on.

In a DFS volume, one shared folder becomes the root folder of the DFS volume. Like any NT-shared volume, the root share can contain additional folders. In addition, the root share can contain links to shared folders on other volumes, either on the same server or on separate servers. These links appear as if they're folders within the root folder.

One of the main benefits of DFS is that it separates the way users view shared network data from the way that data is actually stored on disk. As an administrator, you can set up a DSF volume to create the image of a shared volume organized the way users want the data organized. Then you can spread the data for the DFS volume over several drives and, if necessary, over several servers to improve performance. And as demand for the shared data changes, you can change the physical arrangement of the data without changing the way users access the data.

Disk Quotas

Windows 2000 Server has a new disk quota feature that lets you put a limit on how much server disk space a single user can have. This is a welcome feature, especially on networks that are tight on server disk space and have users who love to collect large sound and video files.

Disk quotas don't have to be absolute. You can establish which actions are to be taken when a user reaches or exceeds his or her quota. For example, you can have a message sent to the administrator to alert the administrator. The administrator can then look at the user's disk usage and decide to enforce the quota. Or the administrator could simply increase the user's quota if it appears that the user has a legitimate need for more disk space.

Printer Improvements

Windows 2000 has several improved printing features, as described in the following paragraphs:

- ✔ Printers are integrated into the Active Directory. Among other benefits, this enables users to search the network for printers based on printer capabilities. For example, a user can tell Windows 2000 to find a color printer that can handle 11-x-17-inch paper. (Good luck.)

- ✔ Internet printing enables you to print over the Internet. If your local copy shop has an 11-x-17-inch color printer that is connected to the Internet, you can now send output to that printer. Be sure to take your credit card with you when you go to pick up your output.

- ✔ If necessary, Windows 2000 automatically downloads and configures the correct printer driver whenever you print to a network printer. Users no longer have to use the Add Printer Wizard to add a network printer before they can print from it.

IIS Improvements

Microsoft has made many enhancements to Internet Information Server for Windows 2000, most of them designed for servers that host large, active Web sites. For example, IIS now lets you host more than one domain on a single server. IIS now includes the ability to monitor and limit the CPU usage of each Web site on the server. And a new Wizard makes it easier to set up secure Web sites for electronic commerce.

Windows 98 User Interface

Windows 2000 Server sports the jazzy Web-based user interface that was first introduced with Windows 98. Yippie!

Chapter 32

Ten Hot Network Buzzwords Guaranteed to Enliven a Cocktail Party

● ●

In This Chapter

▶ Intranet

▶ Client/server

▶ Enterprise computing

▶ Interoperability

▶ Fiber optics

▶ SNA

▶ Groupware

▶ TCP/IP

▶ Broadband

▶ Y2K

● ●

*T*ired of boring cocktail parties where everyone talks about the latest Oliver Stone movie or who's winning the late-night talk-show wars? Here are some conversation topics guaranteed to liven things up a bit or get you thrown out. Either way, they work. Try 'em.

Intranet

What it means: I've grown weary of the Internet, and now I want to create my own little private Internet on my LAN. An intranet uses the tools of the Internet: TCP/IP, HTTP, HTML, and Web-server software, but it isn't connected to the Internet. Intranets are used to create "internal" home pages that can be accessed from the company LAN but not from outside the company.

Used in a sentence: I won't be home for supper tonight, honey. I've got to finish uploading the third-quarter results to the company intranet!

Client/Server

What it means: A computer system in which part of the work happens on a client computer, and part of it happens on a server computer. To be a true client/server application, real work must be done on the server. Any server-based network can be loosely called client/server, but in a true client/server system, at least part of the real work — not just file access — is done on the server. For example, in a true client/server database, a database query is processed on the server computer, and just the results of the query are sent back to the client computer. If you want to know more, get a copy of my very own book, *Client/Server Computing For Dummies,* 3rd Edition, (IDG Books Worldwide, Inc.).

Used in a sentence: I heard that it took your company five years to replace your old mainframe invoicing system to client/server! You should have gotten a copy of *Client/Server Computing For Dummies,* 3rd Edition.

Enterprise Computing

What it means: The complete computing needs of a business enterprise. In the past, computing was too often focused on the individual needs of small departments or workgroups. The result was a hodgepodge of incompatible systems: Marketing had a minicomputer, sales had a NetWare network, and accounting had an abacus. Enterprise computing views the computing needs of the organization as a whole. Very smart.

Used in a sentence: Our enterprise computing effort is sailing along at warp 9; I hear you guys are still stuck at one-quarter impulse. Fascinating.

Interoperability

What it means: Fitting round pegs into square holes. Literally, linking estranged networks together so that they work well together. This one is so hot that a whole trade show called Interop is devoted to making different networks work together.

Used in a sentence: We've finally solved our interoperability problems — we fired the guy who bought the stuff that wasn't interoperable.

Fiber Optics

What it means: The fastest form of network cable, where signals are transmitted by light rather than by electricity. Fiber optics are typically used to form the backbone of large networks or to link networks in separate buildings, where the 500-meter limit of yellow cable just won't do. Fiber-optic cables hum along at a cool 100 Mbps, ten times faster than pokey little Ethernet.

Used in a sentence: What am I going to do now that I've linked three buildings on the campus using a fiber-optic backbone? I'm going to Disneyland.

SNA

What it means: IBM's grand scheme of old to dominate the networking business. SNA is found wherever IBM mainframes are found. SNA stands for Systems Network Architecture and is pronounced *snaw* by mainframers.

Used in a sentence: After we get the link between SNA and Ethernet worked out, our mainframe users will be able to access the advanced computing power of our PCs.

Groupware

What it means: Software that's designed to take advantage of network capabilities to facilitate collaborative work. For example, a word processing program with groupware features enables several network users to add comments or revisions to a document and keep track of who made what change and when. The best-known example of a groupware program is Lotus Notes.

Used in a sentence: Our productivity has shot up so much since we switched to groupware that we've decided to retire and move to Vail. I hear you're still using WordStar.

TCP/IP

What it means: TCP/IP is the protocol for the Internet. It stands for Transmission Control Protocol/Internet Protocol.

Used in a sentence: Don't worry, after you get TCP/IP up and running, you'll be on the Internet soon enough.

Broadband

What it means: Broadband is a new cable TV system that can send more than just TV: It can also handle your phone lines and an Internet connection. And it's lightning fast. In fact, an Internet connection over broadband cable is just as fast as an Ethernet connection on a local area network.

Used in a sentence: No, uh, I don't have broadband yet. Boy, weird weather we've been having lately, don't you think?

Y2K

What it means: Some computer systems, mostly older mainframe computers, are going to have trouble when the clock strikes midnight on January 1, 2000. For years, computer programmers fell into the habit of using only two digits in the year portion of a date. For example, May 16, 1978, was stored as 05-16-78. Unfortunately, when the year 2000 arrives, the two-digit year stored as 00 will cause problems for any software that does arithmetic using the date.

Used in a sentence: I just bought a one-room cabin in Montana where I can hide out during the Y2K crisis.

Glossary

10base2: The type of coax cable most often used for Ethernet networks. Also known as *thinnet, cheapernet*. The maximum length of a single segment is 185 meters (600 feet).

10base5: The original Ethernet coax cable, now used mostly as the backbone for larger networks. Also known as *yellow cable, thick cable*. The maximum length of a single segment is 500 meters (1,640 feet).

10baseT: Twisted-pair cable, commonly used for Ethernet networks. Also known as *UTP, twisted pair,* or *twisted sister*. The maximum length of a single segment is 100 meters (330 feet). Of the three Ethernet cable types, this one is the easiest to work with.

100baseT: The leading standard for 100 Mbps Ethernet. 100baseT uses the same twisted-pair cable in 10baseT. Variations of the 100 Mbps Ethernet standard include 100baseT4 and 100baseTX.

100VG AnyLAN: A standard for 100 Mbps Ethernet that isn't as popular as 100baseT. Like 100baseT, 100VG AnyLAN uses twisted-pair cable.

802.2: The forgotten IEEE standard. The more glamorous 802.3 standard relies upon 802.2 for moral support.

802.3: The IEEE standard known in the vernacular as *Ethernet*.

8088 processor: The microprocessor chip around which IBM designed its original PC, marking the transition from the bronze age to the iron age.

80286 processor: *Computo-habilis,* an ancient ancestor of today's modern computers.

80386 processor: The first 32-bit microprocessor chip used in personal computers, long since replaced by newer, better designs but still used by far too many people.

80486 processor: The last of Intel's CPU chips to have a number instead of a name. Replaced years ago by the Pentium processor.

AAUI: *Apple Attachment Unit Interface,* a type of connector used in some Apple Ethernet networks.

access rights: A list of rights that tell you what you can and can't do with network files or directories.

account: You can't get into the network without one of these. The network knows who you are and what rights you have on the network by virtue of your account.

acronym: An abbreviation made up of the first letters of a series of words.

active server pages: An Internet feature from Microsoft that enables you to create Web pages with scripts that run on the server rather than on the client. Also known as ASP.

adapter card: An electronic card that you can plug into one of your computer's adapter slots to give it some new and fabulous capability, such as displaying 16 million colors, talking to other computers over the phone, or accessing a network.

address book: In an e-mail system, a list of users with whom you regularly correspond.

administrator: The big network cheese who is responsible for setting things up and keeping them running. Pray that it's not you. Also known as the *network manager.*

AFP: *Apple Filing Protocol,* a protocol for filing used by Apple. (That helps a lot, doesn't it?)

allocation unit: Windows allocates space to files one allocation unit at a time; the allocation unit is typically 2,048 or 4,096 bytes, depending on the size of the disk. Also known as *cluster.* NetWare, Windows NT Server, DriveSpace, and FAT32 use different allocation schemes that are more efficient.

antivirus program: A program that sniffs out viruses on your network and sends them into exile.

AppleTalk: Apple's networking system for Macintoshes.

application layer: The highest layer of the OSI reference model, which governs how software communicates with the network.

archive bit: A flag that's kept for each file to indicate whether the file has been modified since it was last backed up.

ARCnet: A slow but steady network topology developed originally by Datapoint. ARCnet uses a token-passing scheme similar to Token Ring.

Artisoft: The company that makes LANtastic.

attributes: Characteristics that are assigned to files. DOS alone provides four attributes: system, hidden, read-only, and archive. Networks generally expand the list of file attributes.

AUI: *Attachment Unit Interface,* the big connector found on many network cards and 10baseT hubs that's used to attach yellow cable via a transceiver.

AUTOEXEC.BAT: A batch file that DOS executes automatically every time you start your computer.

AUTOEXEC.NCF: A batch file that NetWare executes automatically every time you load the server software.

backbone: A trunk cable used to tie sections of a network together. The backbone is often 10base5, fiber-optic (FDDI), or 100 Mbps Fast Ethernet.

BackOffice: A suite of Microsoft programs designed to run on server computers based on Windows NT Server.

backup: A copy of your important files made for safekeeping in case something happens to the original files; something you should make every day.

banner: A fancy page that's printed between each print job so that you can easily separate jobs from one another.

batch file: In DOS, a file that contains one or more commands that are executed together as a set. You create the batch file by using a text editor (like the DOS EDIT command) and run the file by typing its name at the command prompt.

benchmark: A repeatable test you use to judge the performance of your network. The best benchmarks are the ones that closely duplicate the type of work you routinely do on your network.

bindery: The big database where user accounts and other related info are stored on a NetWare 3.2 server.

BNC connector: The connector that's used with 10base2 cable.

bottleneck: The slowest link in your network, which causes work to get jammed up. The first step in improving network performance is identifying the bottlenecks.

bridge: Not the popular card game, but a device that enables you to link two networks together. Bridges are smart enough to know which computers are on which side of the bridge, so they only allow those messages that need to get to the other side to cross the bridge. This device improves performance on both sides of the bridge.

Btrieve: An indexed file access method commonly used on older NetWare networks.

buffer: An area of memory that holds data en route to somewhere else. For example, a disk buffer holds data as it travels between your computer and the disk drive.

bus: A type of network topology in which network nodes are strung out along a single run of cable called a *segment*. 10base2 and LocalTalk networks use a bus topology. *Bus* also refers to the row of expansion slots within your computer.

cache: A sophisticated form of buffering in which a large amount of memory is set aside to hold data so that it can be accessed quickly.

CAPTURE: The NetWare command used to redirect printer output to a network printer. CAPTURE is usually run in a batch file or login script.

CD-ROM: A high-capacity disk that uses optical technology to store data in a form that can be read but not written over.

Certified NetWare Engineer: Someone who has studied hard and passed the official exam offered by Novell. Also known as *CNE*.

Certified Network Dummy: Someone who knows nothing about networks but nevertheless gets the honor of installing one. Also known as *CND*.

CGA: *Crayon Graphics Adapter,* a crude type of graphics display used on early IBM computers.

chat: What you do on the network when you talk *live* with another network user.

Chaucer: A dead English dude.

cheapernet: See *10base2*.

CHKDSK: A DOS command that checks the record-keeping structures of a DOS disk for errors.

click: What you do in Windows to get things done.

client: A computer that has access to the network but doesn't share any of its own resources with the network. See *server*.

client/server: A vague term meaning roughly that the work load is split between a client and server computer.

Clouseau: The most dangerous man in all of France. Some people say he only plays the fool.

cluster: See *allocation unit*.

coaxial cable: A type of cable that contains two conductors. The center conductor is surrounded by a layer of insulation, which is then wrapped by a braided-metal conductor and an outer layer of insulation.

COM1: The first serial port on a computer.

CompuServe: An online information network that you can access to talk with other users about issues such as NetWare, Windows NT, politics, and El Niño.

computer name: A unique name assigned to each computer on a network.

CONFIG.SYS: A file on every DOS computer that contains configuration information. CONFIG.SYS is processed every time you start your computer.

console: In NetWare, the file server's keyboard and monitor. Console commands can be entered only at the server console.

console operator: In NetWare, a user working at the file server's console.

Control Panel: In Windows, an application that enables you to configure various aspects of the Windows operating system.

conventional memory: The first 640K of memory on a DOS-based computer.

CPU: The *central processing unit,* or brains, of the computer.

crimp tool: A special tool used to attach connectors to cables. No network manager should be without one.

CSMA/CD: *Carrier Sense Multiple Access with Collision Detection,* the traffic management technique used by Ethernet.

daisy chain: A way of connecting computer components in which the first component is connected to the second, which is connected to the third, and so on. In 10baseT Ethernet, you can daisy-chain hubs together.

DAT: *Digital audiotape,* a type of tape often used for network backup.

data-link layer: The second layer of the OSI model, responsible for transmitting bits of data over the network cable.

dedicated server: A computer used exclusively as a network server.

delayed write: A disk-caching technique in which data written to disk is placed in cache memory and actually written to disk later.

differential backup: A type of backup in which only the files that have changed since the last full backup are backed up.

digitized sound: A file containing a sound that you can play if the computer has a sound card. See *Clouseau*.

DIP switch: A bank of switches used to configure an old-fashioned adapter card. Modern cards configure themselves automatically, so DIP switches aren't required. See *jumper block*.

directory hash: A popular breakfast food enjoyed by NetWare managers.

disk: A device that stores information magnetically on a disk. A hard disk is permanently sealed in an enclosure and has a capacity usually measured in thousands of megabytes. Also known as *gigabytes*. A *floppy disk* is removable and can have a capacity of 360K, 720K, 1.2MB, 1.44MB, or 2.88MB.

DMA channel: A direct pipeline for I/O that's faster than normal I/O. Network cards use DMA for fast network access.

domain: (1) In a Windows NT network, one or more network servers that are managed by a single network directory. (2) In the Internet, a name assigned to a host computer.

DOS: *Disk Operating System,* the original operating system for IBM and IBM-compatible computers. DOS isn't used as much now that Windows 95 and 98 have taken over.

dot-matrix printer: A prehistoric type of printer that works by applying various-colored pigments to the walls of caves. Once the mainstay printer for PCs, dot-matrix printers have given way to laser printers and inkjet printers. High-speed matrix printers still have their place on the network, though, and matrix printers have the advantage of being able to print multipart forms.

DriveSpace: The disk compression feature of Windows 95 and 98 (and MS-DOS 6.2). DriveSpace compresses file data so that files require less disk space. This compression increases the effective capacity of the disk, often by a factor of 2:1 or more.

dumb terminal: Back in the heyday of mainframe computers, a monitor and keyboard attached to the central mainframe. All the computing work occurred at the mainframe; the terminal only displayed the results and sent input typed at the keyboard back to the mainframe.

DVD drive: A new type of CD-ROM drive with much higher storage capacity than a standard CD-ROM drive — as much as 17GB on a single disk compared to the 600MB capacity of a standard CD.

Eddie Haskell: The kid who's always sneaking around, poking his nose into other people's business, and generally causing trouble. Every network has one.

editor: A program for creating and changing text files. DOS 5.0 and later versions come with a basic editor called EDIT. Other editors are available, but EDIT is good enough for most network needs.

EGA: The color monitor that was standard with IBM AT computers, based on 80286 processors. Now obsolete, but plenty of them are still in use.

EISA bus: *Extended Industry Standard Architecture,* an improved I/O bus that is compatible with the standard ISA bus but provides advanced features. Computers with an EISA bus were often used as file servers until the PCI bus became more popular. See *ISA bus* and *PCI bus*.

e-mail: An application that enables you to exchange notes with other network users.

ENDCAP: The NetWare command you use to stop network printer redirection.

enterprise computing: A trendy term that refers to a view of an organization's complete computing needs, rather than just a single department's or group's needs.

ESDI: An older style of disk drive that's not often used nowadays.

Ethernet: The World's Most Popular Network Standard.

EtherTalk: What you call Ethernet when you use it on a Macintosh.

ETLA: *Extended Three-Letter Acronym,* an acronym with four letters. See *TLA*.

expanded memory: An ancient technique for blasting past the 640K limit. Unlike extended memory, expanded memory can be used with 8088 computers.

extended memory: Memory beyond the first 640K in a DOS computer. The term isn't used with Windows 95 or 98 or Windows NT; memory is just memory.

Farallon: The company that popularized PhoneNET as a cheaper and more flexible alternative to LocalTalk, Apple's cabling scheme for networking Macintoshes.

Fast Ethernet: A new Ethernet standard that operates at 100 Mbps rather than 10 Mbps.

FAT: *File allocation table,* a record-keeping structure that DOS uses to keep track of the location of every file on a disk.

FAT32: An improved way of keeping track of disk files that can be used with Windows 98.

FDDI: *Fiber Distributed Data Interface,* a 100 Mbps network standard used with fiber-optic backbone. When FDDI is used, FDDI FDDI/Ethernet bridges connect Ethernet segments to the backbone.

ferrule: The outer metal tube that you crimp on to attach a BNC connector to the cable.

fiber-optic cable: A blazingly fast network cable that transmits data using light rather than electricity. Fiber-optic cable is often used as the backbone in large networks, especially where great distances are involved.

file rights: The ability of a particular network user to access specific files on a network server.

file server: A network computer containing disk drives that are available to network users.

FTP: *File Transfer Protocol,* a method for retrieving files from the Internet.

full backup: A backup of all the files on a disk, whether or not the files have been modified since the last backup. See ***differential backup***.

fulminic acid: An unstable acid (CNOH) that forms explosive salts of some metals, especially mercury. Used to punish users who write their passwords on stick-on notes stuck on their monitors.

gateway: A device that connects dissimilar networks. Gateways often connect Ethernet networks to mainframe computers or to the Internet.

GB: *Gigabyte,* roughly a billion bytes of disk storage (1,024MB to be precise). See *K*, *MB*, and *TB*.

generation backup: A backup strategy in which several sets of backup disks or tapes are retained; sometimes called grandfather-father-son.

generation gap: What happens when you skip one of your backups.

glass house: The room where the mainframe computer is kept. Symbolic of the mainframe mentality, which stresses bureaucracy, inflexibility, and heavy iron.

group account: A grouping of user accounts that share common access rights.

groupware: A relatively new category of application programs that are designed with networks in mind to enable and even promote collaborative work.

guru: Anyone who knows more about computers than you do.

HTML: *HyperText Markup Language,* the language used to compose pages that can be displayed via the World Wide Web.

HTTP: *HyperText Transfer Protocol,* the protocol used by the World Wide Web for sending HTML pages from a server computer to a client computer.

hub: In Ethernet, a device that is used with 10baseT and 100baseT cabling to connect computers to the network. Most hubs have from 8 to 24 ports.

IACI: *International Association of the Computer Impaired.*

IDE: *Integrated Drive Electronics,* the most common type of disk interface in use today, popular because of its low cost and flexibility. For server computers, SCSI is the preferred drive interface. See *SCSI.*

IEEE: *Institute of Electrical and Electronic Engineers,* where they send computer geeks who've had a few too many parity errors.

incremental backup: A type of backup in which only the files that have changed since the last backup are backed up. Unlike a differential backup, an incremental backup resets each file's archive bit as it backs it up. See *archive bit, differential backup,* and *full backup.*

inkjet printer: A type of printer that creates full-color pages by spraying tiny jets of ink onto paper.

Internet: A humongous network of networks that spans the globe and gives you access to just about anything you could ever hope for, provided that you can figure out how to work it.

Internet Explorer: Microsoft's popular Web browser.

interoperability: Providing a level playing field for incompatible networks to work together, kind of like NAFTA.

intranet: A network that resembles the Internet but is accessible only within a company or organization. Most intranets use the familiar World Wide Web interface to distribute information to company employees.

intranetWare: A funny name that Novell used for NetWare when the term *intranet* was the hottest buzzword.

I/O port address: Every I/O device in a computer — including network interface cards — must be assigned a unique address. In the old days, you had to configure the port address using DIP switches or jumpers. Newer network cards automatically configure their own port addresses so that you don't have to mess with switches or jumper blocks.

IP address: A string of numbers used to address computers on the Internet. Every computer on the Internet must have a unique IP address.

IPX: The transport protocol used by NetWare.

IPX.COM: The program file that implements IPX.

IRQ: *Interrupt ReQuest*, network interface cards must be configured for the proper IRQ in order to work. In olden times, you had to use DIP switches or jumper blocks to set the IRQ. Nowadays, network cards configure themselves.

ISA bus: *Industry Standard Architecture*, the most popular type of expansion bus for accommodating adapter cards. See *EISA bus* and *PCI bus*.

ISO: *International Standards Organization*, whom we can thank for OSI.

ISP: *Internet service provider*, a company that provides access to the Internet for a fee.

JetDirect: A device made by Hewlett-Packard that enables printers to connect directly to the network without the need for a separate print server computer.

jumper block: A device used to configure an old-fashioned adapter card. To change the setting of a jumper block, you remove the jumper from one set of pins and place it on another.

K: *Kilobytes*, roughly one thousand bytes (1,024 to be precise). See *GB*, *MB*, and *TB*.

LAN: *Local area network*, what this book is all about.

LAN Manager: An obsolete network operating system that Microsoft used to sell. Microsoft long ago put all its networking eggs in the Windows NT basket, so LAN Manager exists only on isolated islands along with soldiers who are still fighting World War II.

LAN Server: IBM's version of LAN Manager.

LANcache: The disk caching program that comes with LANtastic.

LANtastic: A peer-to-peer network operating system that was once the most popular choice for small networks, before the built-in Windows for Workgroups and Windows 95 and 98 came along.

laser printer: A high-quality printer that uses lasers and photon torpedoes to produce beautiful output.

lemon-pudding layer: A layer near the middle of the OSI reference model that provides flavor and moisture to an otherwise dry and tasteless fruitcake.

Linux: A public domain version of the UNIX operating system that is becoming popular as a network server.

LLC sublayer: The *logical link sublayer* of layer 2 of the OSI model. The LLC is addressed by the IEEE 802.2 standard.

local bus: A fast expansion bus found on 486 and Pentium computers that operates at a higher speed than the old ISA bus and allows 32-bit data transfers. Two types are commonly found: VESA and PCI. Many 486 computers include several VESA local bus slots, but newer Pentium computers use PCI slots. For best network performance, all servers should have VESA or PCI disk I/O and network interface cards.

local resources: Disk drives, printers, and other devices that are attached directly to a workstation rather than accessed via the network.

local area network: See *LAN*.

LocalTalk: Apple's scheme for cabling Macintosh networks by using the Mac's printer ports. PhoneNET is a cabling scheme that's compatible with LocalTalk but less expensive.

login: The process of identifying oneself to the network (or a specific network server) and gaining access to network resources.

LOGIN: The NetWare command used to log in to a NetWare network.

LOGIN directory: In NetWare, a network directory that's mapped to the workstation before the user has logged in. The LOGIN directory contains commands and programs that are accessible to every computer on the network, regardless of whether a user has logged in. Chief among these commands is the LOGIN command.

login name: In a Windows network, the name that identifies a user uniquely to the network. Same as *user name* or *user ID*.

login script: A file of NetWare commands that is executed when a user logs in.

logon: Same as *login*.

logout: The process of leaving the network. When you log out, any network drives or printers you were connected to become unavailable to you.

LOGOUT: In NetWare, the command you use to log out.

LPT1: The first printer port on a PC. If a computer has a local printer, it more than likely is attached to this port. That's why you should set up printer redirections using LPT2 and LPT3.

Mac OS 8.5: The latest and greatest operating system for Macintoshes.

MAC sublayer: The *media access control* sublayer of layer 2 of the OSI model. The MAC is addressed by the IEEE 802.3 standard.

Macintosh: A cute little computer that draws great pictures and comes with built-in networking.

mail server: The server computer on which e-mail messages are stored. This same computer also may be used as a file and print server, or it may be dedicated as a mail server.

mainframe: A huge computer housed in a glass house on raised floors and cooled with liquid nitrogen. The cable that connects the disk drives to the CPU weighs more than most PCs.

mapping: Assigning unused drive letters to network drives or unused printer ports to network printers. See *redirection*.

MB: *Megabytes,* roughly one million bytes (1,024K to be precise). See *GB*, *K*, and *TB*.

memory: The electronic storage where your computer stores data that's being manipulated and programs that are running. See *RAM*.

metaphor: A literary construction suitable for Shakespeare and Steinbeck but a bit overused by computer writers.

modem: A device that converts signals the computer understands into signals that can be accurately transmitted over the phone to another modem, which converts the signals back into their original form. Computers use modems to talk to each other. *Modem* is a combination of *modulator-demodulator*.

monochrome: Monitors that display only one color, usually green or amber against a dark background. Monochrome monitors are often used on NetWare server computers, where flashy color displays would be wasted on an empty closet.

mouse: The obligatory way to use Windows. When you grab it and move it around, the cursor moves on the screen. After you get the hand-eye coordination down, using it is a snap. _Hint:_ Don't pick it up and talk into it like Scotty did in _Star Trek IV_. Very embarrassing, especially if you've traveled millions of miles to get here.

Mr. McFeeley: The nerdy-looking mailman on _Mr. Rogers' Neighborhood._ He'd make a great computer geek. Speedy delivery!

MSD: _Microsoft Diagnostics,_ a program that comes with DOS 6.0 and 6.2 and Windows 3.1. MSD gathers and displays useful information about your computer's configuration. In Windows 95 or 98, you can get similar information from a program called Microsoft System Information, which comes free with Microsoft Office 97.

MSN: _The Microsoft Network,_ an online service similar to CompuServe or America Online.

NE2000: The standard by which network interface cards are judged. If your card is NE2000 compatible, you can use it with just about any network.

NETBIOS: _Network basic input output system,_ a high-level networking standard developed by IBM and used by most peer-to-peer networks. It can be used with NetWare as well.

Netscape: The company that makes Navigator, the most popular program for browsing the World Wide Web.

NetWare: The chief priest of network operating systems, the proud child of Novell, Inc.

NetWare Directory Services: The cool new feature of NetWare Version 4.0 and later whereby the resources of the servers are pooled together to form a single entity.

NetWare Loadable Module: A program that's loaded at the file server. Also known as _NLM._ NLMs extend the functionality of NetWare by providing additional services. Btrieve runs as an NLM, as do various backup, antivirus, and other utilities.

network: What this book is about. For more information, see Chapters 1 through 32.

network drive: A drive that resides somewhere out in the network rather than on your own computer.

network interface card: An adapter card that lets the computer attach to a network cable. Also known as _NIC._

network layer: One of the layers somewhere near the middle of the OSI reference model. It addresses the interconnection of networks.

network manager: Hope that it's someone other than you.

Network Neighborhood: An icon on a Windows 95 or 98 desktop that enables you to access network servers and resources.

network operating system: An operating system for networks, such as NetWare or Windows NT Server. Also known as *NOS.*

network resource: A disk drive, printer, or other device that's located in a server computer and shared with other users, in contrast with a *local resource,* which is located in a user's computer.

newsgroup: Internet discussion groups similar to discussion forums in an online service.

NIC: See *network interface card.*

NLM: See *NetWare Loadable Module.*

node: A device on the network, typically a computer or printer. A router is also a node.

Norton Utilities: A big box chock-full of useful utilities, all for one affordable price. Get it.

NOS: See *network operating system.*

Novell: The folks you can thank or blame for NetWare, depending on your mood.

NTFS: A special type of disk format that you can use on Windows NT Server disk drives for improved performance and security.

offline: Not available on the network.

online: Available on the network.

operator: A user who has control over operational aspects of the network, but doesn't necessarily have the power to grant or revoke access rights, create user accounts, and so on.

OSI: The agency Lee Majors worked for in *The Six Million Dollar Man.* Also, the *Open System Interconnection* reference model, a seven-layer fruitcake framework upon which networking standards are hung.

packets: Data is sent over the network in manageable chunks called *packets,* or *frames.* The size and makeup of a packet is determined by the protocol being used.

parallel port: A port normally used to connect printers, sometimes called a *printer port.* Parallel ports send data over eight "parallel" wires, one byte at a time. See **serial port**.

partition: A division of a single disk drive into several smaller units that are treated by the operating system as if they were separate drives.

password: The only thing protecting your files from an impostor masquerading as you. Keep your password secret, and you'll have a long and happy life.

patch cable: A short cable used to connect a computer to a wall outlet, or one running from a patch panel to a hub.

PCI: *Peripheral Component Interconnect,* the high-speed bus design found in modern Pentium computers.

PCONSOLE: The NetWare command you use from a DOS command prompt to manage network printing.

peer-to-peer network: A network in which any computer can be a server if it wants to be. Kind of like the network version of the Great American Dream. You can easily construct peer-to-peer networks by using Windows 95 or 98.

permissions: In Windows NT, rights that have been granted to a particular user or group of users enabling them to access specific files.

PhoneNET: An alternative cabling scheme for Macintosh networks, cheaper than Apple's LocalTalk cables.

physical layer: The lowest layer of the OSI reference model (whatever that is). It refers to the parts of the network you can touch: cables, connectors, and so on.

pocket protector: A status symbol among computer geeks.

port: A connector on the back of your computer that you can use to connect a device such as a printer, modem, mouse, and so on.

PPP: *Point to Point Protocol,* the most common way of connecting to the Internet for World Wide Web access.

presentation layer: The sixth layer of the OSI reference model, which handles data conversions, compression, decompression, and other menial tasks.

print job: A report, letter, memo, or other document that has been sent to a network printer but hasn't printed yet. Print jobs wait patiently in the queue until a printer agrees to print them.

Print Manager: In old-style Windows (Windows 3.1 and Windows for Workgroups), the program that handles print spooling.

print queue: The line that print jobs wait in until a printer becomes available.

print server: A computer that handles network printing or a device such as a JetDirect, which enables the printer to attach directly to the network.

PRN: The DOS code name for the first parallel port. Also known as *LPT1*.

protocol: (1) The robot C-3PO's speciality. (2) The rules of the network game. Protocols define standardized formats for data packets, techniques for detecting and correcting errors, and so on.

punch-down block: A gadget for quickly connecting a bunch of wires, used in telephone and network wiring closets.

QIC: *Quarter-inch cartridge,* the most popular and least expensive form of tape backup. See *DAT*.

queue: A list of items waiting to be processed. The term usually refers to the list of print jobs waiting to be printed, but networks have lots of other types of queues as well.

RAID: *Redundant Array of Inexpensive Disks,* a bunch of disk drives strung together and treated as if they were one drive. The data is spread out over several drives, and one of the drives keeps checking information so that if any one of the drives fails, the data can be reconstructed.

RAM: *Random access memory,* your computer's memory chips.

redirection: One of the basic concepts of networking, in which a device, such as a disk drive or printer, appears to be a local device but actually resides on the network. The networking software on your computer intercepts I/O requests for the device and redirects them to the network.

repeater: A device that strengthens a signal so that it can travel on. Repeaters are used to lengthen the cable distance between two nodes. A *multiport repeater* is the same as a *hub*.

resource: A disk drive, disk directory, printer, modem, CD-ROM, or other device that can be shared on the network.

ring: A type of network topology in which computers are connected to one another in a way that forms a complete circle. Imagine the Waltons standing around the Thanksgiving table holding hands, and you have the idea of a ring topology.

RJ-45: The kind of plug used by 10baseT networks. It looks kind of like a modular phone plug, but it's bigger.

router: A device that works kind of like a bridge but can handle different protocols. For example, a router can link Ethernet to LocalTalk or a mainframe.

ScanDisk: A Windows 95 and 98 command that examines your hard disk for physical defects.

scheduling software: Software that schedules meetings of network users. Works only if all network users keep their calendars up-to-date.

SCSI: *Small computer systems interface,* a connection used mostly for disk drives but also suitable for CD-ROM drives, tape drives, and just about anything else. Also winner of the Acronym Computer Geeks Love to Pronounce Most award.

segment: A single-run cable, which may connect more than two computers, with a terminator on each end.

serial port: A port normally used to connect a modem or mouse to a DOS-based computer, sometimes called a communications port. See *parallel port*.

server: A computer that's on the network and shares resources with other network users. The server may be dedicated, which means that its sole purpose in life is to provide service for network users, or it may be used as a client as well. See *client*.

session layer: A layer somewhere near the middle of the beloved OSI reference model that deals with sessions between network nodes.

SFT: *System Fault Tolerance,* a set of networking features designed to protect the network from faults, such as stepping on the line (known as a *foot fault*).

share name: A name that you assign to a network resource when you share it. Other network users use the share name to access the shared resource.

shared folder: A network server disk drive or a folder on a server drive that has been shared so that other computers on the network can access it.

shared resource: A resource, such as a disk or printer, that is made available to other network users.

shielded twisted pair: Twisted-pair cable with shielding, used mostly for Token Ring networks. Also known as *STP*. See ***twisted pair***.

smiley: A face made from various keyboard characters; often used in e-mail messages to convey emotion. :-)

SNA: *Systems Network Architecture,* a networking standard developed by IBM that dates from the mid-Mainframerasic Period, approximately 65 million years ago. Used by fine IBM mainframe and AS/400 minicomputers everywhere.

sneakernet: The cheapest form of network, in which users exchange files by copying them to disks and walking them between computers.

SNMP: *Simple Network Management Protocol,* a standard for exchanging network management information between network devices that is anything but simple.

spooling: A printing trick in which data that is intended for a printer is actually written to a temporary disk file and later sent to the printer.

ST-506: An old type of disk drive interface that's obsolete but still found on far too many computers.

star: A type of network topology in which each node is connected to a central wiring hub. This gives the network a star-like appearance.

SUPERVISOR: The top-dog account in NetWare. Log in as SUPERVISOR, and you can do just about anything.

switch: A super-efficient bridge that can create connections between any number of ports.

SYS: The volume name of the system volume on most NetWare servers.

system fault tolerance: See *SFT*.

tape drive: The best way to back up a network server. Tape drives have become so inexpensive that even small networks should have one.

task: For a technically accurate description, enroll in a computer science graduate course. For a layperson's understanding of what a task is, picture the guy who used to spin plates on *The Ed Sullivan Show.* Each plate is a task. The poor guy had to frantically move from plate to plate to keep them all spinning. Computers work the same way. Each program task is like one of those spinning plates; the computer must service each one periodically to keep it going.

TB: *Terrazzo bytes,* imported from Italy. Approximately one trillion bytes (1,024GB to be precise). (Just kidding about *terrazzo bytes.* Actually, TB stands for *terabytes.*)

TCP/IP: *Transmission Control Protocol/Internet Protocol,* the protocol used by the Internet.

terminator: The little plug you have to use at each end of a segment of thin coax cable (10baseT).

thinnet: See *10base2.*

three-letter acronym: See *TLA.*

time sharing: A technique used on mainframe computers to enable several users to access the computer at the same time.

time-out: How long the print server waits while receiving print output before deciding that the print job has finished.

TLA: *Three-letter acronym,* such as FAT (File Allocation Table), DUM (Dirty Upper Memory), and HPY (Heuristic Private Yodel).

token: The thing that gets passed around the network in a Token Ring topology. See *Token Ring.*

Token Ring: A network that's cabled in a ring topology in which a special packet called a token is passed from computer to computer. A computer must wait until it receives the token before sending data over the network.

topology: The shape of the network; how its computers and cables are arranged. See *bus, star,* and *ring.*

transceiver: A doohicky that connects a network interface card (NIC) to a network cable. A transceiver is always required to connect a computer to the network, but 10base2 and 10baseT NICs have built-in transceivers. Transceivers were originally used with yellow cable. You can also get transceivers that convert an AUI port to 10baseT.

transport layer: One of those layers somewhere near the middle of the OSI reference model that addresses the way data is escorted around the network.

Travan: A newer technology for inexpensive tape backup that can record up to 800MB on a single tape cartridge. See *QIC* and *DAT.*

trojan horse: A program that looks interesting but turns out to be something nasty, like a hard-disk reformatter.

trustee rights: In NetWare, rights that have been granted to a particular user or group of users enabling them to access specific files.

twisted pair: A type of cable that consists of one or more pairs of wires that are twisted in a certain way to improve the cable's electrical characteristics. See *unshielded twisted pair* and *shielded twisted pair*.

uninterruptible power supply: See *UPS*.

unshielded twisted pair: Twisted-pair cable that doesn't have a heavy metal shield around it. Used for 10baseT networks. Also known as *UTP*. See *twisted pair*.

UPS: *Uninterruptible power supply,* a gizmo that switches to battery power whenever the power cuts out. The *Enterprise* didn't have one of these, which is why the lights always went out until Spock could switch to auxiliary power.

URL: *Uniform Resource Locator,* a fancy term for an Internet address. URLs are those familiar "dot" addresses, such as "www-dot-microsoft-dot-com" or "www-dot-idgbooks-dot-com."

USB: A new type of computer interface that may someday become the standard interface for all devices that attach to your computer, including keyboard, mouse, monitor, printer, scanner, and speakers.

user ID: The name by which you're known to the network.

user profile: The way Windows keeps track of each user's desktop settings, such as window colors, wallpaper, screen savers, Start menu options, favorites, and so on.

user rights: Network actions that a particular network user is allowed to perform after he or she has logged on to the network. See *file rights*.

users' group: A local association of computer users, sometimes with a particular interest, such as networking.

UTP: *Unshielded twisted pair*. See *10baseT*.

vampire tap: (1) A whirlygig that enables you to tap into a 10base5 cable to attach a transceiver. (2) What Dracula orders from when he goes to a bar.

VGA: *Video Graphics Array,* the current standard in video monitors. Most VGA adapters these days are actually super VGA adapters, which are compatible with VGA adapters but have extra bells and whistles.

Vines: A network operating system made by Banyan, comparable to NetWare or Windows NT Server.

virus: An evil computer program that slips into your computer undetected, tries to spread itself to other computers, and may eventually do something bad like trash your hard disk.

volume name: In NetWare, each disk volume has a name. Most NetWare servers have a volume named SYS.

Web browser: A program that enables you to display information retrieved from the Internet's World Wide Web.

Windows: The world's most popular operating system.

Windows for Workgroups: Microsoft's first network-aware version of Windows, now pretty much defunct.

Windows 95: A version of Windows that became available in — you guessed it — 1995. Windows 95 was the first version of Windows that did not require DOS.

Windows 98: The successor to Windows 95 introduced in 1998. Windows 98 includes a new user interface that makes the Windows desktop resemble the World Wide Web.

Windows NT Client: Microsoft's advanced version of Windows, designed to operate as a network client.

Windows NT Server: Microsoft's premier server operating system ideal for running dedicated servers in small or large networks.

wiring closet: Large networks need a place where cables can congregate. A closet is ideal.

workstation: See *client*.

World Wide Web: A graphical method of accessing information on the Internet.

WWW: See *World Wide Web*.

Y2K: Either Armageddon or Much Ado About Nothing. We'll find out on January 1, 2000.

yellow cable: See *10base5*.

Index

Discover Dummies™ Online!

The *Dummies* Web Site is your fun and friendly online resource for the latest information about *...For Dummies*® books on all your favorite topics. From cars to computers, wine to Windows, and investing to the Internet, we've got a shelf full of *...For Dummies* books waiting for you!

Ten Fun and Useful Things You Can Do at www.dummies.com

1. Register this book and win!
2. Find and buy the *...For Dummies* books you want online.
3. Get ten great *Dummies Tips*™ every week.
4. Chat with your favorite *...For Dummies* authors.
5. Subscribe free to *The Dummies Dispatch*™ newsletter.
6. Enter our sweepstakes and win cool stuff.
7. Send a free cartoon postcard to a friend.
8. Download free software.
9. Sample a book before you buy.
10. Talk to us. Make comments, ask questions, and get answers!

Jump online to these ten
fun and useful things at
http://www.dummies.com/10useful

For other technology titles from IDG Books Worldwide, go to
www.idgbooks.com

Not online yet? It's easy to get started with *The Internet For Dummies*®, 5th Edition, or *Dummies 101*®: *The Internet For Windows*® *98*, available at local retailers everywhere.

Find other *...For Dummies* books on these topics:
Business • Careers • Databases • Food & Beverages • Games • Gardening • Graphics • Hardware
Health & Fitness • Internet and the World Wide Web • Networking • Office Suites
Operating Systems • Personal Finance • Pets • Programming • Recreation • Sports
Spreadsheets • Teacher Resources • Test Prep • Word Processing

IDG BOOKS WORLDWIDE
BOOK REGISTRATION

Register This Book and Win!

We want to hear from you!

Visit **http://my2cents.dummies.com** to register this book and tell us how you liked it!

✔ Get entered in our monthly prize giveaway.

✔ Give us feedback about this book — tell us what you like best, what you like least, or maybe what you'd like to ask the author and us to change!

✔ Let us know any other *...For Dummies*® topics that interest you.

Your feedback helps us determine what books to publish, tells us what coverage to add as we revise our books, and lets us know whether we're meeting your needs as a *...For Dummies* reader. You're our most valuable resource, and what you have to say is important to us!

Not on the Web yet? It's easy to get started with *Dummies 101*®*: The Internet For Windows*® *98* or *The Internet For Dummies*®*,* 5th Edition, at local retailers everywhere.

Or let us know what you think by sending us a letter at the following address:

...For Dummies Book Registration
Dummies Press
7260 Shadeland Station, Suite 100
Indianapolis, IN 46256-3917
Fax 317-596-5498

...FOR DUMMIES™

BESTSELLING BOOK SERIES